COLORADO MOUNTAIN COLLEGE

W9-CQC-781

DATE DUE		
APR 1 4 1989		

89240

NK4275 .C56 P67 1988
Colbeck, john.
Pottery materials : their
composition, preparation and

Colorado Mountain College
Learning Resources Center
Leadville, Colorado 80461

POTTERY MATERIALS

John Colbeck

POTTERY MATERIALS

their composition, preparation and use

Photographs by
Bonnie van de Wetering

89249

B T Batsford Limited London

Colorado Mountain College
Learning Resources Center
Leadville, Colorado 80461

© John Colbeck 1988
First published 1988

All rights reserved. No part of this publication
may be reproduced, in any form or by any means,
without permission from the publisher

ISBN 0 7134 4695 1

Typeset by Photosetting, Yeovil
and printed in Great Britain by
Richard Clay (Chichester)
for the publishers
B T Batsford Limited
4 Fitzhardinge Street
London W1H 0AH

CONTENTS

ACKNOWLEDGMENT

For their help with this book I am very grateful to Margaret Cole for typing the manuscript with care and involvement, to Thelma M Nye, who proposed the book, for advice, encouragement and patience and to Bonnie van de Wetering for advice and for the care and patience with which the photographs were taken and printed.

INTRODUCTION

This book is an introduction to theoretical and practical aspects of pottery materials: their nature, preparation and application. As an introduction it focuses on the needs of beginners but much of the material should also be a useful reference for those who have more experience.

Beginners are often overwhelmed by the detail of much of the technical literature of ceramics which frequently presumes a background knowledge which many do not possess. So far as theoretical aspects are concerned the book, therefore, aims to provide a clear but simple background and thus form a bridge between an initial interest in materials and the more technical literature which covers theory in greater detail. So far as practical aspects are concerned the aim is to describe those about which beginners most frequently seek information and, therefore, aspects which, in practical terms may prove most useful.

Descriptions of mechanical processes involving electrical or heavy equipment are omitted not through any prejudice against such equipment, which in fact offers time- and labour-saving advantages, but because it is not always available, and where it is the assumption may be made that instruction in its use is also provided.

Descriptions of mechanical processes involving electrical or heavy equipment are omitted not through any prejudice against such equipment, which in fact offers time- and labour-saving advantages, but because it is not always available, and where it is the assumption may be made that instruction in its use is also provided.

Today most potters have ready access to a wide range of prepared raw materials and, increasingly, of ready-to-use mixtures. The existence of ready-made mixtures – of glazes, slips, stains, lustres and enamels as well as clay bodies – might seem to diminish the need for potters to understand the qualities of the various raw materials and the principles on which mixtures may be compounded using these. This is not, however, the case because, if choice is to be made from the actual range of possibilities, it will be found in some areas that available ready-to-use mixtures cover only a small spectrum of the full range. Certainly it is advantageous to use ready-made mixtures, when these are available, to suit specific intentions but, when they are not, the range of possibilities can be extended immensely by using prepared raw materials to compound mixtures for special purposes. In many instances, even without equipment, this need not be prohibitively time consuming. As a basis from which to proceed, there are more recipes and other information available today than ever before.

No idea can take precise form until its materials are defined and no material has inherent virtue until its context of use is specified. Ultimately the content and quality of objects – the ideas they embody – be they one-off or mass produced, functional or non-functional, are the central concerns of work. But ideas, when manifest, necessarily take material form and in doing so the nature and quality of the material becomes an integral part of the idea. While history is full of examples of the creative use of what is available – however little this may be – the challenge today is that there are some new possibilities and that most, if not all, of those which existed at different stages in history are also still available. Even within present material limitations almost anything is possible. The choice is greater than ever. The underlying aims of this book, therefore, are to encourage beginners to understand the materials available, to feel confident in their use and to experiment with their qualities so that selection of materials becomes an integral and an enhancing aspect of the consideration of ideas.

SECTION ONE
CLAY

The one indispensible material of pottery is clay. Deposits of clay usable for pottery occur universally in a great variety of types but all aspects of that variety are not evenly distributed. Deposits of the purest clay – kaolin, china clay – are unevenly distributed. There are, however, few places where a range of clays of varying qualities does not occur.

The two qualities which are of fundamental importance to potters are the forming qualities in the plastic state and the fired qualities: to produce an object at all the clay has to be formable; to produce a durable object the clay has to be able to be fired to a point at which it develops a sufficient degree of strength.

Clay and clay bodies

In any theoretical discussion a distinction must be made between the word 'clay' and the term 'clay body'. Materials definable as *clay* exist in immense variety within a range of materials which have certain chemical and mineralogical characteristics in common. A *clay body* is a particular material usable in some defined ceramic context.

Except for brick, tile and 'coarse' pot making, few naturally occurring clays are used as found. If, however, a clay is used as found it is called a *clay body*. More commonly, bodies are the result of blending. From peasant village to urban industry and from ancient times to the present day the blending of clays has been and still is an almost universal practice. It is done both to minimise natural variations and to modify and improve some aspect of a clay to make it more suitable for its intended use. In addition to the blending of clays together, non-clay materials may be mixed with clay in making a clay body.

Thus a 'clay' may be thought of as an *ingredient* and a 'clay body' as a *usable mixture*.

Types of clay

There are a few types of clay, many subdivisions within types and numerous varieties within subdivisions. Four main types are worthy of mention.

China clays
China clays are the purest form of clay. They are very white firing and refractory but, typically, have poor plasticity. With appropriate additions they can become translucent when fired. In all white bodies they are the vital ingredient.

Used alone, china clays are too refractory to be practicable as clay bodies and are anyway lacking in plasticity. Where whiteness or translucency is the aim the additions which are made to china clay introduce plastic material to make it more workable, and fluxing materials to make it less refractory with as little reduction to its whiteness as possible.

China clays are most usually marketed in powder form.

Fire clays
It is easy to accept that china clay as a white and apparently fine powder is a relatively pure material. Raw fire clays are usually greyish in colour and sandy in texture and seem far less likely to be pure. They are, however, relatively pure clay material and as such are highly refractory.

Fire clays frequently occur as shale and have to be crushed before they can be used in clay bodies. Their most common use is as firebricks and other refractory items required in all industries which use intense heat in their processes. Even when fire clays are crushed they can be quite granular. When crushed and mixed with water into a clay body without other additions some fireclays do develop a good plasticity while others remain short.

As an ingredient in clay bodies, fire clays help clay forms to stand well both in the plastic state and during firing. They increase the refractoriness of bodies. Because of their normally granular nature, fire clays give a somewhat sandy texture to bodies and usually give a colour texture to the fired body. This speckled colour texture occurs because much of the iron impurity present in fire clays is in the form of iron pyrites granules. Speckling is especially evident at stoneware temperatures.

Many fireclays are simply too refractory at normal temperatures to develop the fired strength necessary in bodies but less refractory fireclays exist, with a higher proportion of alkali flux impurities and these develop acceptable hardness at stoneware temperatures. A number of stoneware bodies are composed entirely of fireclay or a blend of two or more fireclays.

Fireclays are sold in powder form and often also in lump form. Fireclays or blends of fireclays intended as complete bodies are usually marketed in a plastic state.

Ball clays
The particular quality which ball clays possess is an exceptional plasticity. This plasticity is due to their extremely fine particle size. The quality of extreme plasticity bring with it a high shrinkage rate which makes the use of ball clay alone impractical.

Typically, ball clays have alkali fluxes, iron oxide and titanium dioxide present as impurities. The fluxes help ball clays to fire to hard bodies within the range of normal temperatures. The iron oxide is rarely present in amounts of more than 2% and does not have a pronounced darkening effect. The titanium dioxide, though only present in amounts around 1% to 1.5%, is the most serious disadvantage of ball clays where white bodies are intended because even small amounts of this are detrimental to whiteness in a fired body.

Ball clays are marketed in considerable variety.

They are usually available in powder form, though a few may be bought in lump form.

Though it is repeated later in various contexts it is as well to say here that ball clays contain largish proportions of free silica and, as silica containing powders which are ultra fine, they should be handled with care taking every effort to avoid the creation of airborne dust. Care should be exercised with *all* clays to avoid the creation of airborne dust but this is especially the case with ball clays.

Common clays
This is by far the largest of the four types of clays mentioned. It could be broken up into a number of subdivisions but in this context that seems unnecessary.

There is an immensely broad range of common clays which can be used as the main constituent of clay bodies, usually in the lower parts of the firing range but not always so. There are clays which are used for brick making, tile making, drainage pipe making and 'coarse' pot making but there are also fine clays and clays which are refractory enough for stoneware temperatures. Most clays in the category are relatively plastic. A few are highly so. The majority of clays in the type fire within the brown range of colour referred to as 'terracotta' or 'red' but some are very pale firing.

Worldwide, common clays have formed and still form the basis of bodies used to make vast quantities of pottery both within and outside concerns definable as 'industrial'. Such clays are usually processed by sieving to remove stones and vegetable debris and are usually blended with other clays or have non-clay material additions and when formed into bodies should only be thought of as different in kind not better or worse than bodies built up from the many ball and china clays and other materials now readily available.

Not all common clays are usable in clay bodies.

Some common clays are available in lump form from clay merchants, but usually common clays, blended or with additions, are sold in a plastic state as complete bodies. A few red earthenware clays are available in powder form.

10

The useful qualities of clay

The two distinct qualities of clay and clay bodies are plasticity and the ability to retain form at the intended firing temperature.

Plasticity is not a quality which is possessed equally by different clay bodies nor is the nature of plasticity consistent from body to body. Plasticity is variable both quantitatively and qualitatively.

Quantitatively, white firing bodies being based on china clays which have relatively poor plasticity, are generally less plastic than buff or red firing bodies which are based on the much more plastic ball clays or common clays.

Qualitatively the nature of the plasticity of a clay body may be very different in different contexts of use. A clay which seems to have a really responsive mobile quality when thrown on a small scale may hold its form poorly on a larger scale and be less useable, less appropriate on that scale than a less immediately responsive clay. A clay which spreads well and is excellent for press-moulding or jigger and jolley may be very poor for throwing. Clays with poor spreadability and poor throwability may nevertheless be very good for handbuilding of one type or another. There is inadequate terminology to describe the many differing attributes – differing aspects of plasticity – which make a clay good to use in the many differing contexts of use. In the general sense and on a crude quantitative scale the meaning of plasticity is clear but in specific contexts, unless the term is qualified in some detail, it is imprecise.

The ability of the previously plastic material to become hard and durable and retain its form when heat is applied to it is also one which is variable.

The word 'fireability' is not one which one hears but the idea is a useful one. For example, some ball clays, if used pure, shrink considerably and distort, often developing surface undulations or cracks on firing. Such mixtures, in practical terms, could be thought of as unfireable. Somewhat similarly many common clays, though possessed of very acceptable plasticity, are not predictably fireable. The aim of firing is to convert the previously plastic material of a clay form to a hard durable material without distortion of the form. A clay body fired as intended may be completely non porous or may retain some degree of porosity. The temperature needed to do this varies considerably from body to body. It is expected that with or without support, whichever is normal for the type of body, the clay body will retain its form during the firing but it is obvious that some forms are more demanding of material than others. Given that the length and atmosphere of firing are important, as well as temperature, the variables are clearly complex and considerable but in any consideration of clay bodies 'fireability' is an idea which has very useful meaning.

The physical and visual qualities of a fired clay body can be altered by making modifications to the body just as can its quality of plasticity. There is a complex relationship between the working and the fired qualities of clay bodies and altering the body to affect either quality will always affect the other to a greater or lesser extent. Just as the working characteristics of a body can only be described in relation to a particular process of forming, so the fired characteristics are only constant in relation to a particular schedule, atmosphere and temperature of firing.

Conditions of clay

Clay passes through three states as it dries from a formable condition to one in which it can be fired: *plastic*, *leatherhard* and *dry*. These three states gradually merge into one another.

1   Plastic clay

The plastic state of clay is that within which clay bodies are readily formable. In this state bodies can be easily impressed with finger tip pressure. Within the plastic state there is a range of conditions. At the softer end of the range the clay is only just sufficiently firm to adhere together in a kneadable mass without a strong tendency to stick to the hands. This is the state when two plastic bodies can be mixed together by wedging and kneading with the minimum of effort. Somewhat firmer – a mid plastic state – is the stage in which most forming is done. In a firmer plastic state a sheet of clay can be thinned somewhat between the fingers but the edge of a sheet may crack with this treatment.

2   Leatherhard clay

In the leatherhard state clay is no longer formable by plastic means but is still impressible by fingernail pressure. It is difficult to make a clear distinction between the firm plastic and early leatherhard state. The definitive leatherhard state is one in which the clay is firm enough to resist the pressure of a knife so an action such as facetting or the turning of thrown forms will produce long clean shavings of clay. After this mid leatherhard state, as the clay approaches dryness, cut shavings have no length. They break up into fragments as they are cut.

3 Dry clay

Dryness is an obvious state: strong fingernail pressure crumbles rather than impresses the clay. Apparent dryness is, however, deceptive for clay is only as dry as the air surrounding it, regardless of whether it has been 'drying' for two weeks, two months or even two years. In an inappropriately fast initial stage of firing, 'dry' clay can explode and shatter because it is damp. True dryness – the elimination of all moisture from the clay – is only achieved through the application of heat.

Refractoriness and vitrification

At some temperature all clays, however pure, soften, deform, melt, run and form glassy material. The higher the temperature a clay can withstand without deforming the more refractory it is said to be.

In the lower ranges of red heat, around and above 650°C, clay becomes irreversibly hardened but, though it is hard in the sense that it can never again be softened into a formable state, it is still scratchable and fragile. In this state it is very porous. In greater heat, at orange to yellow heat, with less refractory clays, and at yellow to white heat, with more refractory clays, the fluxes in the clay become active and begin to melt and flow bonding the clay particles together making the body harder, stronger and less porous.

When a clay has been fired up to a point of non-porosity it is said to be vitrified.

Methodical testing can show that some clay bodies approach vitrification as they are subjected to progressively greater heat, with gradual reductions to their porosity over a long temperature range, while others move from a relatively soft, porous state to being deformed and molten relatively suddenly within a short temperature

range. Clay bodies of the stoneware type, intended for use in the higher temperature range, tend to vitrify across a longer temperature range than clay bodies based on common clay intended for use as earthenware bodies. Indeed, common clays unblended and without refractory additions frequently change from being porous to becoming molten in a short temperature range. The tradition that earthenware has a porous body made impervious to liquids with glaze arose through potters who avoided subjecting clay bodies to temperatures where the risk of loss was unacceptably high.

The classification of clay bodies

The conventional classification of clay bodies, and other aspects of ceramics into earthenware, stoneware and porcelain is one which is clear but limited. *Earthenware* is thought of as ceramics fired in the range of 960° to 1140°C; *stoneware*, fired in the range of 1220°C to 1300°C; and *porcelain* fired in the upper part of, and sometimes somewhat above, that range. *Earthenware* is considered to be soft and porous, *stoneware* hard and non-porous, vitreous, and *porcelain* is thought of as a white body with the hardness and non-porosity of stoneware with the additional quality that when thin and vitrified it develops a degree of translucency.

Clear and convenient as this classification may be, it does not admit the diversity which exists. There are clay bodies which can be fired to maturity within the earthenware temperature range developing the hardness and non-porosity conventionally associated with stoneware. At stoneware temperatures some refractory clay bodies retain the porosity and softness associated with earthenware. Many bodies exist, as do glazes, which work in the non-earthenware, non-stoneware range of 1140° to 1220°C.

This oversimplified classification has arisen partly through standardisation. Production potteries, large and small, for obvious reasons of convenience and economics, tend to standardise materials to work at particular temperatures. Even educational institutions, with their greater opportunity and facility for experiment, tend, for similar reasons, to standardise firing temperatures to one or two for earthenware, and one or two for stoneware and porcelain. Much literature on ceramics inevitably reflects this standardisation.

If the possible diversity is not acknowledged, an

acceptance of the simple classification of clay bodies and the use of standardised temperatures can lead to ignorance of the fact that good ceramic – good in the technical sense of being sound, in which the clay body has developed full strength – only occurs when a particular clay is fired to its optimum temperature. Underfiring of clay bodies, provided it is not excessive, can be justified in some contexts – indeed a degree of porosity is sometimes a desired quality. It is frequently practised as a means of eliminating warping in, for example, large open forms. Underfiring may be achieved by either firing a particular clay body to a lower temperature than that used previously or by firing at the same temperature but altering the body to make it more refractory. This latter alternative results in a new clay body but where firing temperatures are standardised, and the opportunity to fire to a lower temperature is slight or non-existent, it is the more common solution when warping has been encountered in the use of a particular clay body.

The theory of clay bodies

What is a good body?
Even in the purely technical sense it is somewhat harder to define the attributes of a good body than it is to define those of a good glaze. This is because while a good glaze is simply expected to form a glassy impervious coating which adheres well to the particular body it covers, bodies are expected to do many different things. The simple answer to the question is that a good body is one which does what the potter expects of it. While this answer may be condemned as something of an evasion of the question it is, if sensibly pursued, a very useful way of looking at bodies because, in formulating precise answers to the question 'what is expected of a body?', the factors relevant to answering 'what is a good body?' have to be seriously weighed against one another.

Especially if visual criteria are added to technical criteria it will be found that good bodies are often compromises between the fired and the working qualities of a body. This is especially true for non-industrial potters who expect and need bodies to have greater plasticity than is required for industrial forming methods.

In the absolute sense, a good body is impossible to define in precise technical terms. The temptation is to say that a good body is one which has developed full fused strength, but this is not always desired or necessary.

Good bodies are necessarily formable but in the fired state good bodies, depending on their context of use, range through bodies which may be highly porous and still relatively soft, to harder bodies of low porosity in which vitrification has begun, to dense fully vitrified bodies, to bodies which have developed translucency and which, in all these cases, retain their form during firing.

Necessarily a potter uses formable bodies, and it is the responsibility of potters to ensure that fired bodies have qualities appropriate to the particular context.

Bought clay bodies
Clay bodies which are sold have been extensively used and tested so, with due awareness of the contexts for which they have been designed, may be thought of as good bodies. Obviously, though, in relation to the discussion of what constitutes a good body, not all are good for all purposes.

Manufacturers, quite naturally, tend to market clay bodies which they judge to be most salable in relation to the needs of the market at any given time. So even though a great range of bodies is available, individuals may seek bodies of particular quality which cannot be bought.

In this situation an individual has three main options: (1) two or more bought plastic clay bodies may be blended together; (2) various materials may be added into the clay body; (3) bodies may be mixed from dry powdered ingredients.

Blending clay bodies together
This is a relatively simple matter. From knowledge of the individual clay bodies, these are blended in proportions which seem most likely to give the desired working and fired characteristics. Rather than imagining that the first test of considered proportions will be right, it is usual and sensible to test a small number of variations. The proportions are worked out on the basis of observed qualities, the bodies are weighed up and wedged and kneaded together and the resulting bodies are tested for their plastic and fired characteristics.

Adding materials into clay bodies

The actual addition of dry powdered ingredients to a clay body should be undertaken with some caution. Among those additions which may be considered are china clay, ball clay, red clay, fire clay, flint and felspar. It is perfectly possible to *knead* these materials into the clay but while this may be the quickest method it may not be the best. Firstly, the mixing achieved by this means may be far less than intimate and an incompletely integrated material may well not have the effect intended and will certainly have a different effect from that of the same amount of material completely integrated. Secondly, the addition of dry powder to a plastic body, whatever its long-term effect on plasticity may be, has the immediate effect of making bodies shorter. This problem is caused by the incomplete wetting of all the introduced particles of material, and diminishes if the clay is not used for a while. A better method is to *wet the dry material*, sieve it and, using a scraper on some hard surface, blend the wet, sieved material with a small amount of clay body and then wedge this into the remainder of the clay. This method is shown in adding pigment to a body on page 182. Where dry materials are added to a clay body, as far as record keeping goes, the weights of plastic body and dry material additions should be recorded.

The addition of grog is a slightly different matter and is dealt with separately.

Mixing bodies from dry materials

The major physical problem of undertaking this is either mixing the clay body at a plastic consistency or removing excess water from a clay body in a slip state. As well as being used as a term for mixtures of materials which are used to coat clay bodies the word slip is also used when a clay body is in watery suspension – more precisely, clay bodies in this state are called *body slips*.

A second problem, no less major, is of deciding on what basis and in what proportions to incorporate which materials. While some understanding of clay theory is useful, both to the blending of existing clay bodies and deciding on dry material additions to these, it is essential to the compounding of bodies from dry materials.

The parts of a clay body

Very simply, clay bodies consist of two parts: a *clay part* and a *non-clay part*.

Clays occurring naturally also have clay and non-clay parts. Even china clays, often thought of as 'pure' clay, rarely contain much more than 80% clay mineral. In nature it is rare to find a balance between the clay and non-clay parts that enables a clay to become a useful body without some additions.

For useful understanding, the simple picture of a clay body having two parts needs to be extended.

A fuller description of some aspects of chemistry is included in the section on glaze, and reading pages 53 to 57 may make the next few paragraphs clearer to some readers.

The *clay part* of the picture of a body is composed of the oxides of silicon (silica) and aluminium (alumina) combined with each other and with water in fixed proportions (the water is chemically combined water which can only be driven off by firing, not the water which dries out of clays). This mineral, called *kaolinite*, is the one which, when of sufficiently fine particle size, gives clays their particular quality of plasticity. The particular concern about this part of a clay body is its particle size. The particle size of clays is measured in *microns*, a micron being one thousandth of a millimetre. The higher the proportion of clay with particle size of less than 1 micron the more plastic it will be. Well over 50% of the weight of most ball clays is composed of particles of less than 1 micron.

The *non-clay part* of the picture of a clay body can be extended by subdividing it into two parts: a part containing fluxes and a part containing other materials. As long as the particle size of these parts is fine, in sieve mesh rather than micron terms, the chemistry rather than the particle size is the aspect which is most relevant. The fluxes which consist of various oxides (those of potassium, sodium, calcium and magnesium being the most common) are necessary to a body if it is to develop a fused hardness, whether partial or complete, at any chosen temperature of firing. A proportion of fluxes is present in all bodies because to some extent all clays contain fluxes in the form of 'impurities'. Additional material is usually added by incorporating materials which behave as fluxes. The second part of the subdivision of the non-clay part of bodies consists almost wholly of further silica and alumina. Some of this silica and alumina is brought into clay bodies in the form of felspathic or micaceous 'impurity' present as non-clay material in all clays. Other silica and alumina are brought into bodies with materials included because of the fluxes they contain; materials such as china stone and felspar. Some of the silica is brought in as free silica 'impurity' in natural clay and yet more may be specifically added in the form of quartz or flint. The free silica, as well as that present in the clay and other body materials, represents a glass-forming oxide on which the fluxes can react to form a glassy bond within the clay body but silica has other functions as well.

Thus the initial picture of a clay body consisting of two parts rapidly becomes more complex and could quickly be made yet more complex. If, however, the basic picture of a clay body containing a clay part, consisting of silica and alumina, and a non-clay part, subdivided into fluxing oxides and further silica and alumina, can be accepted, this is a sound basis from which to develop a fuller understanding.

Scientific analyses of clays

Analyses are prohibitively expensive to have done, so given a quantity of plastic clay body there is virtually nothing an individual can do to discover its precise nature in scientific terms. However, starting with powdered materials it is possible to construct bodies by methodical testing and to cross check observed results against published scientific data which is available from the companies who market clays in bulk. These companies regularly analyse their clays from various points of view which are of interest to anyone doing work with clay bodies.

Particle size analyses

These show the weight percentages of different clays which are greater or less than certain sizes. A broad comparison of the particle sizes of china and ball clays shows that ball clays have a far greater weight proportion of particles of smaller micron sizes. Broadly, particle size analyses are indications of the degree of plasticity – the greater the proportion of particles of 1 micron size or less the greater the plasticity.

Mineralogical analyses

These show the proportions of the different minerals which occur in clays – micaceous material, felspar, quartz (silica), carbonaceous material and other minerals and the kaolinite which is the pure clay material. Broadly, mineralogical analyses show that china clays contain a far higher proportion of pure clay material than ball clays and that there are considerable mineralogical differences between different ball clays.

Percentage oxide analyses

These give analyses of the percentages of different oxides in clays. The oxides present in significant amounts are silica (SiO_2), alumina (Al_2O_3), iron oxide (Fe_2O_3), titanium dioxide (TiO_2), calcium oxide (CaO), magnesium oxide (MgO), potassium oxide (K_2O) and sodium oxide (Na_2O). The material lost during firing is quoted as LOI – loss on ignition. Though quoted as such, not all the oxides are always present in oxide form, calcium oxide is, for example, often present as calcium carbonate and when this is the case the carbonate, in changing to the oxide form during firing, gives off carbon dioxide. Changes such as this and the loss of chemically combined water from kaolinite account for the 'loss of ignition'. To discover the actual fired analysis of a clay, the loss on ignition is eliminated and the oxide percentages recalculated resulting in all of the percentages increasing slightly. Percentage oxide analyses are useful in indicating the total flux content of a clay and, if the amount of titanium and iron oxides are considered, give a broad indication of fired colour – in china and ball clays the amount of titanium dioxide present is at least as important as iron oxide in indicating how much the fired clay departs from pure whiteness.

Data about non clay body ingredients

Where the data about china stone, felspar, quartz and the various other materials which may be included in clay bodies, is not published in catalogues, details of percentage oxide analyses and sieve mesh size of preparation are usually readily available on request.

The limits to scientific understanding of clays

The simple picture which has been drawn of pure clay as kaolinite, which occasionally exists in nature in relatively pure form as china clay but more usually has felspathic, micaceous, siliceous and other impurities mixed with it, is a considerable simplification of the picture seen by scientists and ceramic technologists. In fact kaolinite is not the only clay mineral, and clay technology is an exceedingly complex field. Scientists themselves do not claim complete knowledge or understanding of the field and disagree about aspects which are still the subject of research.

To a potter, a clay's behaviour and the behaviour of bodies based on it – their formability and their fireability – are paramount. While oxide percentage analyses of clays are attractive as factual information it must be stressed that because of the complexity of the field they should not be accorded too much importance – they are neither an absolute yardstick nor the only one. This is said not to dismiss the importance of theoretical study – indeed, in a complex field it seems important to study all information which may lead to a fuller understanding of particular interests – but is said rather to underline the importance of balancing theoretical study with observed practical understanding.

The relevance of analyses and data in constructing bodies
While a great many potters experiment with glazes to evolve particular qualities and colours, far less such work is done with clay bodies. Moreover, there is far less published material about experimentation with and the principles of constructing bodies than there is with glazes. (Though with industrial bodies this is less true.)

A great many potters use exclusively bought bodies and are entirely content with these. As has been said, many good bodies can be bought. Those who blend bodies together or make additions to bodies are merely blending or adapting good bodies which, in their view, need some alteration to make them more suitable for some particular purpose, and such work is usually based on empirical experiment rather than calculation.

Because pure whiteness of body has for a long time been an aim for the majority of industrial pottery, there is a considerable volume of literature about industrial bodies. Though much of this is concerned with bodies which have unacceptably low plasticity for hand forming methods, this literature is relevant to the principles of compounding bodies. The problems of evolving white firing, low firing bodies with reasonable plasticity immediately become evident from such a study.

For anyone who is interested in evolving bodies, it is important to understand that, while theory and calculation are central to such work with glaze, the relevance of such work with bodies is certainly different and probably less. Bodies which are remarkably different in physical quality can be surprisingly similar as percentage analyses and vice versa.

Those who do mix their own bodies from dry powdered materials usually do so because they find that the working and fired qualities they can achieve are closer to what they want than in bodies they can buy or blend from bought bodies. (Occasionally these bodies are then produced by manufacturers.)

Anyone who embarks on mixing bodies from dry ingredients is treading a fairly lonely path. It therefore seems sensible to consider the work from as many points of view as possible, and the data produced by clay merchants for use in constructing industrial bodies linked to simple calculation procedures can be one of a number of factors considered in this work.

There are no narrow definitive limits of percentage analyses for the construction of bodies to work at different temperatures, and any work of this sort should make as wide a reference to published information as possible.

Factors of relevance to the consideration of whether to buy or mix bodies
Unlike all other pottery mixtures, the mixing of bodies does require either space or quite substantial equipment so the availability of either of these is the first factor to consider.

The second factor, and one of equal importance, is whether or not ready-made plastic bodies exist which have the particular qualities which are desired. But the range of individual wish and intention is such that bodies to suit all needs cannot be bought.

The range of available bodies based on common clay which includes all red earthenwares and some higher firing buff clays is such that, unless some extremely particular body is wanted, it hardly seems worthwhile considering mixing bodies based on these. Furthermore such clays are less commonly available in powder form.

A good range of bodies are available based on fireclays or blends of fireclays and ball clays. Nevertheless the range of bodies of this type is so varied in potential that, good as the range of bought bodies is, the possibilities are such that where they are of interest it is certainly worthwhile to consider mixing bodies of this type.

It is probably in the area of porcelain bodies and the lighter, whiter firing earthenware and stoneware bodies based on ball and china clays that the idea of undertaking the work of mixing bodies is most sustainable. Certainly the range of bought bodies of this type is the narrowest. Furthermore the data on the clays which form the basis of this type is much the most available.

A third and economic factor to consider is that the range of good clay bodies in plastic condition which now exists does so only for those within economic transport distances from clay producing centres. (Moreover, the present range of bodies has not always existed and economic factors may well alter the range.) Transport can increase the costs of all material very considerably so those closest to clay-producing centres are best served. With clay bodies in the plastic state approximately 25% of transport costs are in fact for transporting water. In some places transport costs alone can make the use of dry materials to mix bodies worthwhile. In even more distant places, using relatively local materials is an economic necessity. Thus there are contexts and occasions in which every scrap of empirical and theoretical knowledge is valuable.

A method of mixing clay bodies from powdered materials

As has been said earlier, the mixing of clay bodies without the aid of equipment is an operation not to be undertaken lightly but there is one method by which batches of clay bodies of up to 25 kg of dry ingredients can be mixed without either substantial equipment or very time consuming labour.

A note of caution about mixing clay bodies. Unless specialist scales are available, it is likely that the total weight of particular materials, especially clays, will not fit into the scale pan in one amount. When this occurs it is especially important that a careful and methodical procedure is followed so that no weighing errors occur.

A further serious warning when mixing clay bodies is to take all steps to avoid the creation of airborne dust. Clay bodies rightly tend to be thought of as non-hazardous materials but dry powdered clays, particularly ball clays, contain fine silica dust and these and quartz, as materials frequently included in clay bodies, should be handled with care in the powdered state when they very easily create the hazard of airborne dust.

For the method described below two containers each of about 25 litres and one of about 2.25 litres are needed together with a range of sieves and the drying frame which is described later. 12.5 kg of dry materials are being mixed.

1 The materials are weighed out on scales with a large pan

1

2 One of the two large containers is just over half filled with water. The weighed dry materials are then gently added to the water allowing them adequate time to sink through. It is important to allow materials to sink into the water at their own speed. Stirring in unwetted material simply creates pockets of unwetted material below the water surface which break down very slowly. Subsequent mixing is easier if clays are added to the water before any non-clay ingredients

3 Once all the materials have been added, the mixture can be stirred. Some of the non-clay materials may contain lumps which need breaking up

4 As soon as any large lumps are broken up the mixture can be poured repeatedly from one container to another to wet thoroughly and mix the materials. With the amounts of dry material, and in containers of the size mentioned above, a thin slip will result. Within limits, the more watery the slip the better the clay body will be and the easier it will be to sieve the slip

2

3

4

18

5, 6, 7 In this series of photographs sieving is being done in a specially made fibreglass basin which also doubles as a glazing trough (see also figures 187 and 189–209). A 20 mesh sieve is placed in the basin and the mixture is simply poured through the sieve from where it drains into the container placed under the drainage hole of the basin

5

6

7

8 Non-clay material or any pockets of poorly wetted clay will need a little brushing to ease them through the sieve

9 The slip left in the basin at the end of the first sieving can then be squeegeed into the lower container but at this stage there is no need to clean the basin thoroughly

10 The mixture is then resieved through the 20 mesh sieve. This second time it should pour through easily with very little need for brushing

8

9   *10*

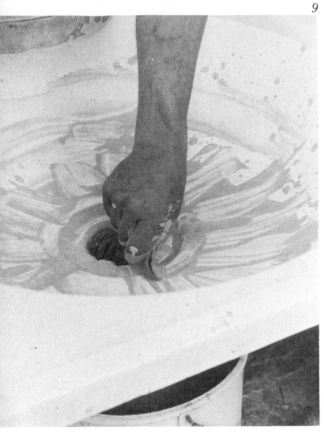 

11 The basin is then cleaned and the sieve quickly washed through from the top with a hose. The additional water can drain into the slip mixture so long as the container is not allowed to overfill. The body slip is then poured from one container to another a few times to make it thoroughly even in consistency

12 Sieving now proceeds through a 60 mesh sieve. Initially, to avoid splashing or spillage it is better to use the smaller container to ladle the slip into the sieve

13 Intermittent brushing will be necessary

14 When the container is about half empty ladling will become awkward and it is simpler to pour the mixture steadily from the large container

12

13

11

14

15

16

15 Finally, the empty container is hosed clean and the mixture is sieved into it through a 100 mesh sieve. Initially, as with the 60 mesh sieving, the mixture should be ladled into the sieve with the small container to avoid spillage and splashing but after about half the mixture has been sieved the larger container can be poured directly into the sieve

16 As might be expected, considerably more frequent brushing is necessary during the 100 mesh sieving

17 The container necessary for drying out clay bodies prepared like this is made of galvanised weldmesh and needs to be lined with a textile bag made up from some strong, finely woven material. Such weldmesh containers can be simply and quite quickly constructed and, in use, are supported on rods which, in turn, rest on trestles or some other convenient support ideally near or over a drainage channel. The container illustrated is of 19 mm weldmesh, made of 14 (British SWG) gauge wire. The entire container can be marked and cut out flat and then folded to shape, the corners being secured with flat metal ties. The top edges are left long so that they can be bent over to locate the metal rods on which the container rests. The textile liner bag should have double sewn seams and it is essential that it is of ultra fine weave. Surprisingly perhaps thin dress lining fabrics work well but have the disadvantage that they tear rather easily if they catch on a sharp projection. The obvious material for a liner is filter press cloth. The bag should be made slightly oversize so that the wire mesh, rather than the sewn seams of the bag, takes the pressure of the weight of the slip body

18,19 Initially, the watery slip mixture is ladled into the container. The cloth tends to fold back on itself so it must be held open. When the large container is empty enough to be controlled safely with one hand, the remaining slip can be poured directly from this. The particular weldmesh container illustrated is 36 cm high, 61 cm wide and 8.25 cm thick and contains the slip from the nearly full 25 litre container with over 5 cm spare capacity at the top. Before the weldmesh container has been completely filled, clear water will start to drip through the textile. The weldmesh container is then simply left for the slip to stiffen up to a plastic state. In the first few hours the level of slip will sink considerably but then the rate of water loss slows down. Before the container is finally left, the top edges of the cloth should be folded down onto the clay which prevents the thin slip on the top edges of the cloth drying out and forming dry flakes of clay. Throughout the drying time the top of the cloth should be kept pressed down onto the clay. If the drying container is left outside it should be covered to keep off any rain

How long the slip takes to dry to a plastic kneadable state is dependent on two factors: the precise nature of the clay body; and the drying conditions in which the container is left. A fine clay with a high ball clay content may take twice as long in the same conditions as a porcelain body with a low plastic clay content. Outside, good drying conditions may exist in winter as well as summer and while the ideal is a hot summer day with a breeze, a cold, dry winter wind has a more drying effect than a still, humid summer day. In good drying conditions the clay will be ready to be removed from the drying container in three to five days depending on the nature of the clay body but in still, damp weather drying time can be up to and over two weeks. Inside buildings drying is as much dependent on air circulation as on temperature, a warm well ventilated building being best. Generally, outside drying is faster than that inside buildings

18

19

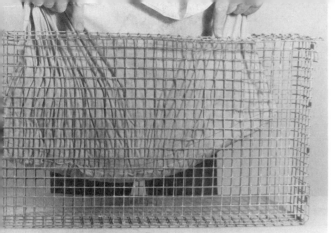

20 The clay body should feel quite firm before it is removed from the weldmesh container. It is removed by easing out the textile liner from the weldmesh frame

21, 22 Obviously the clay body is a very tight fit in the textile bag and removal is easier if the ends of the bag are tapped to reduce the overall length of the mass. The textile can then be peeled back cleanly and the clay removed

20

21

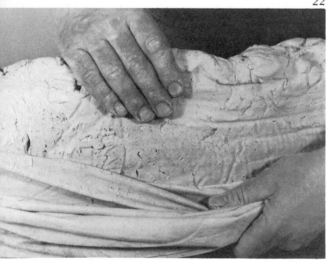

22

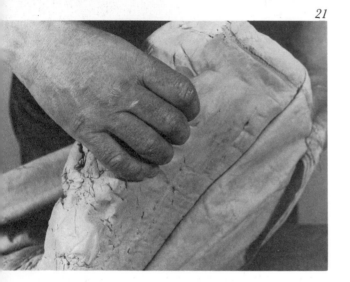

24

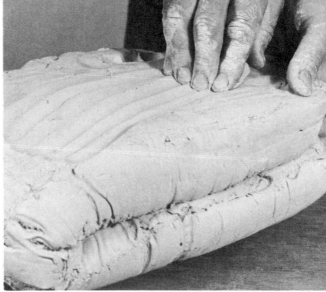

23 It is unnecessary to pug clay produced by this method. Whenever the clay is removed it is of an extremely even consistency and if removed at the right time it can be briefly wedged or kneaded and used immediately

When a batch of clay has been dried the cloth bag should be turned inside out and hosed down to remove any traces of clay so that these neither dry out to become a source of dust nor remain to contaminate the next batch of slip which may be different. If, however, more of the same mixture is to be dried, the bag need not be hosed and can be re-used immediately.

Some further factors of relevance to producing bodies by this method
The dimensions of the weldmesh drying containers used with this method need some consideration. While height and width are relatively unimportant to the function of the containers and are determined by considerations of convenient handling, the thickness is crucial. Drying container thicknesses much over 9 cm start to lengthen the drying times considerably and thicknesses less than 7.5 cm start to be inconvenient to fill and empty. A thickness of about 8 cm seems to be the optimum.

The sequence of photographs showed the mixing of one 25 litre container full of body slip. This required two 25 litre containers. When full, containers much larger than this become difficult to lift and to handle with the necessary control. Larger amounts of body than that shown can obviously be mixed by using additional containers but about 25 kg should be seen as the limit for the method when the body contains a number of different materials. Such an amount would require four containers and to ensure an even dispersion of body ingredients between the two containers which would be full at any time a logical mixing sequence using all four containers must be used: starting with two full and two empty containers the contents of one of the full containers is used to half fill the two empty containers which are then filled up from the remaining full container – this sequence is then repeated several times. With larger quantities than this it is simpler to weigh out separate consecutive batches.

If a number of weldmesh containers are made these can be filled and lined up next to each other

23

with adjacent containers sharing supporting rods. The folded edges on which the weldmesh containers are suspended act as spacers keeping the containers about 10 cm apart. This spacing has no perceptible effect on the drying rate.

As well as the fine bodies for which the method is obviously good, coarser textured fireclay bodies can also be made if powdered fireclay is available. The procedure is to add the weighed fireclay to adequate water and allow this to soak thoroughly. (It will be better if it can be left for a couple of days.) This fireclay slip is then stirred and poured briskly and repeatedly from one container to another until it develops a thin even consistency. The ball clay, together with any other ingredients, is then prepared in the usual way. The two slips are then thoroughly intermixed by pouring from container to container and when mixed put into the weldmesh containers to stiffen. Bodies produced in this way are immediately of greater plasticity than identical bodies produced in a dough mixer.

If grogged bodies are to be produced by this method the grog is mixed in only after the remainder of the body has been slipped and sieved. Thorough grog mixing is achieved by pouring the mixture from one container to another. Some settlement of grog will occur while the slip is stiffening but this can be readily evened out by some brief methodically planned wedging as soon as the clay is removed from the textile drying bag.

The disadvantages of the method are few. In an

89249

Colorado Mountain College
Learning Resources Center
Leadville Colorado 89461

unpredictable climate variable drying time may be a nuisance but if production of bodies occurs ahead of need this should not be a drawback. The settlement of grog can be a problem but it is one which is easily dealt with. The availability of drying space is perhaps the biggest drawback in some contexts.

Perhaps the prime advantage of the method is that it promotes thorough wetting of the clay particles and thereby encourages the formation of all potential plasticity. The resulting clay is far better than dough mixer made clay and at least as good as filter press clay with the bonus that, unlike filter press clay, it is even in consistency without any pugging. While one does have to wait for the clay, production involves no heavy machinery and the actual production time of mixing and weighing is not much longer than that taken to operate machinery.

Mixing small amounts of clay body by hand from powdered material

Small amounts of body can be mixed by hand but the method described and illustrated here is best thought of as being mainly appropriate for test amounts. The method works least well with bodies which contain a high proportion of fine ball clays but works much better with bodies which have a high fireclay content. Because the entire body is not mixed up as a slip, thorough wetting of all particles is not achieved so the plasticity developed is less than that if the same bodies are mixed up as slips and dried out from that state. Bodies mixed by this method do improve with keeping but as part of the point is that usable bodies are produced quite quickly this is only of relevance if large rather than test amounts are mixed.

The principle of mixing bodies by this method is the same as when using a dough mixer, namely that any non-clay ingredients together with as much of the fine clay as will produce a sievable mixture are mixed with the measured amount of water and are sieved and then the remaining clay or clays are added, the clays of coarsest particle size being added last. Deciding exactly how much water to use is largely a matter of trial and error but the aim is to mix the body to a stiff but sticky consistency, firmer than a slurry, not kneadable immediately because this is unrealistic but with as little water as is consistent with reasonably good

mixing. As a rough guide 325 mls of water per kilogramme of dry ingredients is a starting point but some recipes will require less and those high in ball clays will need more.

To clarify the principles involved, the recipe for the body mixed in the sequence of illustrations which follow is

Fireclay (fine)	40
Ball clay	40
Quartz	12
China stone	8

Twelve kilogrammes of the body materials were mixed with 3.8 litres of water.

24 First, all china stone and quartz are added to the water then as much of the ball clay as seems right for the mix to be sievable. If the clay is added until it ceases to be dampened quickly by the water and rests on top in a small dry heap this is usually about right

24

26

25, 26, 27   Rather than pushing the dry powder down into the wet mass which makes pockets of dry material, which are slow to be incorporated, it is better to put one's hand under the dry materials and to spread these out across the surface where they quickly become wetted.

The mixture is then sieved. When the recipe includes non-clay raw materials, sieving should be through at least an 80 mesh sieve.

25

26

27

27

28

29

28 The remaining clay ingredients are then added to the sieved slip, in this case ball clay before fireclay. It is advantageous from this point onwards for the container to be one which is relatively wide in relation to its height

29 The powdered clays are then mixed into the slip by working round the container and repeatedly lifting the slip from the bottom of the container and pushing it down onto the powder. Care should be taken, as always, to avoid the creation of airborne dust

30 After a minute or so the mix becomes strongly resistant and is rather crumbly and it seems as though there may be too little water. Initially at least the temptation to add more water should be resisted and the action of lifting up and pushing down on the mixture should be continued

30

31 As the mixture becomes more homogenous it becomes less resistant to pressure and the sticky mass can be squeezed as well as lifted and pushed

32, 33 When it has become more workable, the hand can be drawn backwards and forwards through the mix which should be lifted and turned over a few times. The material adhering to the sides of the container should be scooped up and blended into the mix.

Spread out onto any clean surface the sticky body will dry to a kneadable consistency quite quickly. If placed on plaster of paris or biscuit drying slabs, it can be kneaded and used in as little as an hour.

Whenever the process is used it is important to use just the right amount of water and to follow the described sequence for the addition of materials and their sieving. The order of addition may be summarised as follows:

– non-clay raw materials (must always be sieved with the water and with as much fine clay as the recipe permits)

– ball clays (and bentonite) (as much as possible should be sieved as a slip)

– red powder clays (as much as possible should be sieved as a slip)

– china clays (as much as possible should be sieved as a slip)

– fire clays (last of the clays to be added)

– grog.

31

32

33

Machine mixing of clay bodies

Industrially, plastic bodies are produced by one of two main methods. They are either mixed from dry ingredients as slips in blungers and then brought back to a plastic state in filter presses which squeeze the water out of the clay body, or they are mixed from clays as dug, or in lump or powder form, in very heavy mills which roll, mix and crush the clays and other body materials during which water is added to bring the body to a suitably plastic condition. In this latter instance there is no excess water to be removed from the body. In both cases the final process is to extrude the clay through pug mills.

Heavy clay mixing machinery rarely exists outside the clay producing industry and though small clay plants - machines incorporating a blunger and a filter press - do exist they too are rare, though a few educational institutions do possess them.

Non-industrial potters who mix their own bodies tend to do so in dough mixers. These are quite substantial machines designed for mixing bread dough. They rarely have the power to mix bodies to anything much firmer than a soft plastic state but drying bodies from this state to a useable condition is not a major problem. When mixing bodies from powdered ingredients in a dough mixer any non-clay ingredient should first be mixed with water and sieved. Where recipes contain two or more different clays the finer clays should be added first. Very fine bodies are not easy to mix well in dough mixers because of the incomplete wetting of all clay particles. Partly for this reason dough mixed bodies benefit from being kept some while before they are used.

Bodies are relatively easy and quick to mix in slip form. The outdoor drying troughs and those situated over the flues of kilns are means more common with the larger scale units of the past and now tend only to be seen in southern countries of Europe. Removing water from a body slip is one of the major problems of producing bodies.

Other aspects of work with clays and clay bodies

The storage and ageing of clay bodies

Prepared clay bodies are best stored, either indoors or under cover in frost-free conditions, out of direct sunlight and well wrapped in polythene. While frost is an advantage in weathering raw clays prior to their use in bodies, plastic bodies should not be exposed to frost because this produces a fine network of cracks in the clay which are filled with ice and when the ice melts the clay needs considerable wedging and kneading or repugging to return it to its previous condition. Over a period of months, polythene bags and sheeting deteriorate in direct sunlight and in frost so prolonged storage should be indoors or well protected from the weather. If protected from the weather and well wrapped in polythene, clay bodies will remain in plastic condition more or less indefinitely.

The plasticity of all clay bodies improves the longer they are kept in plastic condition. A clay body which is freshly prepared is always less plastic than the same body if it has been well stored for a year. This process of improvement in storage is called *souring* or *ageing* and is due to both physical and chemical changes. Water gradually penetrates all the particles of the body more thoroughly - for this reason a dough mixed body will improve more in long term storage than a body prepared from a slip because initial wetting is so much more thorough in the latter case. Chemically the body changes from being slightly alkaline - from the various very slightly soluble 'insoluble' fluxes in the clay and other body materials - to being slightly acidic. This makes the clay particles cling together better. The change occurs because of minute organic growths in the body. The addition of vinegar to the water used to prepare clay bodies speeds up this change to a slightly acidic state. While it is true that all clay bodies improve with keeping there are limits, because the body gradually achieves its full potential plasticity and goes no further. No amount of ageing will make a short body really plastic but it will make it noticeably less short.

Work with found clays

Work with found, as opposed to bought, clay is most likely to be with some type of common clay except in a very few locations or unless some other type of clay has been specifically sought. Only very occasionally can a clay be used as dug, either alone or to blend with other clays.

If a blunger is available, dug clay can be converted to slip easily but if one is not, it is easier to let the clay dry out, break it up into smallish lumps and then add these to water to break the clay down to a slurry. This slurry is then stirred into a slip and the slip is sieved to remove unwanted material such as gravel, sand, and chalk nodules. The fineness of sieving necessary depends both on what is in the clay and what will be required of it. Of the various materials found in clays, sand may be an acceptable 'impurity' but chalk nodules, apart from indicating that the clay may have a high lime content, must be removed and indicate the need for fine sieving. The sieved clay slip has then to be dried out to a plastic state and the result is the found clay in refined form. Experiments then need to be conducted on the formability and fireability of the clay to see what additions it may need to alter and improve these qualities.

Without equipment the preparation of found clay for use in bodies is labour intensive and time consuming on anything other than an experimental scale.

Because comparatively far less is needed, the preparation of found clay for use in slips or glazes is a more realistic proposition. In both these cases the sieved slip of found clay should be dried out completely and crumbled for inclusion in a dry state when slips or glazes are mixed.

Grog
Grog is a very common ingredient of, or addition to, clay bodies. It is added to bodies to alter their plastic or their fired characteristics but though one effect may be more pronounced than the other it always affects both characteristics.

Grog is fired clay which has been crushed. Most frequently it is very high fired and is, therefore, totally or almost totally non-porous. Grog is graded by size and a range is readily available from gravel sized pieces to material graded as 200 to dust (which simply means that it all passes through a 200 mesh sieve). The physical texture of grog starts to become increasingly obvious if additions of grog larger than 60 mesh are made. At 30 mesh the grog gives the clay a fine granular texture and additions of 20 mesh grog and larger make the clay quite coarse. Two different ways of grading grog are used: in one a grading might for example be '20 to dust' which means all the grog passes through 20 mesh and includes superfine dust; in the other the grading might be '20 to 60'

which means all the grog is retained by a 60 mesh sieve and all has passed through a 20 mesh.

The commonest available grog is fireclay grog. Molochite is china clay grog and is used in white or light firing bodies when the inclusion of fireclay grog would detract from the whiteness of the body.

Grog is added to bodies to reduce overall shrinkage in drying and in firing both as an end in itself and as an aid to minimise warping. It also has the effect of speeding up drying time and making firing easier because the inclusion of non plastic material facilitates the passage of water through the body while the clay is drying and in the early stages of firing. Provided the grog is more refractory than the body (which is always the case with fireclay grog and molochite) grog is a way of increasing the refractoriness of bodies. And, though this last factor is related to previous ones, grog improves the stability of more extreme structures and forms both before and during firing.

The effect of grog in a body is dependent on the clay basis of the grog, as mentioned above, and on the sizes and amounts of grog included. The relative amounts of different sizes of grog are very relevant to the effect of the grog. For example, in three trials of adding 20% of grog to a clay body the effects of 20% 30 mesh to dust, of 20% 30 to 50 mesh and of 20% of dust grog are distinctly different on the plastic quality of the body.

For most normal purposes, grog additions range from around 10% to about 30%, though more is certainly entirely possible. Grog can be made from any clay or body.

Knowledge of grog and its uses dates from very ancient times and much, if not most, early pottery shows the presence of grog. In these contexts (and indeed in other much more recent contexts) the practice frequently seems to have been to incorporate grog of the same composition as the body, probably by crushing fired wasters. While this practice clearly does not alter the refractoriness of a body it does alter its forming qualities and, by opening it up, facilitates drying and the early stages of firing.

34 Grog can be added to clay bodies by kneading the clay into the edge of a mound of grog picking it up a little at a time. This is easiest to do if the body is in a somewhat soft plastic state and the grog is dry. In the short term grog can make the body a bit crumbly. This tendency is diminished if the wedging surface is kept slightly sticky with a damp sponge

Wedging and kneading

Wedging and kneading are the two hand processes by which clay bodies can be prepared to an even homogenous state. To some extent the two processes can be used independently but if both are used they are best seen as complementary; wedging being used first to bring the clay quickly to an even state, or at least to one in which such unevennesses as exist become evenly distributed throughout the mass, and kneading being used to bring the clay to a fully homogenous state.

Wedging and kneading both exert considerable strains on a table and therefore necessitate one of heavy construction which can withstand this use. The table surface should be smooth enough to allow perfect cleaning so that white clays are not contaminated but it should have slight porosity so

that the clay readily frees from it. Smooth non-porous surfaces, such as plastic laminate, though much favoured by officials concerned with Health and Safety, in fact make unsatisfactory surfaces for wedging and kneading but there are many surfaces which are satisfactory and are as easy to clean as plastic laminates. Fixed to a smooth backing surface and supported on a heavy structure, a heavy quality linoleum makes an excellent surface for clay preparation. Close grained wood and heavy slabs of marble or slate are also good. A concrete bench supported on brick walls is probably the ideal and a smoothly finished concrete top makes an excellent surface.

The height of a clay preparation surface should allow the palms of hands to rest flat on the surface. It is better to have a bench which is too high than one which is too low because low clay preparation surfaces lead to back ache or more serious back troubles and it is easy enough to stand on boards or a small platform to bring a high bench to a convenient working level.

Wedging

Wedging consists of vertically slicing a piece of clay into two, throwing one half down onto the other, lifting the mass up, turning it round and repeating this cycle a number of times. If the first wedging action is thought of as producing two layers, each action doubles the number of layers; ten such actions producing over a thousand layers and twenty over a million.

The sequence of photographs which follows shows a single wedging cycle.

35 The piece of clay is dropped gently onto the wedging surface, tilting it as it is dropped, so that the part nearest the edge of the surface is raised

36 A cutting wire is passed forwards under the raised half and pulled vertically upwards cutting the clay mass into two halves

37 The detached front half is then picked up loosely between both hands and as it is raised into the air it is pivoted through 180 degrees

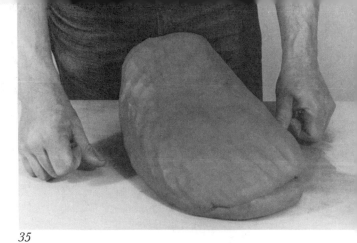

35

36

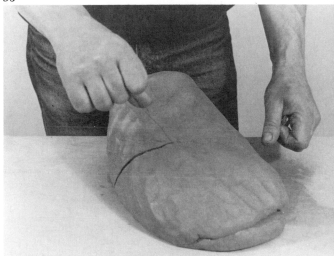

37

38

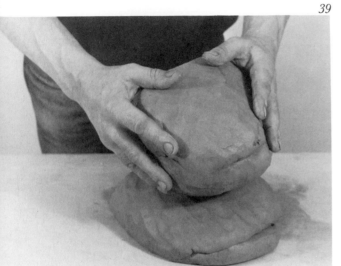

39

38, 39 Top side meeting top side and cut faces in the same plane, the detached half is then forcibly thrown downwards onto the other half

40 This action of throwing the detached half downwards should be strong enough to spread the clay mass leaving it about the same thickness as it was before it was cut

40

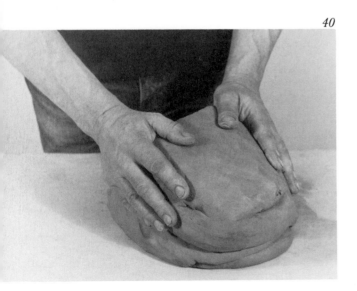

41   For the first few cycles the work can simply be cutting and rejoining but when quite a few cycles have been completed the mass should be tapped at this stage in each cycle to close up the edges

42   The tapped mass is then lifted up, turned horizontally, anti-clockwise in this case, through 90 degrees and dropped back onto the wedging surface with its front end tilted into the air

43   The raised front half is then again detached and the cycle repeated.

Fifteen to twenty cycles of this action make clay which is fairly even, very even.

Wedging is a quick method of mixing two different bodies together and of mixing over firm clay with softer clay to achieve a workable consistency. The slower, more complex, spreading and mixing which occurs in kneading results in a more completely homogenous body but for very many purposes wedged clay is ready for use.

There are other variations of wedging which differ in detail from the cycle described and which are just as effective. The essence of the process is the mixing achieved by the repeated layering and spreading of the clay mass.

41

42

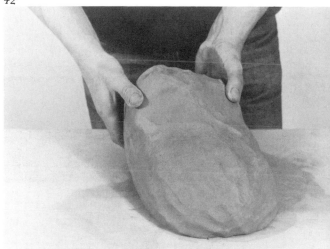

43

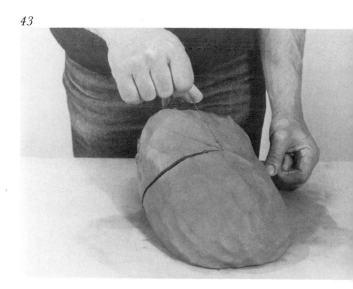

Kneading

For some making processes with some bodies, particularly with more open grogged bodies, kneading is unnecessary, wedging being a perfectly adequate way of achieving sufficient evenness. Where the maximum plasticity is required, especially with plastic and fire clay bodies, kneading imparts the greatest evenness and homogeneity.

Kneading is a skill which some people learn almost instantly but others find frustratingly difficult to acquire. It is a steady rhythmic action and whether it is learnt quickly or frustratingly slowly it is a knack which is acquired from one moment to the next.

Several variations of kneading are possible. The method described is called *spiral kneading*. Spiral kneading can be done by transferring the body weight to the clay through the right or the left arm. The right handed sequence is shown. While any description of kneading necessarily concentrates on what is done with the hands and what happens to the clay, it must be emphasised that kneading is more to do with the controlled application of body weight through the arms than with sheer muscle power. Stance is therefore important and must enable weight to be transferred to the arms when the clay is rolled forward and pressed down and then transferred back to the legs when the clay is being lifted and rolled back to the starting position.

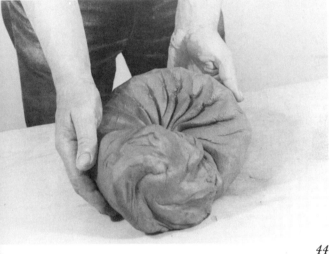

44

45

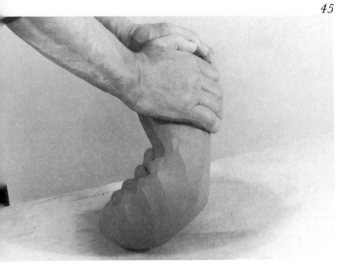

44 The action of kneading imparts a shell-like form to the piece of clay. The near end in this illustration is where the weight is applied. This part is slightly and repeatedly rolled down onto the right hand end which simply revolves steadily clockwise taking the imprint of the edge of each action round until the clay comes round again to the part on which work is actively done. Because force is only applied to part of the mass in any one action it is possible to knead large pieces of clay

45 The action starts with the clay mass raised up, resting on the middle of the ridged rounded part. The right wrist is above the point where the spiral roll of clay meets the rounded ridged part of the clay. The left hand rests on the front spiral of clay as seen in the previous illustration

46, 47   The left hand merely steadies the clay while weight is applied to the clay through the right arm which firmly presses a ridge of clay downwards. The right wrist remains rigid throughout this action of applying downward pressure

48   At the end of the action the spiral of clay is pressed between the kneading surface and the downward application of body weight through the right arm. This pressure lifts the rounded ridged part of the clay up off the kneading surface

From the point of view of spreading and mixing the clay the kneading action is complete at this point and all that remains is to reposition the clay and the hands in readiness for the next kneading movement.

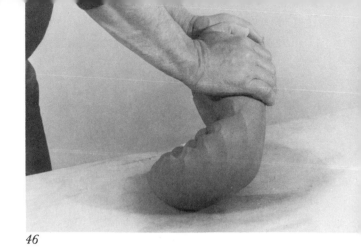

46

47

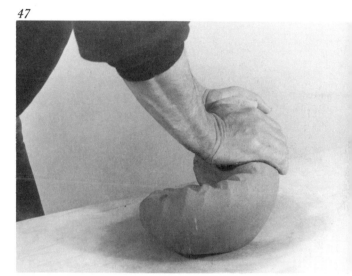

48

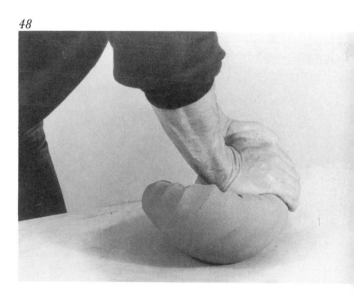

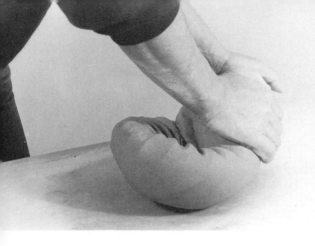

49

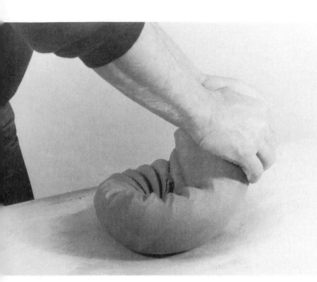

51

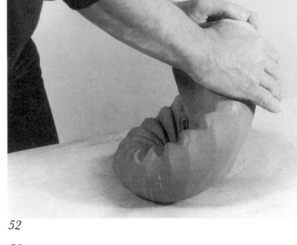

52

53

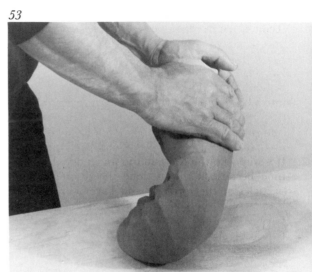

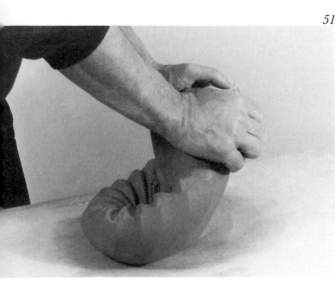

49, 50, 51 As soon as the downward action is complete, the palm of the right hand is raised away from the clay and the right hand finger ends lightly grip the clay so that the palm can be moved further round the spiral roll to be on top of it for the next downward action. The slight containing hold of the left hand is lessened while the right hand moves round the clay roll and the end of the roll rotates in the left palm

52 With the clay almost back to its original position, the left hand resumes its slight containing pressure and, with the right palm now in position, the right fingers extend forwards so that the whole hand is in contact with the clay surface

53 With a continuation of the rolling lift, the clay is back to its original position and a new cycle begins

When a rather uneven mass of clay has to be kneaded it is quicker and more effective if the clay is wedged before it is kneaded.

The reclamation of clay bodies

Clay may need reclaiming for a variety of reasons. Most making processes produce small amounts of clay which are too dry or too wet to use and need reclaiming, and from time to time dry work is accidentally broken or, for some other reason, is not fired. In a small workshop or studio, clay reclamation is straightforward but where many people work together and where half-a-dozen clay bodies are in use, as in many schools, clay reclamation needs to be well organised.

Reclaiming from a dry state

Dry clay forms which are to be reclaimed are, depending on the quantities involved, simply put into a bowl, bucket or bin containing water where they break down to a slurry. In breaking down to a slurry the pieces of clay slowly disintegrate and the particles drop to the bottom of the container. It is important not to add too much dry clay at a time because if this is done the disintegrating particles at the top sink and cover clay at the bottom which may not be fully disintegrated and inhibit the wetting down of this clay. This is especially the case with fine plastic clays. Provided it is not added too quickly, clay can be added until the container is full. When the clay is to be reclaimed, water is poured off the top and the slurry is then reclaimed. The stiffer the slurry the easier it is to reclaim and, for this reason, such reclaim containers should not be stirred as this tends to thin the slurry into a slip. Only when as much water as possible has been decanted should the slurry be stirred.

Reclaiming from a slurry state

Various alternatives exist for drying out slurry to a plastic state but if large quantities are involved most require a fair amount of horizontal space. Drying on plaster of paris slabs is probably the commonest method. The slabs should be 6 to 7 cm thick and of a length and width which enables them to be portable. Plaster, of course, has the problem that, if handled carelessly, chippped fragments can cause contamination of the clay but provided care is taken this should not be a problem. To minimise the problem, all edges should be rounded to minimise the risk of chipping. Dry plaster slabs of 6 to 7 cm have the capacity to stiffen up a 6 to 7 cm layer of slurry. Once the lower layer of slurry in contact with the plaster has stiffened and can be peeled cleanly off the plaster, the whole layer should be turned over to stiffen the soft upper layer. Dry plaster has a very ready power of water absorption but its life is considerably shortened if it remains in a damp condition for long periods, so each time a batch of slurry has been dried the plaster slab should itself be put to dry before it is reused. This both prolongs the life of the plaster slab and makes the drying period of batches of slurry shorter. Gentle heat is not detrimental to plaster but subjecting it to too strong a heat will break it down very quickly.

Porous low fired clay slabs are an alternative to plaster for the drying of slurry. The capacity of these depends, obviously, on their porosity and thickness. A 3 cm biscuit slab of ready porosity has the capacity to stiffen up a 5 cm layer of slurry. Fired clay slabs can be placed side by side to make up the larger area of a single plaster slab. Though biscuit slabs have the advantages that they are virtually everlasting, are not damaged by heat and can therefore be dried out fast and cannot lead to contamination, they are much less commonly used than plaster slabs.

Where plaster or biscuit slabs are used on a wooden bench these should be raised off the bench on wooden battens otherwise dampness can have a detrimental effect on the bench.

Weldmesh and textile drying containers of the type shown, with the preparation of bodies in a slip state, can also be used with slurry. Similarly, slurry can be spread out on canvas placed on a horizontal sheet of weldmesh. In this instance the weldmesh sheet should be supported on stout lengths of wood of about 10 cm × 5 cm, the 10 cm dimension being vertical to allow adequate air circulation.

In contexts where a large amount of slurry has to be reclaimed, heated slurry drying troughs are probably the best alternative. These consist of retaining walls and a hollow base of fireclay slabs supported on brick piers. The heaters, usually gas, play on the underneath of the fireclay slabs. Such troughs have to be carefully managed and it is important that the heat is not excessive otherwise the slurry dries right out where it is in contact with the fireclay slabs and the resulting body is effectively ruined with scraps of dry clay.

Reclaiming from a leatherhard state

On a small scale this can be done without reducing the clay to a slurry state. The pieces should be no more than 12 × 12 cm and should not be thicker than 1.5 cm. They should be sprinkled liberally with water and placed in a bowl covered with a really damp cloth which should be kept damp. The clay should be inspected from time to time to see if it has softened sufficiently or if it needs more water. As soon as it is sufficiently softened it is wedged or kneaded. Clays with grog or a low plastic clay content soften very quickly by this method but fine, very plastic clays are best left overnight.

Large lumps of firm leatherhard clay are the worst problem of all. Of course, with care they should never occur but occasionally a split bag goes unnoticed and its contents become far too hard to use or to cut up into reclaimable slices. Most certainly largish lumps of leatherhard clay should never be put into bins of slurry because immersed in slurry their condition changes only very, very slowly and they make subsequent homogenous reclamation of the slurry difficult, if not impossible. When large really firm lumps do occur it is probably best to let them dry right out and then smash them up into smaller lumps and break them down in water.

54 Clay in any condition between sticky soft and kneadable can be dried to a firmer condition by forming it into a large roll and standing this up in an arched shape on a board. With a large surface area exposed to the air like this, clay will firm up very quickly either indoors or, when weather permits, outside. Outside a strong wind has a remarkably fast drying effect and in such conditions clay should be frequently inspected to ensure it does not become too dry.

54

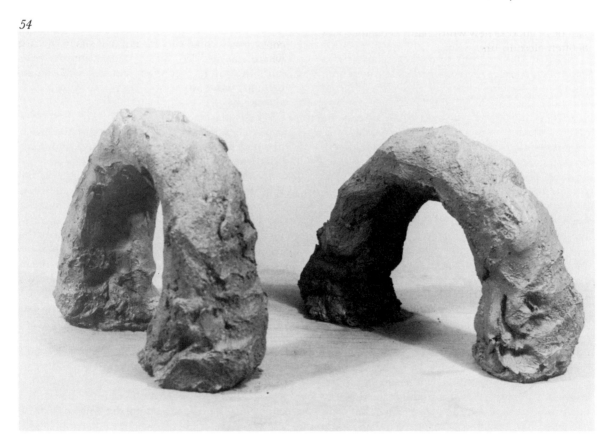

Some general points on the reclamation of clay bodies
On a small scale it is clearly advantageous to reclaim individual bodies separately. In contexts where many people work, and where several bodies are used, the space and time for separate reclamation is rarely available so it is usual to reclaim the various bodies in broad types such as ungrogged red earthenware, grogged earthenware, fireclay based stoneware, ball clay based stoneware and so on. In such contexts it is vital that all who use the workshop understand the system. When several different bodies are reclaimed together as a single body the eventual body will be better if after excess water has been decanted the slurry is very thoroughly stirred. A good slurry bin is not disturbed until it is emptied and thus when it includes several bodies, contains pockets and levels of slurry of different clays. If the slurry is not mixed well, drying either on a porous or a heated surface may affect the different bodies very differently, leading to soft and hard pockets in the reclaimed mixture.

With care and consideration reclaimed clay can be as good as new whilst badly reclaimed clay is often close to unusable.

Contamination of clay bodies with plaster of paris (or other lime based impurities)
Lime of fine particle size is frequently present in clay bodies. It may be present naturally, as in some common clays, or it may be introduced. Fine lime behaves as a flux in bodies and its presence is not considered as contamination. The presence of any lime material in other than a very fine state does, however, constitute a serious problem in clay bodies.

When nodules of lime contaminate a clay body the heat of the firing converts the lime into quicklime. Quicklime very readily absorbs moisture (in this context it does so through the clay from the atmosphere) and in doing so increases considerably in volume. This causes a piece of clay to be pushed out of the clay surface. The craters which can be made by nodules of lime vary from tiny to quite large and depend both on the size of the nodules and their depth below the surface.

It is highly unlikely that lime nodules occur in bought bodies but in workshops chipped plaster of paris moulds or drying slabs can all too easily contaminate bodies. This is particularly the case where clay is dried out or kneaded on plaster of paris slabs and, where these are used, they should be used with care.

41

SECTION TWO

FIRING

It is perfectly possible to buy and successfully operate a kiln with very little knowledge or understanding of the principles of firing or the very varied nature of kilns. Firing a kiln is operating an item of equipment and it is most important to know what works with given materials at certain temperatures. A knowledge and understanding of principles is, however, a great help when practical problems occur but the breadth of the diversity of kilns, clays and glaze materials is such that an aura of mystique frequently surrounds the subject of kilns and firing, especially firing with flame kilns.

This aura of mystique is such that firing is not infrequently expected to endow a pot with qualities its maker has omitted. Some things, it is true, can only occur during firing and cannot be controlled in detail – the extent to which slip or underglaze pigments bleed into a glaze; the fly ash deposits on pots in a stoneware wood firing; the marks of uneven reduction and oxidisation in unglazed brushwood, bonfire or sawdust firings are all examples of effects which may be intended but which cannot be controlled in fine detail. It should be remembered that every fired product is only the result of what is done to it *before* the firing and what occurs *during* the firing. The distinction between a good and a bad firing is not one of divine intervention but is one of the effectiveness of control.

The precise final qualities which any ceramic materials have are dependent on the nature of the firing to which they are subjected. Three major identifiable aspects of this are the rate of temperature rise, the final temperature achieved and the atmosphere of the firing in its different stages.

If knowledge is to be acquired it is risky to rely on memory so careful logs of firings should be kept. Logs should include records of rate of temperature rise, atmosphere at different stages, temperature reached and results. Such records help to dispel unhelpful attitudes of mystique.

The rate of temperature rise

Any kiln is simply a refractory insulated structure into which heat can be introduced either by the combustion of some sort of fuel or by electric elements. Both modern and older types of kilns having the capacity to reach the high temperatures necessary also inevitably have the capacity at low temperatures to increase heat extremely fast, far faster than may be good in the initial stages of many types of firing. The modern use of ceramic fibre, both as a hot face or a back-up insulation material, and of low thermal mass bricks, has made kilns more efficient than was previously the case and such kilns if turned on full, or nearly so, can rise in temperature extremely fast. The first aspect, therefore, is to learn how to operate the kiln so that the temperature rises at the intended rate throughout the firing.

Modern technology makes control easier than it once was. Electric, gas and oil kilns can be fitted with automatic controllers which by various devices permit the selection of different firing schedules which can be designed to be appropriate for the differing needs of different types of firings. Electric kilns without automatic controllers are always fitted with some simple type of controller which permits the heat input to be set at any point between very low and full. The control which can be exercised over gas and oil kilns without automatic controllers depends on the sophistication of the burners. The control of solid fuel kilns depends entirely on the care, skill and experience of the person responsible for the firing.

43

The rate of temperature loss after a kiln has risen to the required temperature is rarely given much consideration. In fact, with very few and rather specialised exceptions, there is little to consider until the kiln is relatively cool. Initially kilns cool down quite fast from the point when firing is finished but as they get cooler the rate of cooling slows down. It is crucial to avoid subjecting the cooling objects to sudden cooling air around 200°C. This is important because cristobalite, a crystalline form of silica present in all clay bodies, undergoes a sudden shrinkage at 220°C. Rushed or uneven cooling at this temperature creates sudden or slight uneven contractions which cause the body to crack. Plates and flat objects are particularly prone to this if a kiln door is left open before the kiln is cool enough. This is partly because they are in close contact with kiln shelves which retain heat longer than the air around them. In practice top vents or spy holes can safely be left open to speed up the cooling of kilns and after 200°C doors can be progressively eased open. The worst thing to do, worse even than removing items from the kiln, which subjects them to sudden rather than uneven cooling, is to leave a kiln door wide open when the objects are still much too hot. This subjects them to uneven cooling.

Ceramic fibre kilns, having a far less mass than brick kilns, gain temperature faster and cool down to cold much faster than brick kilns.

The rate of temperature rise: biscuit firing
It is vital to understand that the initial stages of firing are the final stage of drying. Heat must be applied gradually until the very last of the moisture has been driven out. In practice this means that kiln temperature should rise very gradually to, or just above, 100°C. Water, in the form of steam, not air bubbles as is the common fallacy, is the cause of clay shattering into small pieces in a biscuit firing.

What occurs as the 'dry' clay is progressively heated is that any water which is present emerges from the clay surface as steam, leaving the kiln through the vents of electric kilns or with the burnt gases in flame kilns. The water, as steam, continues to travel to the clay surface and to leave it, until all the water has been expelled from the clay. If the temperature rises too fast a pressure of steam builds up in the clay to a point where it shatters. The clay continues to explode into fragments until these are small enough for the steam to escape.

Obviously objects with thick walls need to be fired more carefully than thin objects as the steam from the middle of the walls has further to travel. Fine textured bodies based on ball or common clays need more care than bodies which have a more open texture because the ultra-fine particles present a more formidable barrier to the escape of steam. In this respect it is the ultra-fine particle size of the clay in the body which is important not its apparent smoothness – porcelain, for example, though smooth to the touch is rarely a problem in biscuit firing for the china clay in it has relatively coarse particle size and it and the non-clay ingredients of the body present little obstacle to the escape of steam.

Flame kilns need especially careful management in the initial stage of biscuit firing because it is surprisingly easy to exceed 100°C by considerable margins extremely quickly even in a large kiln, either locally at the top or throughout the kiln.

From the start of a biscuit firing in an electric kiln, the kiln vents or spy holes, if it has no vents, should be open and the same is true of most flame kilns.

The time taken to warm most clay bodies from cold to safely past the 100°C point should not be less than about two hours. If the objects are very thick, the clay very fine, or if there is any suspicion of dampness, a longer time spent on this phase would not be excessive. The temperature should be allowed to continue to rise at about the same rate for another two hours or so, and after this a temperature rise of between 100°C and 150°C an hour is reasonable.

Kiln vents are usually put in and spy holes closed when the kiln begins to show a dull red heat.

The next point when control of the kiln is important and when the rate of temperature rise may have to be slowed down is between about 850°C to 900°C, and for 100°C above this, though the importance of this varies from clay to clay. This is the temperature at which most carbonaceous material is being burned away. Within this span of temperature the rate of climb should be slowed down to well under 100°C per hour and the kiln should be vented so that all necessary combustion can occur in a clean oxidising atmosphere. Failure to do this may lead to a condition called *black core* in some low maturing red eathenware bodies and can be a cause of bloating in stoneware clays. These precautions are, however, largely unnecessary with porcelain and very white firing bodies which are very open and porous at this temperature and present little impediment to the escape of gases.

When this phase is complete the firing can proceed faster to the intended temperature.

What occurs when the intended temperature has been reached depends upon whether a subsequent glaze firing will be higher or lower than the biscuit. The two practices, therefore, need brief explanation.

Where a biscuit firing is lower than a subsequent glaze firing – often termed 'low biscuit' – the body is fired to a higher temperature in the glaze firing and body and glaze mature simultaneously. This may occur both in the earthenware and the stoneware temperature ranges. The aim of the biscuit firing, as far as the clay body is concerned, in this practice is that it is fired to a point when it is strong and can be glazed using the ready porosity of the clay. Practices vary but such 'low biscuit' firings might be anywhere in the temperature range from 900°C to 1040°C depending on, for example, the clay body concerned, economics, or just preference. When a 'low biscuit' firing reaches temperature the firing is finished and the kiln is allowed to cool.

Where a biscuit firing is higher than a subsequent glaze firing – often termed *high biscuit* – the highest firing the body has is its biscuit. The temperature of this may be anything from a little over 1100°C to over 1260°C depending on the body concerned. The aim of this practice, which is far commoner inside than outside the industry, is to develop full maturity in the body in the biscuit firing. This allows pieces to be supported by various means to minimise distortion losses. The subsequent glaze firing is usually at least 100°C lower than the biscuit so the second firing subjects the body to no risk of distortion and solely occurs to fire the glaze. When a 'high biscuit' firing reaches the required temperature the firing is continued without further rise or loss in temperature. This period of holding temperature is called *soaking* and permits the fluxes in the body to act to mature it more fully. All ceramic fusions are dependent to some extent on time as well as temperature. A soaking period at top temperature usually lasts from half an hour to two hours. When the soak has finished the firing is allowed to cool.

Rate of temperature rise: raw glaze firing
Fuller mention of the practice of raw glazing is made in the section on glaze. As far as firing is concerned, because body and glaze are matured together in a single firing which combines biscuit and glaze firing, all the precautions mentioned in relation to biscuit firing need to be observed.

It is particularly important that all bodies which are not very pale firing are fired slowly in a well-vented kiln around a temperature of 850°C to give all combustibles in the body adequate opportunity to burn away. With darker firing bodies, failure to do this can result in uneven body colour under the glaze in earthenware and bloating in stoneware bodies.

Thorough soaking should also be done to give both body and glaze full opportunity to mature.

Rate of temperature rise: glaze firing
In the firing of glaze applied to biscuit fired clay bodies it might seem that there are no precautions to observe about the rate of temperature rise because the problems of body moisture and combustibles have both been dealt with in the biscuit firing. To some extent this is true and many glaze firings occur fast without ill effects. Three factors do, however, need to be mentioned:

Firstly, if a firing contains vitrified or nearly vitrified biscuit, especially if the objects are thick, initial heating should not be rushed so that any moisture which has seeped into the body has time to escape. Secondly, if fired glazed pieces with nearly vitrified clay bodies are re-glazed these should be thoroughly and slowly dried by warming before they are fired. In this second instance the fired glaze presents a very formidable barrier to the escape of any moisture which may have seeped into the body through crazing or unglazed parts. In either of these instances, though more commonly with the latter, failure to dry out the object before it is fired can lead to cracking or even explosion. Apparently vitrified stoneware, if it has taken in moisture and is re-fired too fast, can explode like damp clay in a biscuit firing. Thirdly, and rather differently, biscuit which has been very low fired or imperfectly oxidised in its biscuit firing should be slowly fired at around 850°C in thoroughly oxidising conditions to allow combustibles left in the body to be released before glazes begin to flux.

Glaze firing should begin gradually but need not be as slow as biscuit firing, apart from where the exceptions mentioned above apply. Two hours from starting the firing to the temperature beginning to rise fast is adequately slow. In this period kiln vents or spy holes should be open to allow moisture from the glazes to escape but once a piece of glass held 5 to 7 cm from the vent or spy hole shows no moisture condensation then the vents or spy holes can be closed. If the kiln is capable of it there is nothing against a temperature rise of 200°C an hour. When the firing is within 40°C to 30°C of the intended temperature the rate of firing should slow down, these last few degrees taking an hour or so. When the intended temperature is reached it should be held for a soak of at least half an hour. Both holding the kiln at top temperature and a slow approach to this gives the glaze materials time to fuse fully. The soaking of high fired stoneware glazes is fairly common practice but earthenware glazes, though rarely soaked in this way, benefit equally from the practice.

Some people, especially those who fire to high temperatures, advocate the 'crash' cooling of glaze firing. This is more achievable with flame than with electric kilns but in all cases depends on the design of the kiln. With some flame kilns firebox entrances can be left open and vents and spy hole bricks removed creating a substantial through current of cooling air. By this means it is possible to cool a kiln from say 1280°C to say 1000°C in less than an hour. 'Crash' cooling can be quite a spectacle but there are some uncertainties about what exactly it achieves. One thing is certain though and this is that crystals need time to form in a molten glaze. 'Crash' cooling, in changing glazes very fast from a molten to a solid state almost totally removes the opportunity for crystal formation and if glazes which have been crash cooled have greater brightness and clarity of colour this is the reason for it.

Setting aside the practice of 'crash' cooling, the normal procedure when a glaze firing has finished is to leave vents and top spy holes open and to let the kiln cool to below 200°C when the door is progressively opened. The precautions mention-ed earlier about cooling draughts are just as relevant with glazed work as with biscuit. The sudden shrinkage of cristobalite occurs every time it is cooled down from over 200°C to normal temperatures.

Some crystalline glazes require a very slow cooling cycle near top temperature keeping the glaze in the molten state for a long period. The only way of diminishing the normally sudden initial cooling, which occurs when a firing finishes, is to continue to fire but at less than full power.

As with biscuit firing, cracks which occur in a glaze firing, as the temperature rises usually open up and distort, while those formed in cooling are fine, hairline cracks with perhaps a bit of spring but with little distortion. In glaze firings, cooling cracks can always be readily distinguished from heating cracks because the glaze on the edge of a cooling crack is sharply fractured while that on the edge of a heating crack is rounded to the edge of the crack.

The rate of temperature rise: on-glaze enamel and lustre firing

These materials are applied to a fired glazed surface using as media oils of greater or lesser viscosity. Enamels are often applied as transfers in which colour and its covercoat are attached to the ware. The initial concern in enamel or lustre firings is to burn off any media or covercoat relatively gradually. While this is occurring, the kiln vents and top spy holes should be open and the temperature should be rising steadily but gradually. A period of about three hours to reach 250°C at an even rate of temperature increase would be a normal schedule. Fumes from the media are unpleasant and should be fan extracted from above the kiln. Normally about three hours is sufficient to burn off the media and covercoat but if fumes are still emerging from the kiln the rate of firing should continue unchanged. When all fumes have gone the speed can be increased until the kiln is on full power. An efficient kiln will reach lustre temperature (and enamel) very quickly once it is on full so, unless the kiln has some sort of automatic cut-out, it should be carefully watched.

If lustre or enamel is fired too quickly in the initial stages of the firing the adhesion of the colour can be affected but, apart from this, there are no special precautions about the rate of firing.

As in all firings normal precautions should be observed during the cooling cycle.

Temperature of firing and temperature measurement

The achievement of intended temperature is of fundamental importance in producing ceramic both of technical soundness and of particular visual quality.

Some materials require firing to precise temperature, to within say 5°C of a defined temperature. to acquire a particular quality, while others may be of more or less consistent quality within a temperature range of say 15°C above or below a defined temperature. In many instances, therefore, the concept of under- or over-firing only has real meaning in relation to a defined result at a particular temperature. Ultimately though it is unwise to isolate the idea of temperature achieved from the rate of temperature rise because it is the heatwork done – the relationship of time and temperature – not simply temperature, which is important. It is important that a given temperature is reached but it is as important that it is reached and held, or reached slowly in the final stages, to give the reactions time to occur fully.

From time to time slight or serious under- or over-firing may occur.

Serious under-firing of clay bodies is evidenced by bodies which are soft and very liable to break – in serious cases the clay can be snapped in the fingers – such bodies when tapped with a finger lack any resonance. Slight under-firing is less easily detected and may be acceptable if the objects are not intended for demanding use – slight under-firing of clay bodies to eliminate the possibility of firing distortion is a relatively common practice. Slight over-firing of bodies is scientifically measurable in increased brittleness and loss of strength but may not be otherwise detectable. Serious over-firing of bodies is often accompanied by slumping of forms as the clay softens, though this may be due to other causes, and by bubbling and bloating within the clay. At certain temperatures – as low as 1150°C for some earthenware clay bodies and well above 1600°C for refractory clays – all clays will slump, melt and flow. Visually, virtually all clay bodies become darker the higher they are fired. Most clay bodies have a wider temperature span than most other ceramic materials in which they develop acceptable qualities but where translucency is intended in bodies the firing temperature is at its most critical.

Serious under-firing in glazes is evidenced by a completely unfluxed glaze layer which is matt and scratchable. Slight under-firing is evidenced by dullness of surface and a lack of depth but this can relate to inadequate soaking as well as inadequate temperature. Slight over-firing of glaze is evidenced by a glassy surface and some tendency to run. Serious over-firing of glaze usually makes it run off the form and may be accompanied by bubbling and uneven, very glassy surfaces. As serious over-firing of glaze is often accompanied by over-firing of the body the symptoms can become confused and confusing.

Temperature measurement is achieved either by the use of pyrometers or cones or bars. Pyrometers measure actual temperature and their use should be related to established, carefully recorded firing schedules. Cones and bars measure heatwork done and, as such, are preferable where schedules vary.

Cones and *bars* consist of a range of precisely formulated mixtures of ceramic materials. Each mixture is given a code number and is designed to soften and bend when heatwork at a particular temperature has occurred. In use, cones or bars are placed so they can be seen through spy holes. Cones are placed vertically and bars are supported at each end and placed horizontally.

Pyrometers consist of a thermocouple and an indicator. The thermocouple projects into the kiln chamber through a hole in the wall and is connected by cable to the indicator on which the temperature can be read. Two types of indicator exist: on one a needle records the temperature on a calibrated scale; on the other there is instant digital read out. The digital read out type has the immense advantage of rises and falls in temperature being immediately recorded.

Both cones and pyrometers have their advocates but ideally they should be seen as complementary. Pyrometers are an invaluable aid to knowing and recording the rate of temperature rise and to maintaining temperature without rise or fall. Firing to a certain cone is, however, a surer indication that known glazes will be fully fluxed.

In practice, where cones alone are used, there should be three. The first should be one or two cone numbers lower than the intended firing and is used to indicate that the temperature rise can be slowed down. The second is the cone for the intended temperature. The third, one cone number above the second, should remain standing, indicating that the intended temperature has not been exceeded.

It is wise to use a particular brand of cone consistently. The fact is not that some brands are more reliable than others but that they do behave differently. For this reason it is useful to record the cone number and brand with glaze recipes as well as the presumed temperature.

Using well designed kilns it should be possible to regulate temperature in such a way that it is even throughout the kiln. With large kilns it is as well to remember that unevenness is possible and that a pyrometer at one point or cones at one spy hole are only indicating what is occurring in that part of the kiln. Where two spy holes exist they should be used at the very least for a visual check on the colour temperature to ensure that top and bottom are the same but it is by no means wasteful to put cones at each spy hole, at least until the behaviour of the kiln is known. Unevenness within kilns is a frequent cause of under- or over-firing and where kilns cannot be evenly fired it is normal to pack the kiln with a mixture of glazes and/or clay bodies which require marginally different temperatures in order to accommodate the unevenness of the kiln.

Atmosphere of firing

It is a common mistake to imagine that atmosphere of firing is only the concern of those who intend reduction and that it is only a concern relevant to flame kilns.

In fact, atmosphere is an important aspect of all firings. In many firings nothing may need to be done about the kiln atmosphere. Where atmosphere is inappropriate it can lead to technical and visual problems.

There is nothing mysterious about kiln atmosphere once one realises it can be observed simply by looking into a kiln. Anyone who has considerable experience of firing kilns will assess atmosphere as quickly as they assess the temperature colour of a kiln. Observing what occurs in a kiln during firing is the quickest way of acquiring knowledge and confidence.

The possible states of atmosphere in kilns are oxidising, neutral and reducing. In an *oxidising atmosphere* unburnt oxygen is available in the kiln chamber. In a *neutral atmosphere* neither oxygen nor unburnt or incompletely burnt carbon are present. In a *reducing atmosphere* unburnt or partially burnt carbon is present and, as there is no available oxygen, the oxygen-hungry carbon seeks out oxygen from those oxides in the clay or glaze which are capable of giving up oxygen.

Two colouring oxides are capable of giving up oxygen in reducing conditions. Ferric iron oxide, Fe_2O_3, is reduced to ferrous iron oxide, FeO. Cupric copper oxide, CuO, is reduced to cuprous copper oxide, Cu_2O. In both these reactions the ratio of oxygen to metal is reduced – hence the name. In the case of iron the ratio reduces from 3:2 oxygen to metal to 1:1 and in the case of copper from 1:1 oxygen to metal to 1:2. Both these changes involve a colour change and both are reversible, unless the glaze containing the oxide fluxes or the clay containing it vitrifies while the oxide is in a reduced state. Though the change of colour which occurs with copper is more dramatic, from green to a pinky red in glazes, the change involved in iron reduction, from tans and browns to pale grey-greens and grey-blues, is the more important because iron oxide is present in virtually all ceramic materials at least as a trace of impurity. These minute amounts of iron make the difference between the yellow-white of oxidised porcelain and the blue-white of reduced porcelain. A further point of importance, particularly with stoneware and porcelain, is that reduced iron oxide is a stronger flux than oxidised iron oxide.

In flame kilns, reduction can be created by reducing the air available for combustion to the point where no free oxygen is available in the kiln chamber. This can usually be done without creating continuous black smoke which is usually a sign that reduction is excessive. Exessive reduction may lead to the trapping of carbon in glazes and is always a waste of fuel (the intermittent black smoke which with some solid fuel kilns coincides with stoking is not necessarily a sign that the prevalent atmosphere in the chamber is reducing). When viewed through a spy hole, a reduction atmosphere has a foggy quality quite different from the clear brightness of an oxidising atmosphere.

In electric kilns and muffle kilns reduction can be induced by introducing combustible material in some convenient form – thin slivers of wood or moth balls, for example – into the kiln chamber through a spy hole so that it falls into a space left beneath the spy hole. Very little material is needed as it only has to burn away the oxygen in the chamber but it needs to be introduced at intervals over a period to ensure complete reduction and to prevent reoxidisation by oxygen slowly penetrating back into the chamber through spy holes and cracks in the brickwork. Reduction will reduce the life of Kanthal element wire but has no effect on silicon carbide elements, kilns fitted with these latter are often also fitted with small gas burners to effect reduction.

Ironically it is at least as easy to ensure a clean oxidising atmosphere in a flame kiln as in an electric kiln. In flame kilns oxidisation can be readily created by regulating the ratio of fuel to air to ensure an adequate air supply for combustion. Viewed through the spy hole the kiln chamber is clear and bright and vision across the kiln is unimpeded when oxidising conditions exist.

Many electric kilns are so well made that they are nearly airtight. Such kilns have a neutral rather than an oxidising atmosphere and, as most clay bodies contain combustible material, the atmosphere can become somewhat foggy if vents or spy holes are not left open while this combustion is occurring. Failure to ventilate electric kilns frequently leads to black core in low firing red bodies and can lead to bloating in oxidised stoneware bodies.

Exactly when reducing or oxidising conditions are necessary depends on the exact context in question. To be reduced *effectively* bodies must be reduced before they vitrify, throughout their thickness while vitrification sets in. Reduction itself hastens vitrification because of the stronger fluxing power of reduced iron oxide, so timing is crucial. Timing is also important because bodies intended for reduction must be reduced before the glazes flux otherwise the melted glaze presents a barrier which the changed atmosphere cannot penetrate. For their own oxides to be reduced, glazes themselves must be reduced before they flux.

The need to establish reduction at appropriate times when this is intended is clear. It is as well to remember also that some ceramic is adversely affected if an atmosphere is not cleanly oxidising when it should be.

Black core

Black core is a condition which occurs mainly in clay bodies based on common red firing clays especially if these are highly plastic, fine textured and ungrogged. In mild cases the condition does not obviously affect objects and may only be evident if an object is broken when a thin seam of blackness will be seen in the wall sandwiched between outer layers of normal terracotta colour. In serious cases the object can distort badly, the clay wall swelling to several times its original thickness. The condition can in fact occur in any body. In paler bodies the core of the wall is greyish rather than black but it is very rare that it occurs in bodies which are not red firing. The condition is caused by overfast or underventilated firings which give the gases generated by all clay bodies inadequate time to escape through the clay before the clay body begins to mature. As the clay body becomes less porous it becomes more difficult for these gases to escape. These gases create reducing conditions in the core of the clay wall and, in bodies high in iron, this reduction vitrifies the clay turning it black – hence the name.

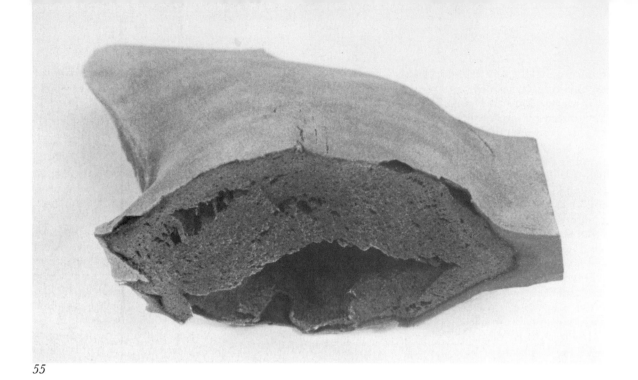

55 This illustration is of an extreme case of black core where the clay wall has swelled to several times its original thickness. The clay body is the same North Devon body shown in colour plate 1(b). The body in fact is an excellent one at temperature up to 1080°C or slightly higher. The example shown was only fired to 1040°C, but the particular biscuit firing was done with the ventilation brick in from 200°C onwards, was very tightly packed and was very fast between 750°C and 1040°C. In fact, in this example black core has become bloating on a grand scale

Generally the condition of black core can be avoided by slower firing particularly in the temperature range 800°C to 950°C and by proper ventilation of the kiln, aiming to achieve very clean oxidising conditions especially in this temperature range when gases are generated and the clay body is still very porous. In bodies prone to black core the addition of dust grog can usually be made without much perceptible alteration to the body and this greatly facilitates the passage of gases through the clay body thereby greatly reducing or eliminating the tendency.

Bloating

Bloating can occur in both oxidised and reduced firings. It is very rare in earthenware where it is almost always a sign of over-firing. In stoneware it can usually be traced to the incomplete control of kiln atmosphere. Bloating is caused by the liberation of gases in a clay body after the body has become resistant to the escape of gases. The pressure of these gases creates small bumps – bloats – on the clay surface which are actually gaseous bubbles in the clay wall. In mild cases there may be only one or two isolated bloats on an object but in severe cases there may be many.

In oxidised stoneware bloating is usually caused by conditions at or near the end of the firing becoming slightly reducing and can usually be cured by opening the kiln vent for the last 100°C of the firing.

In reduced stoneware firings the causes of bloating are more complex but it is sometimes a sign that firing has not been sufficiently oxidised – or has been too fast – in the range of 800°C to 950°C (the biscuit as well as the glaze firing schedule should be considered in relation to this) or, and more usually, that the onset of reduction conditions has been too sudden or too late in the firing schedule. The important thing to ensure in

56

a reduction schedule is that a body is already fully reduced as it becomes vitrified. If a body which is oxidised and vitrified is subsequently reduced, bloating almost always occurs. In oxidising conditions the temperature range within which vitrification occurs and at which it is complete varies from body to body. In reducing conditions, with all bodies to some extent, though varying from body to body, the vitrification range is lowered and shortened and the vitrification point is lowered – this is particularly the case with stoneware bodies high in iron oxide because reduced iron is a more powerful flux than oxidised iron. Thus in all reduction firings the point at which reduction commences is crucial because it must wholly penetrate the body while this has sufficient porosity to allow it. An established reduction schedule which suits one body will not necessarily suit others. It should always be remembered that reduction has to be achieved and sustained through the vitrification point.

56 In this illustration both the bloated surface of the object and the section showing what has occurred in the clay wall are clear. The clay body itself is a sound stoneware body in very common use in reduction firings up to and slightly above 1280°C. The body is shown as *F* in *colour plate* 2(b). This particular example has, in fact, been fired in a reduction atmosphere to 1260°C so over-firing can be dismissed as the cause. However, while reduction of this body normally commences at about 1050°C, in the particular firing it did not commence until 1140°C. Inspection of the section of this example shows a pale oxidised core to the wall sandwiched by a reduced outer skin with the majority of the cavities – the bubbles – existing at or very near the junction between the oxidised core and the reduced outer skin. In this instance it appears that the relatively high temperature at which reduction began caused the outer skin to vitrify before reduction had penetrated the entire wall thickness, thus trapping the gases created by reduction on or near the inner edge of the vitrified clay. As the vitrified clay became softer at higher temperature the pressure of the pockets of gas pushed the wall out into the many bloats which are evident

SECTION THREE
GLAZE

Glaze theory

Glaze is a suspension in water of finely intermixed insoluble materials which is applied to clay bodies as a thin surface coating. When fired to appropriate temperature these materials fuse with one another forming a molten solution which, on cooling, becomes a glassy coating on the clay body.

It is easy, on scanning the range of technical literature on ceramics, to conclude that the subject of glaze is a complex one; and it is as easy on closer scrutiny of that literature – of mathematics to several decimal places, of chemistry and of pages of molecular formulae – to conclude that, as well as being complex, the subject is also a very precise one.

Both conclusions would, in fact, be correct but, accepted too readily, can be both misleading and disheartening. The field of glaze is complex not because of any inherent fundamental complexity but because of the range of possible diversity: both the diversity which occurs from differing proportions of the same materials and that which occurs from the use of differing materials. The field is precise because of the sensitivity of scientific tests evolved for industrial use to evaluate differing properties of glazes – their elasticity, their hardness, their resistance to acids, their resistance to thermal shock and so on.

At the risk of oversimplification, but with the intention of achieving clarity, only the broad pattern of glaze theory is described here. Anyone who wishes to study the subject in detail may refer to the many books on the subject, a selection of which is listed at the end of the book.

The parts of a glaze
Any glaze is composed of three necessary parts fulfilling three needs. The first need is for a *glass former*. Silica is the commonest of these but with a melting point above 1700°C, which is above the melting point of clay bodies and is anyway too high for convenient or economic practice, silica immediately creates a second need which is for a *flux*. The function of the flux is to lower the melting point of combinations of silica and flux to an appropriate point within the range of temperatures at which clay bodies mature. A third part is needed because combinations of silica and fluxes changes from being unmelted to being excessively fluid in a short span of temperature. The oxide of aluminium – *alumina* – makes combinations of silica and flux more stable and viscous.

At this point complexities threaten to flood in and obscure the simple picture of a glaze as a combination of silica, flux and alumina. Firstly, silica is not the only possible glass former. Secondly, quite a large number of fluxes exist. Thirdly, alumina is not the only possible stabiliser nor is its sole effect that of a stabiliser. These facts may be investigated or not but, either way, they should be seen as the diversification rather than the destruction of the simple picture of three parts.

Before embarking on a study of glaze theory it is important to understand that theory is based on the functions of single oxides as they combine with other oxides and that the practice of glaze making uses materials which often contain more than one oxide. A good example of this is potash felspar, a common glaze material at all temperatures. This type of felspar, ignoring minor impurities, contains potassium oxide, which functions as a flux; alumina, the most usual stabiliser; and silica, the commonest glass former. Thus as a single material it contains oxides which provide material for each of the three necessary parts of a glaze. The reason that felspar, if used alone, does not form a glaze is that the oxides necessary for the three essential parts of a glaze are not present within the necessary range of proportions.

The proportions of the parts of a glaze: eutectics
The phenomenom which is the basis for determining the relative proportions of the different parts of a glaze is the eutectic mixture. A eutectic mixture is the proportion of two (or more) oxides or raw materials which melt at a lower temperature than any other mixture of those materials. The temperature at which this mixture melts is called the *eutectic point*. Eutectics are a simple fact of nature. The somewhat extraordinary fact about eutectic mixtures is that their eutectic point is often lower than the individual melting points of the materials in the combination. The eutectic of lead oxide and silica may be given as an example: silica melts at 1713°C, lead oxide melts at 880°C but the eutectic mixture of silica and lead oxide (which is 7.1% silica and 92.9% lead oxide) has a eutectic point of 508°C. Eutectic mixtures exist for all the materials actually used in glazes and for the oxides which exist in those materials and which may or may not be available as distinct materials for the mixing of glazes. The phenomenom of eutectics is not confined to ceramics. Metal alloys are also based on eutectics.

There is surprisingly little mention of the eutectic mixtures of different materials in the majority of ceramic literature which concentrates rather on the functions of different oxides and the recipes and formulae of ranges of glazes designed to be used at various temperatures. Glazes are not eutectic mixtures but contain materials which in particular proportions can form eutectic mixtures. The temperature at which a glaze works and its power of fusion at that temperature is determined by the relationship between the proportions of the materials in the glaze and the proportions of the eutectic mixtures which exist between those materials.

A study of the formulae which exist for glazes at any given temperature reveals that the proportions of the parts of a glaze and of the materials in those parts can be altered within a range, sometimes quite a wide range. Such possible variation provides glazes with different inherent qualities, visual and physical, which are within the limits of technical soundness. It is the possible diversity which gives the subject of glazes its apparent complexity.

Glaze raw materials and frits
Two main types of materials are encountered in glaze recipes: *raw materials* and *frits*. Most suppliers' catalogues list the two types separately.

As supplied, most raw materials have been processed in some way and may be presumed to be of a fineness which requires no further grinding prior to their use in glazes.

Frits likewise are supplied ready for use. Frits may be thought of as man-made raw materials for glaze making. Some understanding of the need for frits and their nature is useful background to a study of the theory related to glaze composition.

Two factors relevant to the need for frits have already been stated: firstly, the relationships between the oxides contributing to the three parts of glazes must exist within certain proportions to work within specified ranges of temperature, different temperatures requiring different relative proportions; secondly, glazes are suspensions of insoluble materials in water.

The need for frits arises simply because insoluble sources of some oxide fluxes do not exist with the oxide fluxes in sufficiently high proportions for glazes to be made, particularly at lower temperatures.

Frits are manufactured by taking soluble fluxes and firing these with silica. Small amounts of other glaze-making oxides are often also included. The resulting glassy material is crushed and ground down and is a ready source of insoluble fluxing oxides in higher proportion than is naturally available. At one time there was a certain amount of trade secrecy about the precise ingredients of frits but most manufacturers now publish full formulae.

Lead frits are an exception to the above description as lead oxide does exist in insoluble form and lead frits, therefore, contain lead oxide in a lower proportion than is otherwise available. Lead frits are manufactured because in glaze suspensions they are much less toxic than lead oxide.

Expressions of materials: elements and oxides
Glaze theory uses the symbols of chemistry and requires simple mathematics. The symbols of

chemistry are a convenient shorthand and the mathematics, though it would be tedious to do longhand, is quick and straightforward with the most elementary of calculators. Some symbols are learnt relatively quickly but there is no need to memorise them because tables showing the symbols and other attributes of ceramic materials are readily available.

Pure substances are called *elements* by chemists. Every element has been given a symbol to represent it. A combination of an element with the element oxygen is known as an *oxide*. Each element combines with oxygen in a particular proportion or in particular proportions. Most elements only form one oxide but the examples of copper and iron oxides, which can exist in more than one form, have already been mentioned in the section on atmosphere of firing, see page 48. The proportions in which different elements combine with oxygen vary; for example, two or one; equal parts; one to two. The particular combination which any element makes is recorded in the symbol given to that oxide. Though the terms 'pentoxide' and 'dioxide' exist, all combinations of oxygen with an element are broadly referred to as *oxides*.

The smallest particle of an element is called an *atom*. The smallest particle of a combination of elements, such as an oxide, is called a *molecule*. Every element has been given a weight – the weight of one atom of that element in relation to the weight of one atom of hydrogen. From the knowledge of atomic weights the molecular weight – the weight of one molecule – of any oxide can be calculated by reference to the symbols for that oxide which shows the proportions of the combination.

What glaze theory does is to give minerals – pottery raw materials – ideal formulae as if they, like oxides, were combinations of elements which always occurred as combinations of fixed proportions. Minerals in fact do vary. The idea, therefore, may seem a crude one and it may seem odd that a subject which expresses itself in atoms and molecules, which are quite precise concepts, and in several decimal places of mathematics, is actually based on a premise which is imprecise. It should, however, be remembered that large mineral deposits are remarkably consistent in quality and that impurities in these, which are not acknowledged in the ideal formulae, are also fairly consistent. In addition it should be said that the theory and the methods of calculations arising from it have stood the test of time.

Aspects of symbols, atomic and molecular weights and ideal formulae may be illustrated using potash felspar as an example:

Potash felspar has the ideal formula

$$K_2O. Al_2O_3. 6SiO_2$$

The symbols in the formula represent the following elements which have atomic weights as indicated

Symbol	Element	Atomic weight
K	Potassium	39
O	Oxygen	16
Al	Aluminium	27
Si	Silicon	28

Three oxides are present in the formula

K_2O	the oxide of potassium (a two to one ratio)
Al_2O_3	the oxide of aluminium – alumina – (a two to three ratio)
SiO_2	the oxide of silicon – silica – (a one to two ratio).

The two full stops separate the three oxides and the figure 6 before SiO_2 indicates that for every one molecule of potassium oxide there is one of alumina and six of silica.

For calculations involving felspar, the molecular weight needs to be known. This is 556. In ceramics the atomic weights used by chemists which are calculated to several decimal places are usually corrected to whole figures. The molecular weights of the oxides in the formula in the proportions which that formula indicates. Each oxide weight is likewise the sum of the atomic weights in the ratio shown by the oxide formula. Whenever calculations are being undertaken, tables of formulae and molecular weights should be used.

Expressions of glazes: recipes and formulae

Recipes

A glaze recipe is the expression of the material ingredients of a glaze. These are listed in terms of mineral materials and manufactured frits. The materials and the amounts listed are crucial to the particular quality of the glaze. The glaze recipe should also state the firing temperature and, with high temperature glazes, the firing atmosphere. (Glazes for temperatures below 1200°C are usually presumed to be fired in oxidising conditions and atmosphere is rarely stated for such glazes.)

A now well-known glaze, the Leach Cone 8 glaze, published by Bernard Leach in *A Potter's Book* has the memorably simple recipe:

China clay	10
Whiting	20
Flint	30
Felspar	40

(in its original form the materials listed were limestone not whiting, and quartz not flint, but the material form above is in common use.)

Recipes are usually, as here, given as percentages which are then simply multiplied into whatever units are in use for weighing out the glaze. Recipes do not always appear as actual percentages because, when adjustments to a recipe are made or colour additions included, the list is rarely corrected back to a true percentage. The fact that a recipe does not total one hundred does not necessarily mean that there is an error.

Glaze formulae

There are two ways of chemically expressing the parts of a glaze: the molecular unity formula and the percentage formula.

The molecular unity formula

This expresses the oxides in a glaze using their chemical symbols, the relative amounts of different oxides being shown as molecular parts. The oxides are all grouped by their functions: fluxes on the left, stabilisers in the middle and glass formers on the right. The parts of the whole expression relate to the fluxes which are grouped together in fractions which add up to one – hence the name. By this unification the ratio of fluxes to stabilisers to glass formers, the three parts of a glaze, can immediately be seen and is a basis for comparison.

The unity method uses the ideal formula for materials which ignore minor impurities.

If the Leach Cone 8 glaze, used as an example above, were expressed as a unity formula it would appear as:

$$K_2O \quad 0.27$$
$$\qquad\qquad Al_2O_3 \quad 0.41 \qquad SiO_2 \quad 3.72$$
$$CaO \quad 0.73$$

In relation to the literature of the subject this formula permits a comparison between this and other glazes using the same oxides designed for the same or similar temperatures.

The identity of the unity method as a notional one is clear from the apparently highly precise unity formula above because, in reality, fractions of molecules cannot exist.

Partly perhaps because percentages are closer than fractions of molecules to most people's experience, and partly because calculations can easily include recognition of known impurities, percentage formulae are an alternative with some supporters.

Oxide percentage formulae

As an aspect of quality control, raw material merchants regularly undertake and either publish or will provide recent typical analyses of their raw materials. These are expressed in percentage amounts of oxides present and, unlike ideal formulae, do acknowledge minor impurities.

The Leach Cone 8 glaze, shown above first as a recipe then as a unity formula, is shown below as an oxide percentage formula based on raw material analyses:

SiO_2	68.59
Al_2O_3	12.01
Fe_2O_3	0.17
CaO	12.81
MgO	0.08
K_2O	5.36
Na_2O	0.97

The calculation is corrected to two decimal places. In addition to the percentages above, traces of phosphorus, manganese and titanium oxides in amounts between ten and forty parts per million are present.

The relevance of glaze recipes and formulae and the relative merits of unity and percentage formulae

The relevance of glaze recipes is clear. Provided all the materials stipulated are available, a glaze suspension can be made directly from a recipe and applied to objects.

The relevance of formulae is less clear. Certainly a glaze cannot be mixed up directly from a formula because formulae have first to be translated into real materials by mathematical calculation. (For details of glaze calculation procedures see Appendix 3.)

Glaze calculations come into their own when an individual wishes to experiment with different qualities and types of glaze. Thousands of glaze recipes exist but simply to go to recipe books and endlessly mix up recipes can be a great waste of time because what is never completely clear from a recipe is how similar or different glazes are to one another. Even glazes with the same raw materials in different percentages may be significantly different in their oxide make up – and, therefore, for example in their colour response, fluidity and other qualities – and this difference is far clearer if the receipes are translated to one or other of the types of formulae. Glaze theory has no relevance if it stays on paper. It is the fired results of glazes tested after theoretical calculations that is the point of understanding and undertaking work in theory. The prime relevance of glaze theory, glaze calculations and formulae, is as a time, material and effort saving exercise when a particular study of glaze is being undertaken.

Excellent glazes, excellent in the technical sense of being well fitting, tough and hard, quite apart from their visual qualities, were made long before modern scientific analysis of glaze was possible. The empirical method by which these were devised is still a perfectly possible means of evolving modifications to glaze or indeed of actually evolving glazes but to become involved in such work without investigating at least the simpler facts of glaze theory is to risk much time wasting.

The relative merits of the oxide percentage method and the molecular unity method are debatable. The disadvantage of the unity method is that to many it seems so remote from the actual practice of glaze making and so inherently complex that initial confusion is sometimes never overcome. The advantages of the method are that the ratios of fluxes to silica and alumina are immediately evident and, importantly, that the majority of ceramic literature uses the method. The corresponding disadvantage of the percentage method is that most ceramic literature does not use it. Percentage analyses are not always readily available for bought materials. Where such analyses are available the oxide percentage formula of a glaze has the advantage that it can be used to show the amounts of all oxides present not just those theoretically present. While the method does allow comparison of the percentages of particular oxides in one glaze with those in another it does not permit the ready comparison of the proportions of the parts of a glaze which is so easy with the molecular unity method.

It is probably best to see the two methods as complementary: to use the unity method for general comparison and classification and the percentage method for studying the detail of what is actually present.

As a rider it should be said that the unity method can be used with the full oxide analyses of materials. This is far less frequently done than with the ideal formulae of materials and considerably lengthens the mathematics involved.

Finally, it should be stated again that valuable as theory is to those with a mind for solving problems and originating or modifying glazes, the apparent complexity of the subject can be avoided by those with no wish to become involved: glaze recipes abound and more than ever before a large and increasing variety of glazes can be bought ready made.

The nature of fired glaze
When glazes melt they form solutions, the various glaze oxides dissolving into one another. Because they are solutions with qualities similar to liquids at normal temperatures, glazes are sometimes referred to as supercooled liquids.

Just as some materials cannot be dissolved in some liquids at normal temperature the same is true at glaze temperatures. A few non-reactive materials do not form eutectics with other glaze materials and do not, therefore, enter the solution of the glaze. An example of such a material is tin oxide. Its much used opacifying, whitening effect is due to its presence in the glaze solution as a fine, white, evenly distributed and undissolved powder. While many of the materials added to glazes to colour them, in fact dissolve in the glaze melt forming solution-colours, some do not, and some glaze stains are specifically formulated to remain suspended in the molten glaze solution.

The adhesion of fired glaze to clay bodies
All glazes in their most molten state, at top firing temperature, are active solutions seeking out further appropriate material to dissolve. The stickiness of the molten state helps glazes to adhere to clay bodies but the eventual strength of the adhesion occurs because glazes have an affinity for the oxides in clay bodies. This is to be expected because many of the same oxides occur in glazes and in clay bodies. In the heat of the firing glazes melt into clay bodies very slightly and form a minute layer which is neither completely glaze nor completely body. This layer is known as the *interface layer*. It may be scarcely formed if the oxides in a particular glaze and particular body do not have a strong affinity for one another and if, for example, the glaze is low firing and the body very refractory and only low biscuited. But if the oxides have strong affinity and if body and glaze are matured together and, therefore, simultaneously in an active state, a very strong and substantial interface layer is formed as is usually the case with porcelain.

Theoretical and practical aspects of glazing

The need for glaze materials to be insoluble
Glazes are suspensions of insoluble glaze materials in water.

Various factors make it necessary for the materials used in glaze suspensions to be insoluble. Firstly, the highly caustic nature of some soluble fluxes is eliminated when these are fritted. Secondly, the problem of soluble fluxes being absorbed by porous biscuit, rather than being deposited on the surface where they are needed, is eliminated by fritting. Thirdly, the loss of flux material by the discarding of water from an over-fluid glaze suspension, which would occur if soluble fluxes were used, is impossible with fritted materials. Lead oxide if fritted even though it is not soluble because fritted lead is much less toxic

in glaze suspensions than unfritted lead oxide.

It should be noted that though materials such as felspar, nepheline syenite, china stone and frits are said to be insoluble they are, when finely ground (as is always the case with glaze materials), very slightly soluble and small amounts of flux do become dissolved. This small amount of solubility can be ignored from the point of view of fired glaze quality and of glaze application but it may affect the quality of a glaze suspension leading to a tendency for a glaze to settle.

The glazing of clay bodies in a porous biscuit state
Pouring and dipping are the commonest methods with this state of clay. With glazing of this type the porous clay absorbs water from the glaze suspension leaving a layer of the glaze materials deposited on its surface. The longer the porous clay is in contact with the fluid glaze the thicker the layer of glaze deposited on the surface will be up to the point when the porous clay is saturated with water when its power of holding the glaze layer in fact diminishes.

What precisely is the correct consistency for glaze suspensions is a question which considerably troubles the less experienced. What is even more vexing is that there is no simple answer to the question. The application behaviour of different glaze suspensions used with porous biscuit can vary considerably: some with a high percentage of plastic clay material, such as ball clay or red clay, may quickly seal the biscuit surface and leave only a thin layer of glaze on the surface; others, with no plastic clay, may quickly build up a surprisingly thick layer. Glaze formulae obviously give no clue to the nature of glaze suspensions but the materials listed in the recipe do give a clearer indication. The only certain way to judge the likely application behaviour of glaze suspensions and to know, therefore, what consistency they need to be is through practical experience.

Four factors are relevant to the controlled application of glaze onto porous biscuit fired clay by dipping or pouring; firstly the time that the fluid glaze and the biscuit are in contact – the time taken to apply the glaze; secondly, the porosity of the biscuit; thirdly, the consistency of the glaze suspension; and fourthly, the materials used in the recipe. The last two of these factors need to be related to each other and together related to the particular porosity of the biscuit for the first factor

– the time taken to apply the glaze – to be of convenient duration to achieve control.

The glazing of clay bodies in a non-porous state

With the glazing of non-porous biscuit the theory of application is less neat and is simply that the non-porous body dipped into a creamy suspension will, purely by virtue of the consistency of the suspension, retain an even coating of glaze. Being non-porous the body has no power of water absorption so time and the presence or absence of plastic clay in the suspension are both of less relevance than with porous biscuit. The consistency of the glaze suspension is the crucial factor in this case. The consistency must not be so thick that suspension lacks the mobility for an even layer to be possible but must not be so fluid that the layer left on the piece divides into watery rivulets before it dries.

Industrially, all china bodies and most white earthenwares are fired to a non-porous biscuit and the majority of this is glazed by dipping. Spray glazing tends to be done on items such as sanitary ware which is too large to handle easily. Much research has gone into the nature of the glaze suspensions used for dipping but an experienced specialist glazer will adjust the fluidity of his glaze if the feel is not quite right. Industrially dipped glazed items are placed onto a moving belt which carries them into heated drying cabinets which speed up the drying of the glaze.

Outside the industry the glazing of non-porous biscuit, other than by spray glazing, tends to be thought of as highly problematic. In fact, provided sensible experiment is made with glaze consistency, it is far less of a problem than it may at first appear.

Raw glazing

When clay bodies are glazed in the unfired state they are said to be raw glazed.

As with several aspects of ceramics the same term has somewhat different meanings to different groups of people. Within the industry the term 'once-fired ware' is applied to the process defined above and within the industry 'raw glazing' means using glazes in unfritted form.

The procedure of raw glazing offers the economic advantage of achieving glazed work after one rather than two firings. Despite the potential savings of ever-rising fuel prices it is not, however, a widespread practice.

The theory of raw glazing is that the glaze suspension contains sufficient plastic clay material for the glaze layer to adhere to the clay body and shrink with it before and/or during the firing until the point when the glaze adheres through its own fusion.

The commonest time for raw glazing to be done is while clay bodies are in the leatherhard state. When glazing occurs at this time it is usual to use recipes which contain ball clay or, where appropriate, red clay. These clays assist the adhesion of the glaze layer as the clay body dries and ensure that the glaze layer shrinks with the clay body during firing. As the leatherhard clay body has virtually no power of absorption, the glaze suspension needs to be of a thickish cream-like consistency to adhere in a sufficiently thick coating.

Somewhat surprisingly, it is possible to raw glaze some clay bodies in the dry state. Clay bodies which are very open in texture or low in plastic clay content, which includes porcelain as well as many coarser bodies, may be suitable for this treatment but close textured highly plastic bodies will crack at edges, especially if these are thin. Glazes need to be somewhat thinner suspensions than those appropriate for glazing leatherhard bodies.

With fine, complex or delicate objects the idea of raw glazing is impractical.

With raw glazing the application of glaze differs depending on whether the clay body is leatherhard or dry. Raw glazing leatherhard clay is very similar to applying slip and the procedures followed are the same. With dry clay bodies it is important that the inside and outside of forms are glazed more or less simultaneously so that the shock of sudden dampness is equalised. To glaze only part of a dry form may cause cracking which would not occur if both inside and outside are glazed.

Some problems of raw glazing

Two aspects of what occurs when glaze is applied to biscuit fired bodies are often taken for granted. When problems arise in the firing of raw glazed bodies these aspects are the more appreciated.

Firstly, in a biscuit firing the clay body undergoes either all, as in a high biscuit, or some, as in a low biscuit, of its shrinkage. In the subsequent glaze firing, the unfired glaze layer is, therefore, on a form which is dimensionally stable throughout the important period – high biscuited work, anyway, shrinks no more and by the time low biscuited work does begin to shrink further, the glaze layer is attached to the form by the start of its own fusion. In a raw glaze firing the unfired glaze layer is on a form which is subject to shrinkages before the glaze achieves adhesion by fusion. This can create one of the problems of raw glazing in that glaze flakes off during the firing leaving bare patches on the form and glazed patches on the kiln shelves. The possible cures to be tried are to increase further the plastic clay content of the glaze, using clays of the highest available shrinkage, or to scrap the idea of a particular glaze and to try others. More radically, the body may have to be altered to make it shrink less or shrink later by the addition of non-plastic material or more refractory clays of lesser shrinkage.

Secondly, a biscuit firing burns off the combustible material in clay bodies so that in the subsequent glaze firing, the glaze layer is on an inactive body as well as one which is dimensionally stable. A problem which can occur in raw glazed work is that if the glaze layer begins to fuse before the gases from combustible material have emerged from the clay body, then black core or bloating may occur. The problem is more common with earthenware because the temperature range when earthenware glazes begin to fuse tends to overlap with the range when gases from carbonaceous material are emerging from the clay body. To avoid black core in earthenware, and bloating in stoneware bodies, the period of oxidation, mentioned as being necessary in the section on firing, should be extended in time and maintained across a wider temperature range to encourage the complete combustion of all combustible material at as low a temperature as posssible. Highly grogged open bodies and those with low plastic clay content tend to be fairly immune to these problems.

Undoubtedly in both earthenware and stoneware traditions raw glazing was a more common procedure and its lack of present popularity is certainly partly due to the lack of recent traditions and a consequent lack of widespread first hand experience. To imagine, however, that it is easy with all types of glaze and body, or that a change can be made to it with few problems, would be somewhat optimistic.

All making of ceramics represents a system with inter-related aspects and changing one aspect may necessitate changing others.

The strength of an unfired glaze layer
One aspect which the nature of glaze materials affects is the strength of the dry coat. Glazes high in clay tend to form a strong layer which can be handled before firing with little fear of damage, while glazes low in clay tend to form fragile, dusty coatings which have to be handled with care. If coatings of a particular glaze tend to be rubbed off or chipped, even with careful handling, then it can save a lot of trouble to incorporate one of the proprietory glaze hardeners, sold by most suppliers, into that glaze as a matter of routine.

The behaviour of different glaze suspensions
It might be thought that once a glaze has been mixed and sieved it can be stored in a covered container and be used at any future time with little more being necessary than a thorough stir. Sometimes, certainly, this is true but some glaze suspensions suffer acutely from a problem known as *settling*, which is both irritating and time consuming. Settling is not the separation of a glaze suspension into a water layer on top and a thicker suspension of glaze materials underneath but occurs when the glaze materials sink to the base of a container and go out of suspension forming a dense layer of material which is highly resistant to remixing. A settled layer of glaze has the tough resilience of hard rubber. If the layer is prized out of the container and broken up it will be found, in relation to the water on top of it, to be somewhat mysteriously dry. The reasons for some glazes settling, and others not, are complex and are the result of both chemical and physical factors.

Buckets of settled glaze are a nuisance but large bins present a daunting problem. The quickest way, and it is none too quick, of returning a settled glaze to a usable state is to pour off all liquid and, bit by bit, break the solidified layer into small pieces, returning these to the liquid and stirring constantly. The glaze can then be resieved.

Glazes with a high proportion of clay tend to suspend well and not settle but those high in felspar, flint and some frits can settle badly and quickly. Industrially, very close attention is paid to factors influencing glaze suspension. Outside the industry, where sophisticated control is not possible, it is important to learn the different suspension qualities of glazes in use through practical experience. Whenever settling appears as a problem the cure is to use appropriate amounts of a glaze suspender. Glaze suspenders are readily available from pottery suppliers.

Crawling

Crawling is the parting of a glaze layer during firing resulting in bare, unglazed areas. In mild cases, a few unglazed splits may occur, while in extreme cases, the entire glaze layer may divide up into small areas giving a snakeskin-like effect.

Crawling is often attributed to dusty biscuit but, while this can cause it, it is usually an inherent problem of a particular glaze due either to the physical nature of the glaze ingredients or to the viscous nature of the molten glaze.

When a glaze layer develops a network of cracks as it dries this frequently leads to crawling. Thick applications of glaze always aggravate crawling. How crawling can be cured depends very much on what can be identified as the cause.

Where a glaze layer and the physical nature of the ingredients is, therefore, suspect, the theoretical cure is to reduce the wet to dry shrinkage of the glaze. This is done by substituting materials of lesser shrinkage for those of greater shrinkage – thus china clay could be substituted for ball clay or calcined china clay for china clay. This does not always work, and sometimes the opposite, ie to substitute ball clay for china clay, does in fact work. In theory this is illogical for the glaze layer should then have greater shrinkage. When it does work, two factors can be advanced as possible reasons: firstly, despite its high shrinkage, ball clay does have a strong power of adhesion and this improved adhesion could be a reason for a diminished tendency to crawling; secondly, despite their theoretically identical formulae ball clays are higher in flux and silica and lower in alumina than china clays and these facts will make a glaze slightly more fluid and less viscous and, therefore, tend to reduce a crawling tendency.

Tin oxide and other opacifiers can transform a clear glaze which never crawls into an opaque glaze with a strong tendency to crawl. When this occurs the problem can usually be cured by diminishing the amount of alumina present in the glaze thus in effect increasing the relative amounts of flux and silica. Rather like alumina, though their total effect is different, opacifiers act as stabilisers in glazes by diminishing flow. When a perfectly sound glaze has an opacifier added and begins to show crawling tendencies it has simply become too viscous.

A great deal of industrial research has been done on crawling and the subject is a complex one. Usually one or other of the solutions mentioned, where possible combined with a thinner application of glaze, will work but if the problem persists it may be better simply to seek an alternative glaze.

Crazing

Crazing is not necessarily a glaze fault as such and is caused by too great a difference between the thermal expansions and contractions of a body and a glaze.

Crazing occurs when, on cooling, a body does not shrink more than the glaze on it and is evidenced by a network of cracks in the glaze which occur as the glaze fails under tensional stress.

A study of crazing is part of the larger study of glaze fit. In broad terms the subject is apparently simple but investigation in any depth reveals considerable complexity.

Very simply most materials, fired glaze and clay bodies included, have greater compressive than tensional strength. A fired cooled glaze may be smaller than, the same size as, or larger than the body to which it is attached. If it is smaller, crazing occurs because the glaze being attached to the body is under tensional stress. If it is slightly larger, no crazing occurs because the glaze is put under slight compression by the smaller body to which it is attached – the body, correspondingly, is put in slight tension but this is not sufficient to affect it detrimentally. If, however, the glaze layer is too large, the tension in the body can cause this to fail at edges where compressive and tensional stresses are complex and slivers of glaze and body can be pushed off the edges of forms and any sharp projections – this rather dangerous and unpleasant problem is fortunately rare which is one reason why it has various names of which *shivering* is the most common. In more severe cases, where the glaze layer is too large, the object may shatter either into car windscreen-like fragments or larger pieces, depending on the form of the object and on the clay body.

Solely from the point of view of the glaze, the tendency to crazing is diminished by increasing the proportion of silica in a glaze at the expense of the fluxes. For shivering and shattering exactly the opposite is the case.

Crazing needs to be considered in relation to clay bodies as well as glazes. The important factor to remember here is the role of *cristobalite*. Cristobalite, a crystalline form of silica, undergoes a contraction at about 220°C, a temperature far below the point at which even the lowest firing glazes have any molten softness which might accommodate this movement. Cristobalite is formed quite slowly, at temperatures above 1020°C, from the free silica which exists in bodies. It is not found in glazes because glazes contain no free silica – all the silica in glazes, whether the proportion is relatively high or low, reacts with the fluxes to form the glaze solution. Thus bodies in which cristobalite has developed undergo a contraction at 220°C as they cool while glazes do not. It is this contraction of bodies which helps in the prevention of crazing by putting the cooling glaze under compression. Thus to diminish the tendency of a glaze to craze on a particular body, any steps which assist the formation of cristobalite are beneficial. In earthenware bodies particularly, a longer firing above 1020°C and, in the case of body/glaze combinations where the practice is to have a high biscuit, a higher biscuit will assist the formation of cristobalite. Adding silica to the body will increase the free silica in it which is available to form cristobalite.

Shivering and shattering may indicate that a body has too much free silica and, therefore, cristobalite, but these conditions usually indicate that the parts of a glaze are seriously imbalanced and the glaze, rather than the body, should be the initial suspect.

While glaze and body are equally more or less likely to be at fault with crazing, making adjustments to a body is a much more serious step to take and it is easier to try adjustments to a glaze or to use other glazes, so this is usually the first step where crazing has to be avoided. Thick layers of glaze are always more prone to crazing than thin

layers and one option is always to apply the glaze more thinly.

Crazing in some glazes is impossible to cure by any known means. Some fluxing oxides have very different contraction rates to others and, when a glaze flux is used alone with pigmenting oxides to create a particular colour, alterations to the glaze to reduce crazing can destroy the colour. This is particularly true with glazes based on frits high in sodium oxide, and the turquoise and mauve colours which can be achieved in such glazes cannot be achieved without crazing.

Secondary crazing is the term given to crazing which occurs a long while after objects emerge from a kiln – weeks or months. This can occur with porous bodies which emerge from the kiln with uncrazed glaze but subsequently absorb water, causing the body to expand fractionally, thereby putting the glaze into lesser compression or into tension. When this latter occurs secondary crazing develops.

Weighing and mixing glazes from frits and raw materials

Because of the very differing densities of the various raw materials and frits used in glazes, the liquid volume of glaze which a given weight of material will make is very variable. Obviously it is important to have containers which are sufficiently large. As a rough guide, a small bucket of 4.5 litres capacity will hold about 5000 g of most stoneware glazes but over 8000 g of a lead frit earthenware glaze, both at an average useable consistency. The wateriness of the glaze suspension is a further factor which is variable.

Plastic buckets and bins are the obvious containers for glaze storage. These, however, are of variable quality. Three criteria are important: one, the container should have a lid to prevent contamination and to minimise water evaporation; two, the form should be such that access for mixing and stirring is easy and the glaze can be cleanly poured; and three, the material should be strong enough to withstand the pressure of sustained storage and the various forces exerted by repeated stirring, lifting and pouring. The first two criteria are relatively easy to meet (where containers are not supplied with lids, polythene sheet tied over the top is a cheap and effective substitute) but the third criteria is much more problematic. Whatever their quality as household buckets may be, many types of these are short lived as glaze containers as they tend to split. The harder, more rigid plastics are particularly prone to this while more flexible polythene buckets generally last much longer. The black polythene buckets sold as builders' buckets are very durable (but are not sold with lids). The best bucket sized containers (and they exist somewhat smaller and larger than buckets) are second-hand plastic containers originally sold with various materials such as masonry paint and various granular or liquid chemicals. Perhaps because of the value of their original contents these are extremely durable and, though they are usually a rigid type of plastic, they outlast household buckets many times over. Larger second-hand containers are not so readily available and, with bins, the choice is between household plastic dustbins and fermentation bins sold for home brewing. Rather, as with buckets, dustbins of the rigid plastic type tend to split, so fermentation bins designed for liquid storage give much better service. The strength and durability of glaze containers is important because a large batch of glaze, especially of earthenware glaze, represents a not inconsiderable investment and, if dispersed over the floor from a split container, creates a considerable and rather unhealthy mess.

Though extensively used before plastics were common, galvanised iron containers tend to react with some glaze suspensions and for this reason it is preferable not to use them for glaze storage. Their use as temporary containers during glaze application is not a problem.

In the description of mixing which follows, a smallish batch – 3000 g of the Leach Cone 8 glaze mentioned earlier (page 56) – is made.

Having decided on the amount of glaze to be made, the next step, working from the recipe, is to do the simple mathematics. Firstly, to determine the batch factor (the amount by which each of the individual materials specified in the recipe is multiplied, to give the amount of each needed) and secondly, to determine the batch weight of each material.

Weighing can then proceed.

57

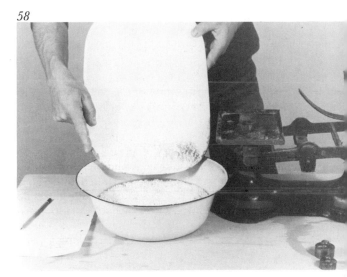

58

57, 58 As each of the materials is weighed it is gently slid from the scale pan into the water. For the initial wetting of glaze materials containers which are wide in relation to their height are best as the surface area of the water is greater and more thorough wetting is more quickly achieved. (Wide containers become less possible with very large batches of glaze.) Several types of scales exist: the *balance* type, as here, in which the scale pan is counter balanced by a platform on which weights are placed; the *beam* type in which the weight required is set by moving a small weight along a calibrated arm; and the *dial or digital* type in which the amount of material on the scale pan is read off on a dial or, with electric scales, digitally. For convenience the dial or digital type is best; for trouble-free durability the balance type illustrated is probably best

59

60

×30

elspar	40	1200	✓
lint	30	900	✓
hiting	20	600	✓
hina cl.	10	300	✓

59 When each material has been added to the water it should be ticked off on the sheet on which the batch calculations were made. To avoid mistakes this simple procedure should always be followed. If there is an interruption it is all too easy to forget which materials have been added and which not and, because most glaze ingredients are relatively similar white powders, this procedure is a simple safeguard against mistakes

60 Whether the calculation of batch weights is done in a notebook or on a sheet of paper, as here, matters little. Most glaze recipes are expressed as percentages so calculation of the batch factor, 30 in this case, is very straightforward. The calculation of batch weights with the recipe illustrated is obviously extremely simple but whether simple or more complicated those not confident of their mathematics can quickly check for multiplication errors by adding together all the batch weights

61 When the materials have sunk into the water any apparent excess of water should be poured off before the mixture is stirred

62 The mixture is then stirred and any lumps of material are broken up. For large batches of glaze a portable electric hand blunger greatly facilitates this work and speeds up the initial stages of sieving

61

62

63 Sieving then proceeds. The aims of sieving
are:
1 to promote intimate mixing of the glaze
  materials
2 to remove any particles of foreign matter
3 to promote evenness of consistency to assist in
  glaze application.

Glaze sieving is normally done through a 120
mesh sieve but the work of sieving is facilitated
and the life of the finer sieves is extended if full use
is made of a range of sieves starting with a 40 mesh
followed by a 60 or 80 and, finally, proceeding to a
120 mesh. In the first sieving much of the mixture
will pour through the coarse mesh but as the
lumpier, less well wetted materials are reached
these accumulate in the sieve

64 From this point on the unsieved mixture has
to be added a little at a time and has to be assisted
through the sieve with a brush. At this early stage,
and with a coarse sieve, a household washing up
brush with nylon bristles works rather better than
a sieve brush and will not damage the sieve. Such
brushes have the advantage that they retain far
less material than sieve brushes

65 Brushing need only be gentle and should
methodically cover the entire surface of the mesh

63

64

65

66 When the first sieving is complete there is usually a build up of thick material on the underside of the mesh. This is best removed by sharply tapping the side of the sieve and then decanting some of the more watery sieved mixture and running this through the sieve. Sieves should not be tapped vertically as this tends to break the fixings between the wider and narrower cylinders. The once sieved mixture should then be thoroughly stirred, mixing it to as even a consistency as possible

67 The next sieving is through a 60 or 80 mesh and from this point on a standard pottery sieve brush should be used

68 The sieve brush is held vertically and brushed over the mesh surface with a circular motion, its many bristles easing the material quickly through the mesh

When the glaze has been sieved once through a 60 or 80 mesh it should be thoroughly mixed by pouring it forcefully from one container to another which brings it to an even consistency. If it is decidedly too thick some additional water can be mixed in. The final 120 mesh sieving will be easier if the glaze is sieved a second time through the 60 or 80 mesh – second sievings through any mesh size are always quicker than first sievings and improve the evenness of consistency.

Illustration of the final sieving is unnecessary as it follows the same procedure of the 60 or 80 mesh sieving and after the final sieving the glaze is brought to its right consistency by the addition of extra water. If too much water was added initially the sieved glaze can be allowed to settle and excess water can then be carefully decanted. The mixed glaze should be stored in a container and clearly labelled with a complete recipe and its firing temperature.

Some further factors relevant to glaze mixing

To avoid specking in coloured glazes very fine sieving is sometimes necessary. Sieving large batches of glaze through a fine sieve is slow and boring work and thankfully is not necessary. A far quicker procedure is to mix and sieve the glaze in the normal way but without its pigmenting addition. A very small amount of glaze is then decanted from the main batch, and the weighed pigments together with some additional water are then added and the mixture is ground in a pestle and mortar (or a ball mill if one is available). This ground mixture is then sieved through the finest available sieve – a 200 mesh will eliminate colour specking. Any material retained by the sieve is then reground until it is all finely sieved. When all the pigment with its small glaze addition has been finely sieved it is added to the remainder of the unpigmented glaze and this is then poured forcibly from one container to another a few times and poured through an 80 mesh sieve twice to distribute the pigment evenly. The small amount of glaze added to the pigment, which is then ground and finely sieved, is a crucial aspect of the process as this serves to suspend and disperse the pigment during grinding and sieving. Omitting this addition can result in specking because the pigment does not so readily disperse when it is added to the large batch.

When glazes containing found materials, which have not been as finely prepared as bought materials, are mixed up, and in addition contain bought materials, a particular sequence of mixing should be followed. First, all the bought materials should be weighed, mixed and sieved as usual through a 120 mesh. Then the found materials should be added and the complete mixture should then be sieved again through whatever mesh, coarser than 120, is appropriate to the original preparation of the material. To avoid subsequent confusion, if the glaze needs resieving for any reason, this sieving detail should be recorded on the container label.

The mixing of ready-made glazes, which are available in one of two forms, is very straight-forward. The two forms are glazes supplied as *fluid suspensions* and glazes supplied in *powdered form*. Glazes supplied as fluid suspensions are either of the brush-on type, which require only to be thoroughly shaken before use, or can be used for pouring, dipping or spraying. These latter need to be brought to an appropriate fluidity by the addition of water. Such glazes usually suspend very well and, to guard against overthinning the entire amount, it is best to keep back some of the glaze in its delivered fluidity so that the diluted glaze can be easily and quickly thickened should this be necessary. Glazes supplied in powder form need only to be mixed with water and to be sieved through a 120 mesh sieve to be ready for use. Obviously the powdered glaze will need to be weighed in relation to any additions of pigmenting oxides or stains.

Sieves and sieve brushes

Sieves and sieve brushes have one serious drawback. However thoroughly they are washed both tend to retain small amounts of material. If a powerful pigment, such as cobalt oxide, is contained in a mixture it is possible and likely that future sievings of unpigmented mixtures will lead to contamination with occasional blue specks. The identical problem can occur with other pigmenting oxides and with prepared colours, but cobalt oxide is notoriously pervasive. If much work is done with unpigmented mixtures, and if it is important that these show no signs of contamination, it is essential to have two sets of sieves and two brushes – one for unpigmented mixtures and one for pigmented.

Immediately after use sieves and sieve brushes should be washed under a running tap and then hung up to dry. The final rinsing of sieves should be from the underside to flush out any materials retained by the mesh.

The application of glaze to biscuited forms by pouring and dipping

Glaze can be applied to forms in a number of ways which are directly graphic in intention. As a book dealing with aspects of materials and their use, the concentration here is simply on applying an all-over even layer of glaze.

While photographs and writing cannot completely describe the unhurried fluency which is an essential part of efficient glazing they can describe the sequence of actions which are fundamental to achieving that fluency. The fluency cannot be

69

70

achieved by watching videos, films or actual demonstrations any more than by looking at photographs but comes through experience and practice.

The sections which follow show possible sequences of actions with a number of forms. In all cases the clay body has had a biscuit firing leaving it porous. Many of the sequences would also be relevant were the clay body non-porous. There is rarely only one possible sequence. With small forms there are usually several alternatives. With larger forms particular factors, such as the size of available containers or the amount of glaze available, may limit the possibilities. To choose the best way of glazing a particular form it is an immense advantage to be aware of the possible alternatives. To choose the best way of glazing an unusual or complex form it is helpful to know the sequences with simpler forms as these will give clues to methods which may be modified or extended to suit the particular instance.

The examples which follow show possible sequences with a number of basic forms.

Glazing a small form by pouring the inside and dipping the outside

69 The glaze is poured into the form. Glaze is less inclined to dribble over onto the outside when it is poured out if the form is not filled much above half way but this does depend on the detail of the edge

70 The form is tilted and is rotated as the glaze is poured out of it thereby coating the whole of the inside. Tilting and emptying begins as soon as the glaze has been poured in. The form may be rotated once, which is usual with small forms, or several times. The glaze layer will thicken the longer the glaze is being swilled steadily round the inside. The one problem likely to be encountered is glaze running back over the edge onto the outside. Whether or not this is likely to occur is largely dependent on the form and the detail of its edge but it is more likely to occur if the glaze is poured out in an uncertain trickle rather than a steady stream. Cylindrical forms tend to empty rather quickly and are difficult to rotate more than once without running the risk of unwanted dribbles on the outside. A more even coat of glaze can often be applied to the inside of more ovoid

forms by using more watery glaze and rotating the form three or four times. The aim here in glazing the inside is to end up with a neat edge of glaze at the top and no glaze on the outside. In this sequence the form is put to one side for the very short time the glaze takes to become touch dry

71 The moment the inside is touch dry the very edge is dipped into the glaze for 10 to 13 mm

72 The form is then put down immediately and, avoiding the wetness of the edge, is picked up by the inside using a firm outward pressure with the tips of the fingers on the dried, glazed surface

73 It is then plunged down into the glaze to overlap slightly the dipped line. Ideally the top dip should still be wet when the main outside dip meets it. When this is the case no perceptible thickening at the overlap will occur. When the pot has been held steady, long enough for sufficient glaze to adhere, it is lifted out and put aside to dry

This sequence, when adequate containers and quantities of glaze are available, is as relevant with large forms as with small and is not limited to cylinders. A major factor governing the possibility of the process is whether or not an adequate grip can be achieved inside the form for the final dip because large forms are surprisingly buoyant and require a firm downward pressure.

71

72

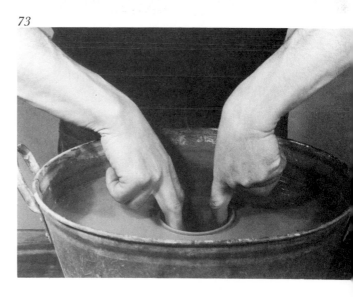

73

75

76

Glazing a small form in a single dip using tongs

74　Glazing tongs can be bought. Any pair, however, tends inevitably to be useful with only a small range of forms and they do not exist in great variety. Glazing tongs are less easy to make than glazing claws but if the trouble is taken to make them they can greatly facilitate glazing some forms. It is essential, of course, that the tongs grip the form securely. With small forms the type shown with one and three prongs is adequate. For large forms tongs with two sets of three prongs are usually more secure. It is important that the tongs not only hold the form safely but that they hold it in such a way that it can be manoeuvred easily in and out of the glaze at the angles that the particular form necessitates

75　The form is securely gripped with the tongs

76　It is lowered into the glaze with the top held so that glaze will immediately be able to enter the inside which eliminates the buoyancy which would occur if the base was immersed first

77 Lowered like this it sinks in quickly and easily. As the form is immersed it should be tilted back sufficiently far towards a vertical position to ensure that no air is trapped inside when it is finally submerged. If air is trapped, part of the inside is likely to be unglazed. This is obviously easy to avoid with a cylinder but fuller, more enclosed forms, would need both more tilting forward initially to allow glaze into the inside and then more tilting back to allow air out

78 The form is held under the glaze surface for as long as necessary. The edge of the form should emerge from the glaze first so that air can enter the inside

79 As soon as the top edge is out of the glaze the form should be so tilted that the glaze empties out, lightening the lift. The lower edge will be the last part to emerge from the glaze. In this example the base had been previously resisted with banded wax

77

78

79

80

80 The tong grip should be strong enough to allow the form to be gently shaken to remove excess drips from the edge, which might run back causing unevenness. The form can be put down immediately onto a work board and if the tongs are removed before the surface begins to become touch dry they leave no mark. Forms with unwaxed bases which are to remain so, can be put down onto stilts

Two slight problems can arise with tongs. Firstly, if the biscuit is very porous and the form is not put down quickly the tong points can leave tiny crater-like imprints in the glaze surface which will show with some glazes. When this occurs the marks should be left till the glaze is dry and then each mark should be very lightly rubbed once or twice with a finger, filling the hole of the tiny crater with glaze powder. Secondly, glaze running off the tongs can run onto the form causing dribbles of glaze. This is partly a question of the design of the tongs and partly one of fluency. Once it can be seen why the problem is occurring some way of overcoming it should be possible.

This use of tongs is not the only way of glazing outside and inside simultaneously but it shares with the other possibilities the advantages of the speed of a single process and the elimination, in that single process, of the inevitable overlap occurring when inside and outside are glazed separately.

Glazing a plate using glazing claws

81, 82 Although they are extensively used industrially where dip glazing is done glazing claws are not readily available. They are, however, relatively easy to make. Thick mild steel wire can be bent to form reasonably strong tongs and claws. Depending on overall size 8 or 10 gauge (SWG) 4 mm or 3.25 mm thick, is suitable. Like tongs, no shape of claw can be expected to work with every form, and the aspects which vary are overall length, claw shape, and the curve between the claw and the finger hold. The two basic types are those illustrated. One single and one double ended tool will hold most small plates, while two double ended ones are needed for wider plates

83 The grip afforded by claws should be secure enough for the plate to be tilted and shaken with complete confidence and should be comfortable enough for it to be maintained and repeated because, although it can be used for single items, it is a process with relevance to repetition glazing. Very importantly the grip should enable the form to be held so that the hands and all parts of the tools except the claws are safely clear of the plate surface. Forms are always held across the top rather than the bottom surface so they can be put down as soon as glazing is complete

84 Prior to immersion the plate is tilted towards the middle of the glaze container and the leading edge is slid into the glaze

82

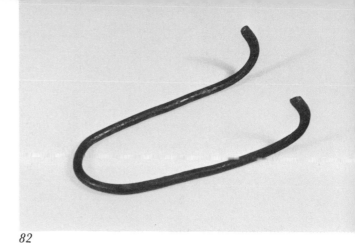

83

81

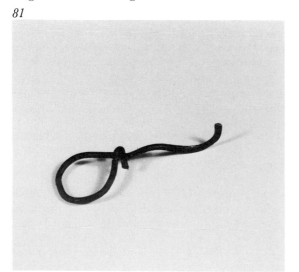

84

85

86

87

85 The tilt ensures that no air is trapped under any foot projections on the base and is maintained as the plate slides further into the glaze

86 Once entirely submerged the plate may briefly be held stationary but, for thinner glazing or with very porous biscuit, the movement through the glaze should be smooth and continuous, the leading edge being tilted upwards and those parts which entered the glaze first, leaving first

87 As the plate emerges from the glaze it is tilted further so that no glaze remains to be poured out of the recess of the plate. Once out of the glaze a gentle shake should remove any drips from the trailing edge and the plate can be put aside on a stilt to dry. As soon as the pulling tension between thumb and fingers is released the claws leave the plate. Just as with tongs, there may be tiny marks to rub lightly later if the particular glaze makes this necessary. The fingers should submerge in the glaze as shallowly as possible during glazing as this minimises what is the major problem with the process – drips of glaze from the fingers falling onto the plate surface as it is put down horizontally. A dextrous shake as soon as the plate has left the glaze helps to eliminate this problem

If the one problem, that of drips, can be overcome, either by experience or a design of claw that means the fingers do not enter the glaze, but more especially by dextrous fluency, this process can result in beautifully even glazing. In theory each part of the plate can be in the glaze for the same length of time. The co-ordination of the tilting motion with a sideways sweeping motion as the plate is lowered into and raised from the glaze should hardly disturb the glaze surface.

This same sweeping and tilting action is basic to the next three sequences and is always one of the alternatives when any type of open, wide form is being glazed.

Glazing a bowl by dipping, using stilts

88 Stilts are not designed to be used for glazing but can be very useful for this and are available in a great variety of shapes and sizes. One size or another can usually be found to hold a form. They have considerable physical as well as refractory strength

89 With open forms of this type the most convenient hold is between two hands with the stilts placed on the outside near the top. Firm pressure is required for steadiness but very large forms can be glazed like this if appropriate containers and amounts of glaze are available

90 So that the glaze has immediate access to the inside the form should be steeply tilted as it enters the glaze

88

89

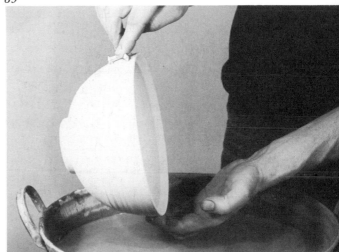

90

91 As soon as the recesses of the foot are submerged the bowl is tilted through to a more horizontal position to glaze the rest of it

92 In a continuous smooth tilting movement the leading edge emerges from the glaze

93 As the bowl emerges from the glaze the tilting action should proceed so that no glaze remains to be poured out of the inside. The whole smooth motion has taken the bowl from one end of the glaze container to the other with minimal disturbance of the glaze surface

91

92

93

94 As the bowl emerges from the glaze one hand is directly above the other and is over one side of the glazed surface. The bowl should not be shaken in this position. Either the bowl should be rotated so the hands are level or the bowl should be tilted back to a horizontal position. In both instances this should be done quickly and the bowl should not be shaken until it has been done

95 Once the bowl is horizontal any drips from the hands do not fall on the glaze surface. One shake clears the glaze clinging to the stilts and the bowl can be put down. Like tongs, stilts leave little or no marks if removed while the glaze surface is still very wet. Any marks left should be treated as for tong marks. If too shallow a shape of stilt is selected, and this is removed only slowly from a fast drying pot, the arms of the stilts can leave a bad blemish on the surface so care should always be taken to ensure that there is adequate clearance between the stilt arms and the bowl surface for any glaze which may cling there to be shaken out. When a foot has not been waxed, saddles, as here, can be used and these mark the wet glaze only minimally

96 Saddles, like stilts, are made to support glazed ware during firing. They also constitute extremely useful supports on which to place glazed bases and feet to dry, and leave only minimal marks which, like stilt marks, can be quickly and simply rubbed over when the glaze is quite dry. Used for this purpose saddles are frequently more stable and convenient than stilts. Once stilts or saddles have been used with wet glaze it is better that they are kept solely for this purpose. If, however, they are subsequently used for supporting ware during firing it is very important that they are washed thoroughly

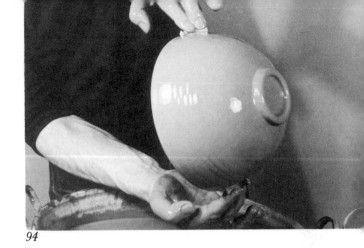

94

95

96

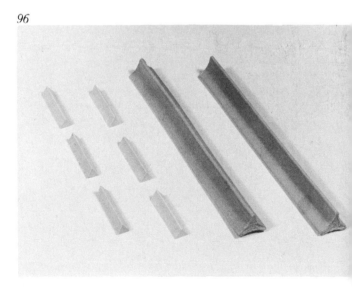

97

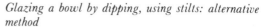

98

Glazing a bowl by dipping, using stilts: alternative method

Bowl forms which do not have fairly vertical sides cannot be held by the previous method. They can, however, be held between the thumb and fingers of one hand with one stilt inside and one outside. To achieve the tilting action, though this is less pronounced with more open forms, and to minimise the hand surface which could make drips on the inside, the thumb should be inside and the fingers outside. One hand does not have the strength to hold and manipulate large forms like this. However, the method can be used with two hands but, even with two hands, the leverage involved in holding a large bowl at one edge imposes a limit on its size.

97   With small forms the grip is a very safe one and the process is best confined to such forms

98, 99, 100, 101   The sequence of actions follows the same pattern as with the previous examples

99

100

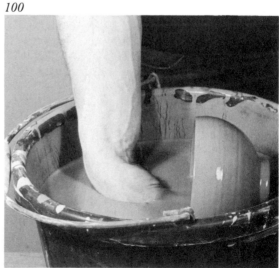

102 As the bowl emerges from the glaze the wet hand is below it so no drips can fall onto the surface of the bowl

103 The moment the glazed bowl is placed on the saddles the dry hand takes over from the thumb gripping the inside stilt. The larger area of the wet hand from which glaze might drip is outside the bowl

104 There are drips of glaze beside the outside of the bowl but, because of the speed and sequence of actions, none is on the bowl inside or out

102

103

101

104

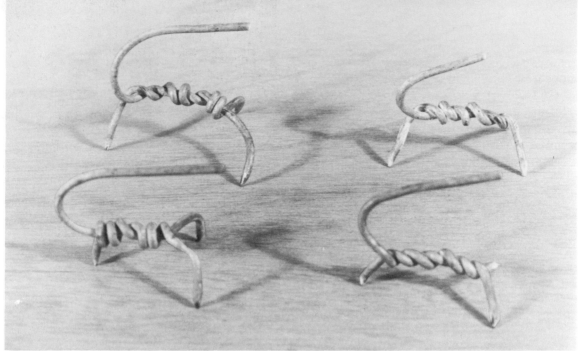

105

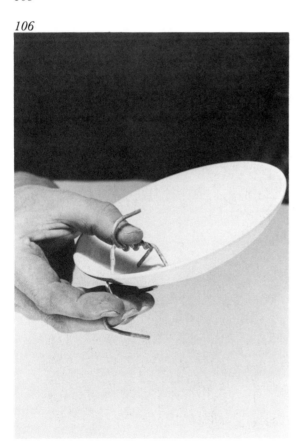

106

Glazing forms using wire holders
In all of the sequences shown using stilts, wire holders can be substituted. As these cannot be bought they have to be made. They are somewhat less comfortable to hold than stilts but have the advantage that they are easier to remove and can be made to virtually any width and depth.

105   To make wire holders 10 gauge steel rod (SWG) is needed. Each holder is made of two short lengths of wire which are twisted together very tightly so that there is no movement in the tiny structure. Three of the ends are bent downwards and the points are sharpened and the fourth end is turned over upwards

In use the holds are virtually identical to those used with stilts

106   Shallow open forms can be held with one holder inside and one outside

80

107, 108 Deeper open forms and more vertical forms are held between two hands with one holder on each side of the form

107

108

109

110

111

Glazing bowls, finger held, by dipping

Well performed, finger holding by edges with appropriate glazes can be a very efficient method. Inevitably it produces unevenness where the fingers touch and the unevenness occurs where it can be most obvious, but some glazes are much more sensitive to variations of thickness than others and, provided an appropriate glaze is used, the process has a decided advantage of speed over glazing with tongs, claws, wire holders or stilts.

Small forms can be held between the thumb and a finger of one hand while larger forms should be held between two fingers of one hand, for steadiness, and one finger of the other hand.

109 The fingers which actually grip the pot should be well covered with wet glaze

110, 111, 112, 113 The immersing, sweeping, tilting sequence is the same as with claws and stilts but, as the hand has to be over the bowl to place it down when glazing is done, the fingers should be immersed as shallowly as possible

114 The bowl should be put down as quickly as possible when it is removed from the glaze so that the finger holds can be touched up before the glaze begins to dry. This touching up is done with a finger dipped in glaze. Rather than actually dabbing glaze onto the bowl the finger is passed over the finger holds, barely touching the actual surface, smoothing out the marks at the edge of the finger holds as much as adding glaze. Some people prefer to let the glaze become touch dry and then touch up marks with a brush but this is a real interruption as the quality of the whole process is its fluency. A common mistake is initially to grip the edges with dry unglazed fingers. This should never be done. To do this will leave a bare patch with a ridge of drying glaze around it which is much more difficult to touch up effectively and quickly

112

113

114

115

116

117

Bounce glazing

This process has a number of different names such as wave glazing, flop glazing, or double dipping, all of which are partly descriptive. Like so many processes in pottery there are several ways it can be done but while details and sequences are variable, there is a common principle. This principle is that once the whole rim of an inverted pot is lowered below the glaze surface a sharp upward and downward movement causes the glaze within it to shoot upwards, by virtue of the suddenly changed air pressure inside the pot. The aim is to cause the glaze inside the pot to well up and coat the whole of the inner surface. Some sequences aim to shoot the glaze up one side and down the other while others, more vertical in action, aim to create a water spout effect which shoots the glaze centrally up to the inside bottom of the pot from where it spreads out and drains back down the walls. Either before or after the sharp bouncing action, the pot is lowered into the glaze to coat the outside to the intended level. The process presupposes that the base of a pot can be firmly gripped and is most usually used when the bottom 12 mm, whether or not this constitutes a turned foot, is to be left unglazed. Though the width of the top of a pot does impose limitations on this process, the application of bounce glazing is not limited to small bowls. The process depends on timing and practice. The fact that the inside is invisible makes it rather difficult to show the sequence in photographs and the speed of the sudden bounce adds to this difficulty but the important thing is to clarify the principles and a possible sequence.

The process can be practised with a cylindrical drinking glass in a bowl of glaze which has the distinct advantage that the behaviour of the glaze inside the form can be observed. If this is done one can see that, as well as sending glaze shooting up the inside walls, the bouncing action displaces air from the inside of the form and leaves a large proportion of the inside volume filled with glaze held there by air pressure.

115 The normal grip is between the thumb and first two fingers of one hand. A securer grip is made if the fingers are first dipped into water

116 Some people lower the form horizontally and complete the entire sequence with purely vertical movements but in this sequence the bowl is lowered into the glaze at a slight slant. As soon as the upper edge enters the glaze the bowl is returned to a horizontal position. This motion has, therefore, trapped a small amount of glaze inside the bowl. If the bowl were now to be raised a little the weight of the glaze within it would cause a reduced air pressure inside and, as always, if the bowl were to be lowered the air pressure inside would be increased

117 The bowl is being raised here to begin the first of two double bounces. The bounces are sharp movements but are not extensive – 25 mm of vertical movement is quite enough. Each of the double bounces is one slight movement to begin the wave of glaze followed by a sharp one to push the glaze up the side. In the first double bounce the bowl is tilted to the right and in the second to the left which sends two waves of glaze over the inside one after the other in opposite directions

118 Because there is no sudden change of air pressure on the glaze outside the bowl the effect of the bounces on the outside is much less extreme, and here the effect of the two actions on the outside can be seen

119 Immediately the bounce or bounces are complete the bowl is lowered into the glaze to coat the outside, and is held steady for as long as is judged necessary. As it is raised up in the glaze a fast but small rotary action helps to swill further glaze round the inside

120 To minimise splashing by the sudden release of the glaze held inside, the bowl should be tilted as it is removed from the glaze. It should be held upside down and shaken gently to remove drips of excess glaze and when the danger of runs of glaze has disappeared it can be turned right way up and slid onto the edge of a workboard

Whichever sequence is followed it is the timing and fluency of the bounces which are central to the success of the process. On forms which do not permit a secure grip at the base or on the foot an alternative hold, with forms which are not too large, is to grip the form between the index finger on the top edge and the thumb on the base. This alternative has the slight disadvantage that the finger mark on the edge has to be touched up in the usual way. Once the knack of the bounce is acquired the process is excellent for the speedy glazing of small forms.

118

119

120

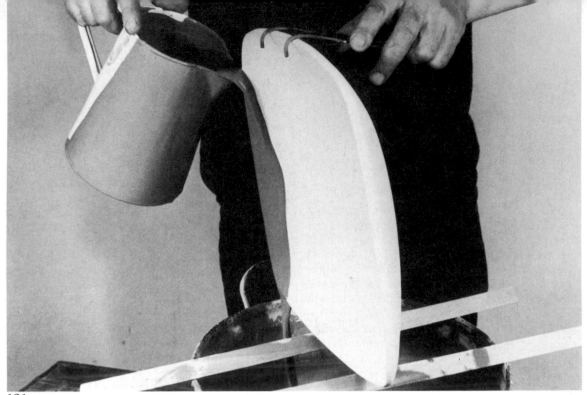

121

Split glazing
Some shallow forms can be quickly, easily and evenly glazed by this method but if evenness is the intention it is limited to shallow forms which have no relief which would divert the even flow of the glaze over the form.

121   The shallow form is supported in a vertical position over a container, its lower edge supported on two triangular section lengths of wood and its upper edge held with a glaze claw or some such convenient tool. Starting at one side the glaze is poured so that the centre of the poured stream of glaze is split by the edge, half glazing the front of the dish and half the back

122   The jug is moved across the top edge steadily pouring a stream which is split by the edge

123   To eliminate the possibility of unglazed streaks, the aim should be to sustain a full, steady stream of glaze from beginning to end. It is advisable to have rather more glaze than might seem necessary

The process has two drawbacks. Firstly, the glaze layer tends to thicken towards the supported edge. This can be partly overcome by dampening the area with a sponge before the glaze is poured but if the edge is thin this must not be overdone. Secondly, when thrown plates or dishes have prominently defined feet, the stream of glaze tends to form unevennesses as it passes over and round the foot. There is little that can be done about this. But with forms such as that illustrated it is very effective.

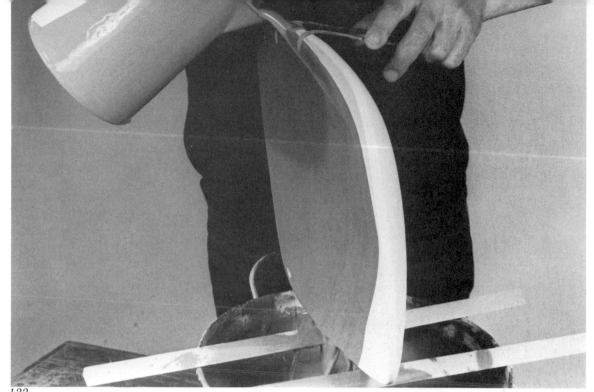

122

123

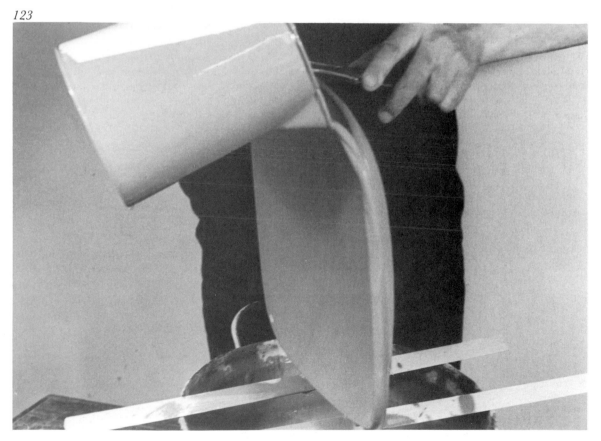

124

Glazing tiles by dipping

Tiles may be glazed either by pouring in the same way as illustrated for slip or they may be dipped. Pouring has the disadvantage that either the margin of the base and the edge have to be resisted or that those parts have to be scraped and sponged clean of glaze.

124   As with all dipping, the glaze should be kept well suspended by frequent stirring. The tile is lowered upside down towards the glaze at an angle until the lower edge is immersed

125   The tile is then tilted until the entire surface is submerged

126   When it has been held steady long enough for a sufficient thickness of glaze to build up, the edge which touched the glaze first is raised first and then the whole tile is removed, gently shaken, turned over and put aside to dry

One small problem with the process is that bubbles on the surface of the glaze suspension can transfer themselves to the glaze layer on the tile causing unevenness and even bare spots. This can be avoided simply by wiping away any bubbles which appear to the edge of the glaze container.

It takes very little time to acquire this simple, fluent process which will give a run-free, even layer of glaze with the great advantage that the base needs no cleaning. With many glazes the partially glazed edges may be left but with the very fluid glazes sometimes used on tiles the edges have to be scraped clean. Even in this case the saving of time in not having to scrape and sponge the base is considerable.

The sequence should present no problems with flat tiles but tiles which contain relief should be bounced just as the whole surface touches the glaze to expel air pockets from the relief.

125

126

127

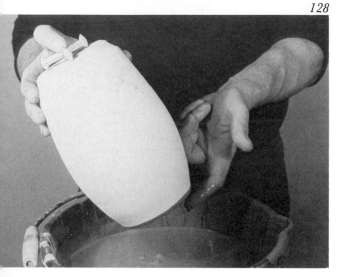

128

129

Glazing larger vertical forms

Glazing larger vertical forms by a single total immersion in which outside and inside are simultaneously glazed tends not to be possible using any of the procedures outlined with smaller forms. In theory, identical procedures will work if sufficient glaze and suitably large containers are available but this is rarely the case. It should be remembered that containers not only have to be large enough to contain the form but also must allow it to be tilted and manoeuvred about in the ways necessary. In practice, therefore, unless containers and quantities of glaze permit it, inside and outside are glazed separately rather than simultaneously. The inside is glazed first and, with or without a brief interval, the outside is then glazed by dipping or pouring or a combination of both.

Because of the need to divide the glazing of larger forms into clearer phases than is the case with smaller forms, procedures tend to be more variable. This section therefore includes four examples which show different aspects or details. For the sake of clarity and continuity some duplication of illustration between the examples has been retained.

127   The inside is glazed by filling about half the form with glaze and rotating the form as the glaze is poured out. As always, pouring out should be positive enough to avoid dribbles of glaze running onto the outside

128   As soon as the inside is glazed the form is inverted ready to be dipped. A single finger hold at the top edge is sufficient for medium sized forms but two are safer for larger forms. The stilt on the base is only necessary if the actual base is to be glazed. With unglazed bases the stilt is dispensed with and the form is either simply dipped to a line or dipped fractionally over a banded wax line. The poured edge should still be wet when dipping commences and the finger, or fingers, on the top edge should be wet with glaze

129   The form is held as vertically as possible and lowered quickly but steadily into the glaze. The air trapped inside gives forms a degree of buoyancy and after they are half submerged they have to be firmly pushed down

130 If the base is to be glazed it is unnecessary to do more than just submerge it. The top of the stilt can still be seen. This illustration clearly shows the judgement of glaze amounts which is necessary if this method is to be used successfully. Obviously the container has to be an adequate depth for the height of the form and it has to be wide enough for the arm as well as the form. These two aspects are easy enough to measure before glazing commences. But when relatively large forms are being glazed in relatively small containers the judgement of the amount of glaze to have in the glaze container is crucial: if too much the submerged arm and form will displace glaze over the top edge of the container, if too little the top of the form will reach the bottom of the container before it is completely submerged

131 If the base has, as here, been glazed it is important to tilt the form as soon as the flat base is clear of the glaze surface so that any excess glaze runs off the base into the glaze suspension, rather than in a streak down the side of the form, which occurs if the form is not tilted until later. The form is then removed from the glaze and held momentarily over the container at a slant to allow excess glaze droplets to gather on one side of the edge. It is then shaken to remove these droplets and turned to an upright position

132 With glazed bases it is convenient to use a fairly tall stilt as this facilitates placing the form down on a work surface quickly so that the finger-hold mark on the top can be touched up while the glaze layer is still wet

The following sequence is probably the next best method to that of the previous example with forms of this broad type and should be considered next when the previous one is impracticable.

130

131

132

91

133

134

133 When glaze is poured it can tend to gather somewhat on underhanging surfaces. The best solution is to dampen the areas where glaze may gather a bit too thickly. This can be done by quickly dipping parts of the form into water but it is often simpler to sponge the relevant areas with a very wet sponge until the wetness on the biscuit surface dries noticeably slower than at first. In this instance the sponging is wettest at the base and decreases towards the widest point. Were this form to be supported on its edge and poured upside down the shoulder, not the lower part, would be the relevant area to sponge

134 Forms of this shape are easier to glaze inside with proportionally less glaze than more cylindrical forms because the glaze can be swilled round to glaze the inside evenly before any is actually poured out. The form therefore is only about one quarter filled with glaze

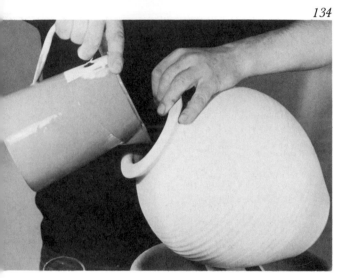

135 The broad edge of the form is glazed by the rotating motion of pouring out the glaze. A form with an edge detail such as this is extremely easy to glaze inside without any risk of making runs or splashes on the outside

135

136 Immediately the glaze has been poured from the inside, and as a continuation of this action, the form is inverted and dipped to just below the top edge. The precise movement of this dipping is extremely important. While it is being dipped the form is being lowered deeper and deeper into the glaze. This gradual dipping produces a layer of glaze which diminishes in thickness down the form. It is the gradation of this layer which allows an even layer to be poured

136

137

137 As soon as the top of the form has been dipped for an adequate length of time it is stood right way up over a bowl, and resting on two triangular sectioned lengths of wood. The bowl rests on a banding wheel so that the form can be rotated. Pouring commences as quickly as possible into the glaze immediately below the top edge which is still very wet. In this illustration the wetness of the glaze on and under the top edge can be clearly seen as can the gradation of wetness – and in fact of thickness – to the dry thin layer of glaze left at the deepest point of the dip. This is the whole point of the gradually deepening dipping action because the thin dry layer does not show once glaze has been poured over it. If the form had been dipped to a level and held stationary a thick dipped edge would have been formed which the pouring would not have concealed

138 Throughout the pouring action the banding wheel is steadily rotated and the jug is held close to the form, pouring from as high up under the edge as possible. Care must always be taken that the jug's spout does not touch the glaze surface because it will leave a mark of thinner glaze. Several rotations pouring with a thinner glaze will always give a more even layer than fewer rotations with a thicker glaze

Once the layer of glaze has become touch dry it is possible to apply a second layer. This can be of the same glaze, simply to increase the total thickness of the glaze or, if the slats and containers are replaced with clean ones, can be of a different glaze, the two particular glazes one over the other, giving a further result. In this latter instance it might well be appropriate, if a precise demarcation is required, to band wax on and just under the top edge to give a line to pour to, or, if the top edge is re-dipped, to band a broad wax line inside the top of the form.

138

139

140

139 In the continuation of this example the dry and very even glaze from the initial pouring sequence can be seen. The top edge has not been re-dipped and the same glaze is being used simply to build up greater thickness. Poured, as is shown, just under the broad top edge, the creation of obvious variations of thickness can be avoided

140 As with the initial sequence, pouring should continue for a number of rotations to even out the second layer of glaze

Three points should be made about pouring second layers of glaze. Firstly, glaze thickness may be built up relatively more quickly on a touch dry layer of glaze than on biscuit, especially if the particular glaze has a low or non-plastic clay content. Secondly, sudden pouring of glaze from some distance can tend to wash away the initial layer, especially if the biscuit is not very porous. Thirdly, the second pouring should occur very shortly after the initial layer has become touch dry because, if the initial layer becomes too dry, the sudden wetting caused by the second layer can make the initial layer bubble up from the biscuit surface which frequently leads to crawling.

In this next example the sequence is very similar to the previous one with the main difference that the inside and outside are glazed with different glazes so the smooth continuity of pouring the inside, and dipping and pouring the outside, is necessarily interrupted.

141 The inside is glazed normally

141

142 To give a safety margin for the application of wax the outside is then dipped to 12 mm

143 The whole of the inside of the edge is banded with wax and, to achieve a precise demarcation, the wax is continued just over the edge to about 2 mm down the outside. Care must obviously be taken that no wax gets onto the unglazed biscuit of the outside which would cause unglazable marks

144 The 12 mm of glaze with the 2 mm of superimposed wax are then cut through with a suitable thin pointed knife leaving a precise line of waxed glaze at the edge. The thin residue of dipped glaze is then wiped clean with a barely damp sponge

145 Because of the time delay of working on the top edge, any sponging of the outside to reduce the possibility of overthick glazing on the underhang should be done now rather than before the inside is glazed. The sequence then follows that of the previous example

143

144

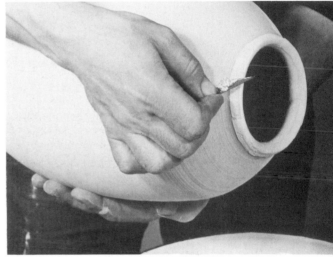

142

145

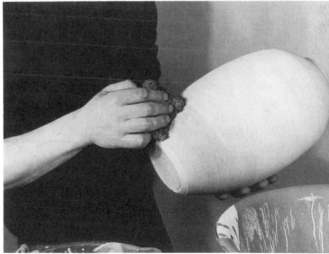

Continued on page 98

Body A 1040°C	Body A 1120°C	Body A 1200°C	Body A 1280°C
Body B 1040°C	Body B 1120°C	Body B 1200°C	Body B 1280°C
Body C 1040°C	Body C 1120°C	Body C 1200°C	Body C 1280°C
Body D 1040°C	Body D 1120°C	Body D 1200°C	Body D 1280°C

PLATE 1(a)

All the tests were fired in an oxidising atmosphere. Body A is a fine fireclay based body; Body B is based on fireclay and has quite coarse fireclay grog; Body C is based on ball clay and a fine fireclay; Body D is based on china clay and ball clay. The clay tests show the darkening effect of increased temperature which is typical to a greater or lesser extent of all, except white, bodies. The subtle colour changes which are discernible in white bodies become most obvious when these are vitrified. In a porous state white bodies have a chalky, very slightly pinkish white appearance whereas once vitrified they show a creamy white when oxidised and a bluish white when reduced, that difference being due to the different effect of oxidation or reduction on the iron impurities which, as a fractional percentage, are always present.

Plates 1(a) and 1(b) show the effect of temperature on the colour of clay bodies. Change of colour is of course only one of a number of effects which different temperatures have on clay bodies.

Staffs 1 1080°C	Staffs 1 1130°C	Staffs 1 1180°C	Staffs 1 1230°C	Staffs 1 1280°C
Staffs 2 1080°C	Staffs 2 1130°C	Staffs 2 1180°C	Staffs 2 1230°C	Staffs 2 1280°C
N Devon 1080°C	N Devon 1130°C	N Devon 1180°C		

The three clay bodies shown here are all common red earthenware bodies. Those in the top two rows are from Staffordshire and that in the bottom row is from North Devon. With the exception of the two samples fired at 1280°C, which were reduced, all the tests were fired in an oxidising atmosphere. The effect of different temperatures on these bodies is obvious.

Conventionally red 'earthenware' clays are thought of as being useful up to and not much above 1100°C but some are more refractory than this, as is the case with the two Staffordshire clays shown here. While very high temperatures are clearly excessive for such bodies they can be mixed with others to produce sound, dark firing, dense bodies at temperature well in excess of 1100°C. The North Devon body shows a behaviour which is typical of many bodies based on common red clays. At 1080°C it is a very sound, slightly porous but strong body. At 1130°C it is glassily brittle and, in fact, distorts badly. At 1180°C it is fluxing quite strongly and beginning to flow. Such behaviour usually indicates the presence of lime in the body. Such bodies can be very strong and durable but clearly their temperature of firing is more crucial than with some other bodies in which the transition from porosity to instability occurs across a wider firing range.

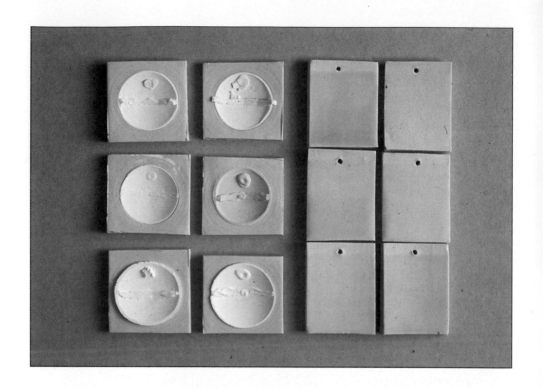

Molochite (Calcined China clay)	Whiting	Woolastonite 48·23 / Molochite 32·31 / Flint 19·46	Whiting 35·15 / Molochite 27·31 / Flint 37·54
China clay	Woolastonite	Whiting 35·15 / Alumina 12·55 / Flint 52·30	Whiting 33·66 / China clay 30·4 / Flint 35·95
Flint	Alumina	Woolastonite 48·23 / Alumina 14·94 / Flint 36·92	Woolastonite 45·83 / China clay 35·68 / Flint 18·94

PLATE 2(a)

This plate demonstrates the phenomenon of a eutectic. On the left are six tests of prepared raw materials and on the right are six mixtures of these materials. The material tests and the mixtures are all applied to the same white body and all are fired to 1260°C in a reducing atmosphere. Not one of the tests of materials shows any tendency to flux, even weakly, yet the mixtures, all of which contain only particular proportions of the materials on the left, are all glassily shiny. This underlines the fact that particular combinations of materials react and melt at lower temperatures than the constituent materials. The basis of these tests is the lime: alumina: silica eutectic. The oxide percentage formula of this is lime (Ca O) 23.25%: alumina ($Al_2 O_3$) 14.75%: silica ($Si O_2$) 62.0%. Expressed by the molecular unity method the formula is

$$Ca\ O \quad Al_2\ O_3\ 0.35 \quad Si\ O_2\ 2.48$$

The mixtures were all calculated using the ideal formulae for the six raw materials, and the molecular unity method of calculation. By this method the mixtures are theoretically identical. The mixtures on the right are, however, subtly different. Using percentage analyses of the actual raw materials, if further calculations are done starting with the recipes of the six mixtures, the amounts of the minor impurities which lead to the subtle differences can be identified.

Body E Unglazed	Body F Unglazed	Body G Unglazed	Body H Unglazed
Body E Glaze 1	Body F Glaze 1	Body G Glaze 1	Body H Glaze 1
Body E Glaze 2	Body F Glaze 2	Body G Glaze 2	Body H Glaze 2
Body E Glaze 3	Body F Glaze 3	Body G Glaze 3	Body H Glaze 3

PLATE 2(b)

All the tests were fired at 1280°C in a reducing atmosphere. The lower half of the glazed tests has a thicker glaze layer than the upper half. The differences of colour, texture and tonality of each of the three glazes on the four different bodies should be noted.

This illustration shows the limitation of thinking of a glaze as having precise qualities outside of its use on a specified body or type of body. This factor should be considered when making glaze tests and, to some extent, applies to all glazes across the whole temperature range.

146 The top is dipped with gradually deepening action into the glaze

147, 148 The outside is poured. In these two illustrations it is noticeable that the initial pouring, before the banding wheel was turned, made a vertical mark but that, as the banding wheel is turned, the glaze stream falls diagonally down the surface. This phenomenon is most noticeable in the first rotation and the speed of rotation and the flow of glaze should be co-ordinated so that the diagonal curtain of falling glaze reaches the bottom without splitting. Once the entire surface is covered with wet glaze, the stream of glaze falls more vertically down the unresisting surface and the volume of the flow can be reduced because, while the surface is wet, there is less chance of the stream splitting and creating streaks of uneven thickness. With this form, unlike the previous example, the top edge offers no barrier to the glaze actually being poured into the form, so the action has to be very steady and controlled. For a really even layer the graduated dipping action must be well done and the pouring action must be as high up on the dipped part as is possible and safe

146

147

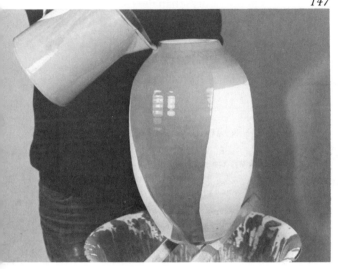

148

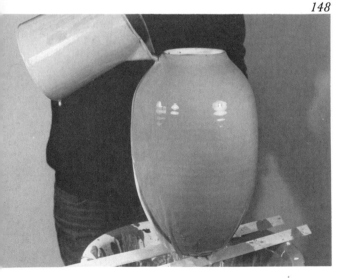

149 When the bases of forms and any chamfers at the bases are to be unglazed, waxing these parts is much quicker than the alternative of scraping and sponging but it can lead to one slight problem in that the banded wax tends to hold a thickish roll of glaze immediately above it. If the particular glaze tends to be fluid when fired this additional thickness can make it run during firing and, if the roll is anyway rather thick, it is liable to be accidentally chipped off in places before it is fired. The problem is easy to cure. As soon as pouring is complete a soft brush, wet with glaze, should be held against the side of the form resting half on the waxed chamfer and half in the gathered roll of glaze, and the form should be slowly rotated for one or more full revolutions. This effectively reduces the roll to a reasonable and even thickness

In this last of the four examples of glazing larger forms the particular form is wider at the top and the outside is glazed with the form upside down. It has been glazed inside and the edge has been waxed and cleaned up as in the previous example. The base and the chamfer to the base have been waxed. The procedure could be done without waxing the top edge as a more or less continuous action of pouring the inside and then the outside, but the scars left by the supporting sticks tend to be quite large if this is done and can only be touched up when the glaze is touch dry.

150 To glaze the outside, the form has been placed on lengths of wood of triangular cross section placed across a bowl which is placed on a banding wheel. Wood of this cross section sheds the poured glaze well. Square or rectangular battens should not be used as these allow glaze to settle on their surface which causes thicknesses to gather near the top edge of the pot

151 The problem with this example is that for the initial slower and more deliberately poured rotation the shallow chamfer does not offer a large surface to pour against. The danger is that some glaze might, in the initial slow rotation, shoot across the base and cause a run down the opposite side which could begin to dry before the pouring reached it. To overcome this problem the initial pouring is onto the base and the form is rotated fairly quickly until the entire surface is glazed

149

150

151

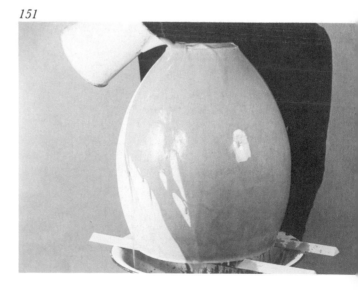

99

152

153

152 During subsequent rotations a lesser flow of glaze is poured onto the chamfer to even out and build up the thickness of glaze

153 The moment pouring ceases any glaze on the waxed base is mopped up with a sponge before it has any chance of running off down the evenly glazed sides. Where there are considerable puddles of glaze on the wax the sponge action to gather them up should be inwards from the chamfer. Once any pools have been gathered up the wax can be wiped clean of droplets of glaze with a clean sponge

154 Finally, larger drips at the top edge are absorbed by a soft brush

154

Glazing larger open forms

Like larger vertical forms the glazing of wide bowls can follow the sequences relevant to smaller forms if large containers and quantities of glaze are available. As this is rarely the case, the sequence of actions is split up so inside and outside are glazed separately, the inside invariably being glazed first.

The two examples which follow are essentially different only in the way the form is supported for the outside to be glazed.

155 So that a circular, thicker layer of glaze does not occur in the middle the bowl should be tilted as the glaze is poured in, and the glaze should be poured in quickly. Sufficient glaze is needed for the radius from the edge to the middle to be covered as the bowl is tilted and rotated

156 So that a defined area of thickening is not created, there should be no pause between pouring the glaze into the bowl and starting the rotation. The line formed by the glaze as the bowl is rotated should be kept as near to the edge as possible and as neat and precise as possible. The steady fluency of tilting and rotating may take a little practice to acquire but it is fundamental to creating an even layer of glaze

157 With glaze of a thick consistency, and a biscuit of only slight porosity, a single rotation will give a reasonably even coating, but with thinner glaze and a more porous biscuit two, three or more rotations, as particular conditions may allow, will result in a more even layer of glaze. It is always best to adjust the glaze consistency to allow this. Accidental runs of glaze over the edge onto the outside should be avoided as much as possible. If they do occur they should either be left to be scraped off with a metal kidney or palette knife before the outside is glazed or, while still wet, they can be smeared off with the fingers if confidence is such that this does not interrupt the continuation of the glazing of the inside

155

156

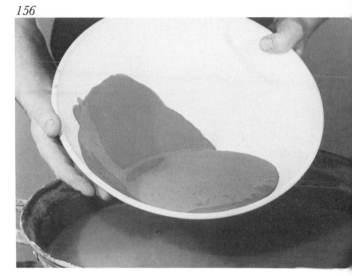

157

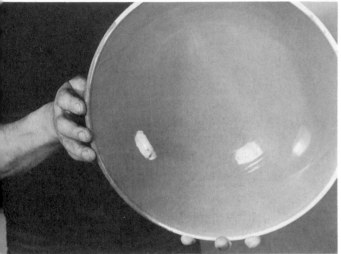

158   When a sufficient number of rotations are complete the glaze should be tipped out fairly sharply so there is no danger of the glaze running back round the edge onto the outside. It is then gently shaken, not hard enough to disturb the whole layer but sharply enough to dislodge drops from the edge

159   Then, most importantly, before the glaze has begun to dry, the edge where the glaze was poured out is wiped with a finger. This smearing action does not clean the edge, it merely removes the thickness of glaze which would create a considerable additional thickness when the outside is glazed if it was not removed. Any runs of glaze on the outside can now be scraped off with a palette knife or metal kidney. These do not need sponging, the important thing being to remove the layer of glaze. Only if the edge and outside are to be glazed with a different glaze do the edge and any runs have to be sponged clean. If and when this sponging is done the sponge should be barely damp so that the porisity of the biscuit in those parts is only minimally affected

160   When the inside glaze is touch dry the outside is glazed by a combination of dipping and pouring. The sequence of actions in the dipping stage is important. If the foot is at all deep the whole bowl should be slightly tilted as it enters the glaze so that no air is trapped but if this would result in a large eccentric dipped area, as would be the case with many deep footed but shallow forms, or if the foot is deep and angular, then the whole bowl should be gently bounced as it enters the glaze to displace glaze into and to cover the inside of the foot. The bowl is then lowered into the glaze for about a third of its height. It should not be held steady but should be moved up and down slowly so that no thickening edge line of glaze can build up, exactly as has already been described in the glazing of larger vertical forms

161 The bowl is turned upside down as quickly as possible. It may be supported directly by the fingers but a folded towel or other suitable cloth does protect the glaze layer inside from inadvertent damage

162 When pouring the outside commences, which should be done as quickly as possible, the thicker glaze near the foot will still be very wet and the thin glaze at the extreme edge may be drying slightly. Pouring should be into the wet glaze and as the edge of the dipped mark is thin it will not show as a line. Most of the movement is done by the hand which is pouring the glaze but for a really smoothly efficient action the supporting hand, limited though its possible motion is, must co-ordinate. It can do this firstly by tilting the bowl appropriately as the pouring hand moves round it, secondly by rotating the bowl through the 40 degrees possible so that in pouring right round the bowl in separate consecutive actions there is never need to pour glaze over the supporting arm, and thirdly by moving as necessary with the pouring hand so that the glaze stream pouring off the bowl returns into the container not onto the table. Each of the separate pouring actions commences on the inside of the left arm (with the right hand pouring and left hand supporting, as in this sequence) with the bowl rotated as far to the left as possible and, as the pouring hand moves round the bowl, the bowl itself is rotated to the right so that the point of initial pouring is reached before the outside of the left arm. The method involves an overlap in each of the separate actions but as long as conditions allow for two, three or more consecutive actions, without excessive thickness occurring, and as long as the whole glaze layer is wet throughout the pouring actions, no unevenness will occur or show

163 A final pouring rotation can be nearer to the edge and it is important that the flow of glaze is gentle, and not, therefore, from any great height, as a sudden rush of glaze into a poured glaze layer can displace glaze, leaving unevennesses

161

162

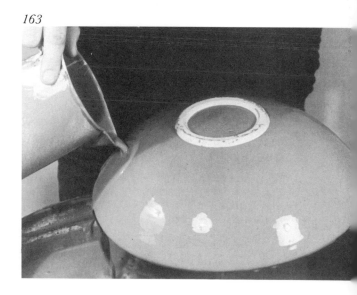

163

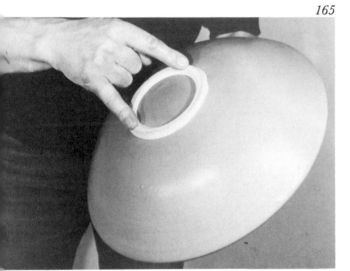

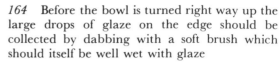

164 Before the bowl is turned right way up the large drops of glaze on the edge should be collected by dabbing with a soft brush which should itself be well wet with glaze

165, 166 The droplets of glaze on the banded wax on the foot can be sponged away and when all danger of runs from the edge has gone the bowl can be turned right way up. Although drying, the outside glaze is not yet touch dry. Waxed feet are not very easy to grip securely and it is safest to check that the grip is not slippery by pushing firmly on the foot before turning the bowl over, held between the inside hand and the fingers on the foot, and sliding it onto the edge of a workboard or table

167 Whether or not outside and inside layers of glaze meet or overlap when this process is used, is largely governed by the precise form of the actual edge. A tendency to overlap can be avoided with the use of wax. Where glaze layers do not quite meet, as here, the fine bare line should be touched up as soon as possible, preferably while the outside glaze is still just wet. A soft brush filled, but not overfilled, with glaze should be used and the action is one of gentle touching. As much as adding glaze, the brush spreads out the wet glaze already on the edge

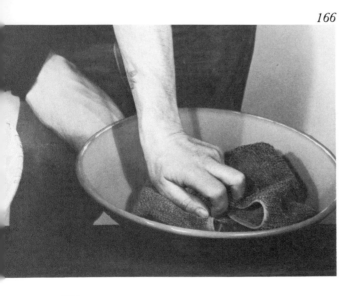

164

165

166

167

This next example is similar to the previous one and the description is, therefore, abbreviated. The major difference is that rather than being hand held, the bowl is supported over a banding wheel for the outside to be poured.

168 The inside is glazed in an identical way to the previous example

169 As soon as the middle of the inside is touch dry the lower part of the outside is dipped identically

170 The bowl is then placed onto a previously prepared rest. The improvised rest on a banding wheel should allow the banding wheel to be moved right up to the glaze container so that the bowl edge will project well over the container. Any stable object of the right height can be used to raise the bowl sufficiently but a folded towel or a piece of dry sponge foam should be used to prevent damage to the inside glaze. The bowl should be central on the banding wheel and stable on its rest. Clearly the process is only relevant to wide bowls

168

169

170

105

171 The rest should be ready for immediate use after dipping and the bowl is transferred quickly to it and, as before, pouring commences into the wet and thicker layer nearest the foot

172 Glaze does not always travel evenly or well over wide edges and any bare areas left after the first pouring action tend to remain bare as each new pouring follows the shapes made by the first, because there is less resistance in these. To overcome this tendency, when the bowl has been poured for one or two rotations, pouring should be stopped and the edge should be banded with a broad glaze-filled brush. This does not leave an adequate coating but it wets the whole edge by spreading the glaze

173 If pouring is then continued the glaze will flow back across the whole edge leaving an even coat. In this illustration the glaze can be clearly seen pouring off the inner, not the outer, edge. When pouring is complete the final action, as before, is to remove any drops from the edge with a brush

This sequence has advantages over the previous one in that pouring in a continuous rotation can be more even than with separate repeated rotations; that the glazing of the edge can be more controlled and that a wide bowl does not have to be hand held and therefore, rather awkwardly manipulated. It has the disadvantages, however, that, with the removal of the possibility of tilting the bowl while glaze is being poured, unevennesses of glaze from pouring can settle on the more horizontal part of the form near the foot and that the bowl cannot be moved to one side until it is touch dry.

171

172

173

Glazing a stem bowl

This example is included because it shows how processes used with simpler forms can be combined and adapted in relatively more complex contexts.

For the sake of photographic clarity different glazes have been used inside and out.

174 The inside of the bowl is part filled on a slant as usual and is glazed up to the highest part of the edge with a number of rotations

175 The glaze is poured out relatively slowly as the bowl is slowly rotated twice, thereby glazing evenly the entire circumference of the edge. Holding the stem of such a bowl makes this an easily controlled action. A few small runs of glaze on the outside may occur because of the slow rotations used to glaze the edge

176 The edge is then waxed to 25 mm down the inside, across and just over the wide edge but keeping a safe margin between the wax edge and the unglazed biscuit

177 The wax and glaze are then cut back to a clean edge and any small runs of glaze are scraped off

175

176

174

177

178

179

180

178   The runs and the scraped edge are then sponged clean

179   The edge of the foot is then waxed and glaze is poured into it. Because of the difficulty of part filling this, tipping it round and pouring it out without splashing glaze onto the outer part of the bowl, the whole form is held vertical and the foot is filled to just short of the edge. A clean, dry jug is then held upside down just over the edge of the foot

180   In one quick swinging action, keeping the bowl and the jug in the same relative positions, the two are turned over ejecting the glaze from the foot into the jug. Because it is necessarily a fast action the position at the end is shown. The action is one which can be useful in a variety of contexts

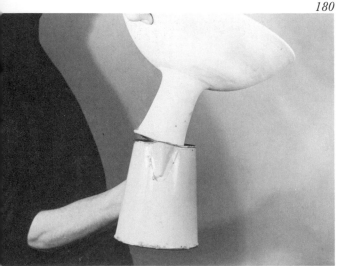

181   The outside of the stem is then glazed by dipping it up to its junction with the bowl and tapering the thickness just onto the bowl in the usual way

182   A towel is then placed in the bowl to prevent damage to the surface in the final pouring

183   The whole form is then inverted and glazed in much the same way as a normal bowl. The junction of dipped and poured glazes is convenient both to the pouring process and visually for while there should be no unevenness, any which does occur is in the least obvious place. In this illustration note how neatly the glazes meet as the glaze poured onto the base of the bowl extends a short way up the stem to overlap into the still wet dipped layer

181

182

183

184

185

184 Droplets can then be sponged from the foot

185 Drips at the wax line can be collected on a soft brush. If there is a thicker roll of glaze at the wax line this can be brushed gently to thin it while still wet

186 Finally, droplets can be sponged from the waxed top edge. While waxing has obvious advantages in creating a crisp division between two glazes it also has obvious applications in achieving an even overall layer of one glaze

186

Glazing forms by rolling them in glaze

Rolling forms in glaze is particularly relevant with larger forms because it enables them, in effect, to be dipped where either the amount of glaze or the available containers, or both, do not allow the form to be completely immersed. A fairly wide container which permits good access is needed.

187 In the three sequences which follow the fibreglass container, illustrated in figures 5 to 16 as a sieving rest, is used as a glaze container. The tapered outlet is blocked by dropping in a small conical plastic container. The container is then filled with glaze

188 Forms which are being rolled can be held by any of the holding devices shown previously where they are appropriate, or can be finger held, but wire supports can be made which are particularly useful for holding the tops of some forms. These must be thick enough not to bend in use and 8 gauge (SWG) wire, 4 mm thick, is sufficient to ensure this. All that is needed is a straight wire but in use this is difficult to hold and the round wire can tend to roll on the top edge of forms so it is better, as shown, to form a bend in the wire and to flatten its roundness slightly. This makes such tools much easier to hold and prevents any tendency of the wire to move. Tools of different lengths are needed because it is important that the tool is not so long that it inhibits the movement of the form when it is in the glaze

187

188

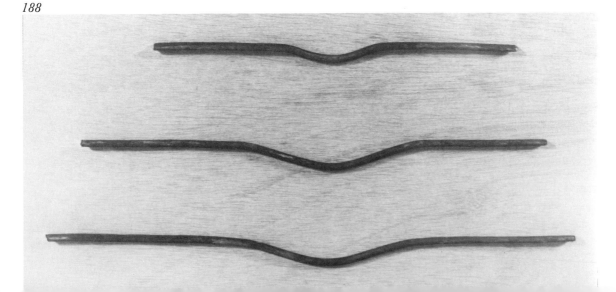

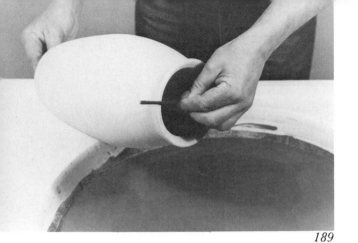

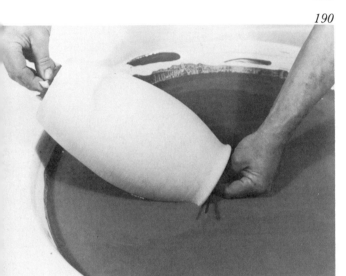

189

190

Rolling a vertical form

189   In use the wire tool is simply placed across the top edge of the form and pressure between the two hands affords a very secure hold

190   A stilt is used in this instance on the base and, in fact, whatever may be the final state of the base, glazed or unglazed, but especially if it is waxed, a stilt offers a secure hold for rolling the form. The form is lowered into the glaze edge first so that glaze flows into the inside

191, 192, 193   Once it is about half submerged, using wrist and finger movement the form is rolled in the glaze by rotating it backwards and forwards as far as the hands can manage

191   *192*

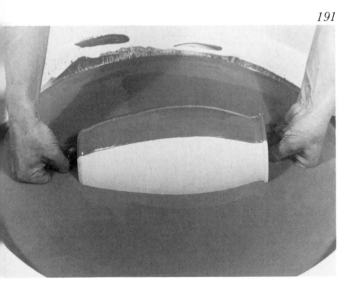

112

194, 195 When an adequate layer of glaze has been achieved the form is removed base first so that no pool of glaze is left inside the form when the edge leaves the glaze

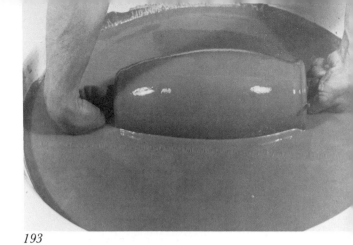

193

194

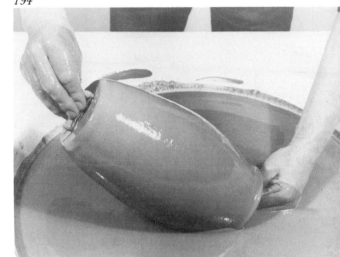

195

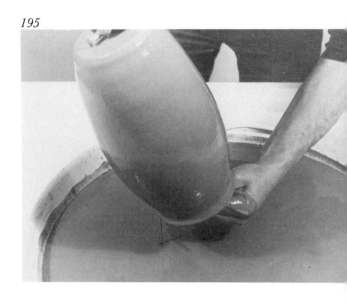

196

Rolling a stem bowl

196   Here a form similar to that shown in figure 174 is being glazed. Being open at top and bottom it is most conveniently held between two wire supports. When forms can be held like this, support is securer if the wires are at right angles to one another, as here

197   Being open top and bottom the form is lowered horizontally into the glaze

198, 199   Using identical hand actions to the previous example the form is rotated backwards and forwards in the glaze

197

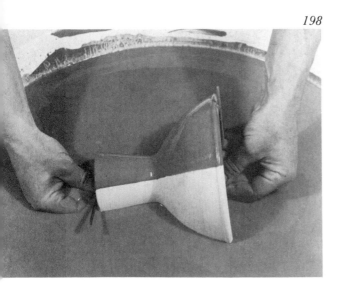

198

199

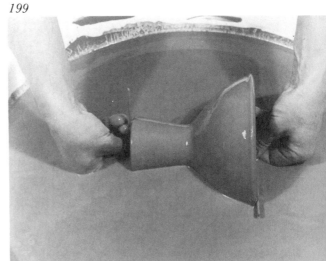

200 So that no glaze is left in either the bowl or the foot, the form must be raised from the glaze surface as horizontally as possible

201, 202 It can then be tilted and rotated to disperse any droplets of glaze. Because of the way the form is held during glazing it is particularly important that an appropriate arrangement of saddles or stilts is laid out before glazing begins so that the form can be put down safely when glazing is complete – though this is obviously not necessary if the foot is waxed or is to be cleaned

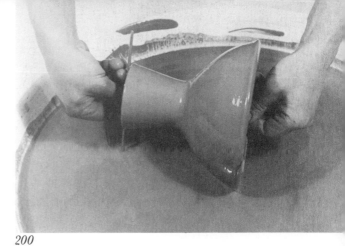

200

201

202

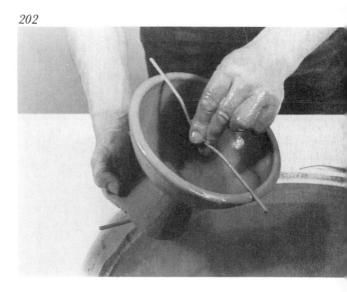

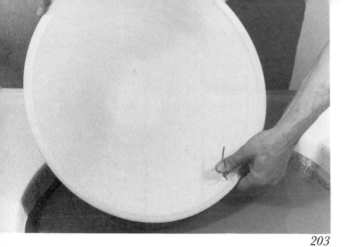

203

204

Rolling a large open form

203 In this instance the form is finger held on one side and held between two wire holders on the other side. It is lowered into glaze fairly vertically

204, 205 As soon as the form has entered the glaze it is gradually lowered to a more horizontal position and the rotation begins

205

206

206, 207 The form is only lowered from the vertical sufficiently for the glaze to cover the area from the submerged edge to beyond the middle. There is no need for any great amount of the form to be submerged as it is in the tilting and rotation – the rolling – rather than the depth of immersion which coats the form with glaze

The form can be taken through however many rotations seem necessary for an adequate layer of glaze to be achieved.

208 Before it is removed from the glaze the form is tilted back to a more vertical position so that there is no pool of glaze to be tipped out

209 While still in the vertical position the form should be rotated backwards and forwards through a few degrees to disperse droplets of glaze on the edge

In all glazing by rolling the submerged part of the form should not be allowed to scrape on the base or sides of the glaze container as this will mark the glaze layer. To avoid this, forms should be immersed only so far as is necessary for the rolling action to cover the entire form.

Rolling is a versatile method quicker and more direct than glazing by pouring or dipping with many larger vertical or open forms. It does, however, have two drawbacks. Firstly, and obviously unlike most of the earlier sequences with larger forms, it is limited to occasions where the same glaze is wanted on the inside and outside of a form. Secondly, dipping by total immersion is rarely an option with larger forms and rolling does require larger quantities of glaze than the interrupted sequences described earlier which can often be very well done with small quantities of glaze.

207

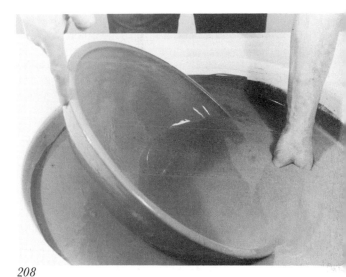

208

209

Glaze spraying

Where spraying equipment is available many beginners steer clear of applying glaze by dipping or pouring and choose spraying which they see as an easier and better option. If time is taken to achieve some confidence and acquire some fluency with dipping and pouring it is un-questionable that, certainly in some contexts and probably in many, these processes are quicker and better than spraying. Spraying, of course, has its uses and there are many contexts where it is better. Some large forms and very fragile objects are impossible to glaze well by pouring and, with these, spraying is the obvious method. When considering the relative merits of different ways of applying glaze it should be remembered that a very considerable amount of dipping (dipping rather than pouring) is still done industrially. This is the case simply because for many objects it is better. Automated spraying may well replace dipping, but manually performed spraying is most unlikely ever to do so. Industrially, spraying is mainly used on large forms and for reglazing blemishes on fired glazed ware.

The application of glaze by spraying in thicknesses which grade from thick to thin, allowing the blending of one glaze into another, has decorative possibilities quite separate from its use for the simple application of glaze and totally different from qualities which can be achieved by glazes applied by pouring and dipping.

Wood ash

Wood ash is sometimes used in glazes, mostly at high temperatures, because it brings a particular quality to glazes which is difficult to achieve by other means. In small quantities, of say 10% or less, it is not a dominant ingredient and can usually be replaced with felspar or even omitted without noticeable effect. But in amounts over about 25% it usually contributes distinct colour and texture.

Recipes which simply specify 'wood ash' usually mean ash from a general mixture of woods. But even when batches of ash are blended there may be a considerable variety of glaze result from one batch to another. Anyone who becomes interested in the effects which can be achieved with wood ash quickly learns that it is a variable material.

The power of wood ash as flux material ranges from strong to weak and while, for example, beechwood ash will have a similar fluxing power, from batch to batch there can be noticeable differences between beechwood ash from one source and that from another, and there is virtually always a difference between ash from twig wood and ash from log sized branches. Experimenting with different wood ashes can be fascinating but it is not worth doing, except out of academic interest, unless worthwhile quantities are available. Burning wood or other vegetable matter specifically for ash for glazes can be a somewhat disheartening activity because there is over a 90% weight loss from wood to wood ash and there can be a further weight loss of around 20% or more from wood ash as gathered to prepared useable wood ash.

Because of the somewhat variable nature of wood ash, ash glaze recipes need to be treated with a degree of caution. Because it is pro-hibitively expensive to have chemical analyses done, calculations using glaze theory are not of use. Anyone who wants to pursue the use of wood ash extensively should, therefore, be prepared to do empirical testing.

The wet preparation of wood ash for use in glazes
Of all the materials which are not used indus-trially, but which are found in published glaze recipes, wood ash is the one which occurs most commonly. Wood ash can now be bought in ready-prepared form but many people prefer to prepare their own.

There are three main sources from which wood ash may be collected: *outdoor fires* where trees have been felled and their branches burned; *demolition sites* and *domestic fires*. Where ash is collected from outdoor fires care should be taken not to scoop up earth or sand with the ash. Where ash is collected from demolition sites some contamination with metal fastenings, such as nails and screws, is inevitable. The cleanest ash is likely to come from those who have log fires or wood burning stoves.

One very serious note of caution concern-ing ash collection is the **danger of fires**. Incompletely burned embers can smoulder for several days in ash and if disturbed by collection can kindle sufficiently to char a hole in a cardboard box or melt a hole in a polythene bag which may allow ash to flow out thus exposing more embers to the air and if all this happens on a wooden floor or table a fire can all too easily develop. Whenever wood ash is collected this should be done in a non-combustible container which is kept on a non-combustible surface or, if it is collected in cardboard or polythene containers they should be placed preferably outside, where there is no risk of a fire spreading.

Ash contains a significant proportion of soluble material and the wet method of preparation combines washing to remove the majority of the soluble material, with sieving to remove the coarse material. The method is simple if a little time consuming but proportionally it takes only a little longer to prepare large amounts.

Outside space, where a hose can be used, is ideal for the preparation of ash but if this is not available a large sink and a sufficient number of large containers are essential.

In the series of photographs which follow, four galvanised containers, of which the smallest is a large bucket, are used to prepare two bucketsful of ash.

210 The two shallowest and largest containers are about two thirds filled with water and the dry ash is tipped into these. The ash is allowed to settle into the water and more water can be added if necessary

211 When all the ash is thoroughly wet the mixture is stirred, the aim being to disturb the charcoal lumps so that these float to the surface. The soluble material in wood ash can be quite caustic so anyone with sensitive skin should either stir the mixture with a length of wood or use rubber gloves. At such an early stage the mixture is not very caustic

210

211

119

212

212 A hose running at full strength helps to float the charcoal. This particular ash was from the branchwood of a felled tree which explains the large amount of charcoal – much less is usually present in ash from domestic log fires or wood burning stoves

213 A coarse garden sieve with 6 mm or larger mesh is then used to scoop up and skim off the floating charcoal

214 The hose can be used to wash fine ash off the charcoal which is then discarded

213

214

215, 216, 217 The watery ash mixture is then stirred and (particularly when the container is nearly empty) poured immediately but gently into a new container, the aim being to retain in the first container all the material which has sunk. This material will include sand, earth and any metal wuch as nails or screws, all of which is also discarded.

215

216

217

121

218

219

220

218, 219　When the two original containers of ash have been similarly processed the ash is then stirred again and divided equally between the four containers. All four containers are then filled from a fast running hose. At this stage the water becomes frothy, a sure sign that the soluble material is in solution. If a finger and thumb are dipped into the liquid and rubbed together a distinct soapiness will be felt. The mixture is allowed to settle for ten minutes or more until the ash has sunk to a level leaving clear liquid on top. Small particles of charcoal will float

220　When the ash has settled the clear liquid is gently poured away. To avoid blocking drains this liquid should be poured away through a 20 mesh sieve to retain the particles of charcoal, which are then discarded

221　All four containers are then refilled from a fast running hose and are stirred

222　This will again cause frothiness and at this stage the mixture is at its most caustic

This sequence of adding water, stirring, allowing the mixture to settle, pouring off clear liquid and then adding water again is repeated a number of times. Five or six repetitions are a minimum to ensure efficient washing out of the soluble material but few people who use ash aim to achieve complete washing. When the feeling of soapiness of the ash water has diminished considerably the cycle of washings may be stopped.

221

222

223

224

223 When washing is complete, water is decanted from all four containers and the ash is concentrated into two; the two empty containers being washed out with the hose in readiness for sieving

224 The ash is allowed to settle further and then excess water is discarded

225, 226, 227 The ash is then run through a 20 mesh sieve. All the upper layer of the ash suspension will run through this very easily and only minimal use of the sieve brush will be necessary. Further sieving will be easier if the sieve is washed before the lower layer is sieved

225

226

227

228

228, 229, 230 The lower layer of ash will tend to sit in the sieve. Initially it should be brushed gently but the final action is to wash the residue retained by the sieve with a hose. This frees and washes through the finer particles. The material remaining in the sieve is discarded

229

230

The sieving sequence is then repeated each time working with a finer grade of sieve.

231, 232 Each time the upper layer of ash will pour through the sieve quite easily requiring very little brushing

233 From 40 mesh sieve upwards it is worth keeping the material retained by the sieve as the majority of this can usually be very quickly crushed in a pestle with a mortar and be added to the mixture in the final sieving. Except where ash is being used in the deliberate creation of unevenly textured finish, it should be sieved through a minimum 80 mesh and preferably a 120 mesh sieve

231

232

233

Continued on page 130

127

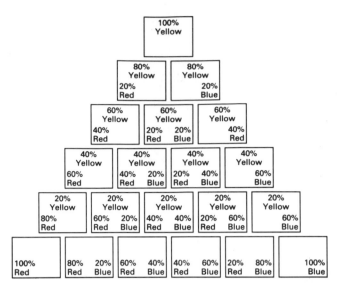

PLATE 3(a)

This illustration demonstrates the principle of a triaxial blend. Three ready-to-use bought glazes were used and mixed together in the proportions shown. Except perhaps for demonstration purposes triaxial blends are very rarely done in the complete form shown here and their use is very rarely concerned with colour. Scientists and ceramic technologists make very considerable use of experiments based on the principles of triaxial blending when studying the effects of alterations to the composition of bodies and glazes. In such work the steps of the blend, which can be decided quite arbitrarily, are much finer, 1% perhaps or 2.5%, rather than the 20% in the simple example shown here and actual experiments would only be made of a selected area of the blend.

It should be noted that in this example only the six tests in the middle of the triangle in fact contain all three glazes. The mixtures of two materials around the outside of the triangle are line blends.

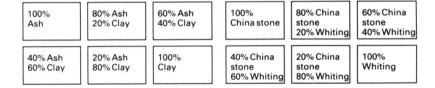

PLATES 3(b) and 3(c)

These two illustrations show two line blends used to find or demonstrate the eutectic mixture of the materials. All the samples were fired at 1280°C.

In plate 3(b) a mixed hardwood ash is used with a common red firing clay from Gloucestershire which is stable at 1100°C but which deforms badly and softens in temperatures over 1220°C. The 60% ash: 40% clay mixture is the one which has melted most strongly and is, therefore, near the eutectic mixture. To evolve a glaze this proportion of the ash and clay could then be tested with additions of different amounts of china clay and flint—the tests could be entirely empirical or the principles of triaxial blending could be used.

Plate 3(c) shows an identical line blend between china stone and whiting. Eutectic mixtures of two materials are very rarely suitable as glazes but, in this case, because of the particular balance of oxides in these materials, the mixture of 80% china stone and 20% whiting is the mixture which is clearly closest to the eutectic and is also a well known 1280°C glaze recipe, memorable in that it contains only two materials. (An alternative glaze recipe is 85% china stone and 15% whiting.)

It is wise to do material and eutectic tests on tiles which are recessed, not flat, as this allows the reacting materials to pool in the recess rather than run off the tile onto kiln furniture. The trailed line across and the dot on the side of the recess make additional thickness of the test materials or mixture (evident in illustration 2(a) as well as 3(b) and 3(c)) not essential but they give a very useful guide to the relative fluidity or stiffness of fluxed mixtures.

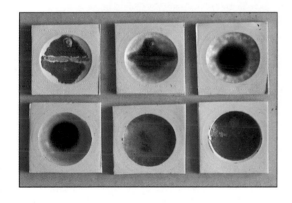

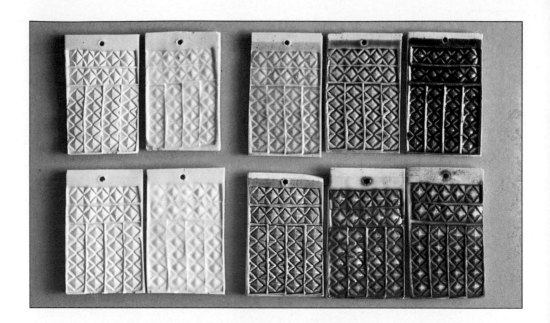

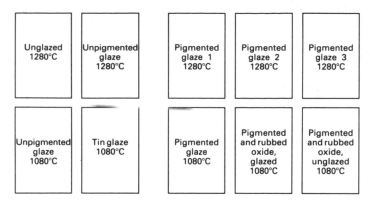

Unglazed 1280°C	Unpigmented glaze 1280°C	Pigmented glaze 1 1280°C	Pigmented glaze 2 1280°C	Pigmented glaze 3 1280°C
Unpigmented glaze 1080°C	Tin glaze 1080°C	Pigmented glaze 1080°C	Pigmented and rubbed oxide, glazed 1080°C	Pigmented and rubbed oxide, unglazed 1080°C

PLATE 4(a)

This illustration shows ten tests all made of white clay, all impressed with rouletted relief and each one differently finished—five at stoneware temperature and five at earthenware. The relevance of these tests is not that any are intrinsically better than others but that all have a very different visual effect on the rouletted relief. It is arguable that the relief is most clearly evident when it is revealed by light and shade alone, as in the unglazed 1280°C test. It is arguable, too, that where the finish creates strong tonal contrast on the relief the actual awareness of the relief is lessened. An awareness of the effect of some particular finish frequently governs some aspect of work at an earlier stage.

Simple tests of slip, glaze, painting pigments, bodies and so on are of obvious value but ultimately it is important, as here, to begin to relate tests to specific contexts.

Glaze P + 0·75% cobalt oxide	Glaze P + 2% copper oxide	Glaze P + 6% iron oxide	Glaze P + 2·5% manganese dioxide	Glaze P + 1·5% copper oxide and 1·5% manganese oxide	Glaze P + 0·5% cobalt oxide and 1·5% manganese dioxide	Glaze P + 5% mauve glaze stain
Glaze Q + 0·75% cobalt oxide	Glaze Q + 2% copper oxide	Glaze Q + 6% iron oxide	Glaze Q + 2·5% manganese dioxide	Glaze Q + 1·5% copper oxide and 1·5% manganese oxide	Glaze Q + 0·5% cobalt oxide and 1·5% manganese dioxide	Glaze Q + 5% mauve glaze stain
Glaze R + 0·75% cobalt oxide	Glaze R + 2% copper oxide	Glaze R + 6% iron oxide	Glaze R + 2·5% manganese dioxide	Glaze R + 1·5% copper oxide and 1·5% manganese oxide	Glaze R + 0·5% cobalt oxide and 1·5% manganese dioxide	Glaze R + 5% mauve glaze stain

PLATE 4(b)

This illustration demonstrates the effect of different glaze fluxes on the colour produced by additions of differing pigmenting oxides. In all cases the white clay body is the same as in the firing temperature of 1080°C. Each of the tests show two differing thickness of glaze, the lower half being the thicker. In glaze P the major glaze flux is a lead frit; in glaze Q the major glaze flux is a soda frit; glaze R is a bought ready-to-use glaze of unpublished formulae but designated a 'low solubility glaze' which by implication means it contains lead and other oxides as its fluxing oxides.

The effect of different glaze fluxing oxides on identical amounts of the same pigmenting oxide or oxides is very variable both in terms of colour and of tonality. With other glaze fluxing oxides and combinations of oxides, and with glazes fired at lower and higher temperatures than this example, the variation of response to pigmenting oxides and stains is considerably extended. This illustration simply exemplifies the fact that, while general rules can be formulated for the colour and tonal response of specified amounts of pigmenting oxides and prepared stains, the precise response can only be determined in the actual context of use.

129

When sieving is complete the ash should be allowed to settle, and clear water should be poured away.

234 When the thick mixture shows little sign of settling further it can be poured and spread out to dry on a flat gently sloping surface, here on a slate slab

235 Water will flow out of the mass quite quickly especially if rough channels are stroked into it. As it starts to dry the material can be scraped back up the slope and further narrower channels stroked into it

236 On an airy warm day drying will occur quite quickly and the mass will develop cracks

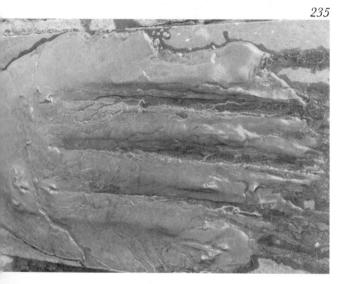

234

235

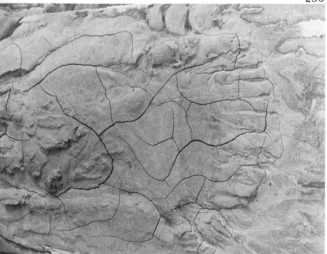

236

130

237

237 As soon as cracks develop drying will be speeded up if more of the material is exposed to the air so it should be scraped up and turned over

Once the material is dry it should be stored and labelled. Included on the label should be the size of mesh through which it has been sieved.

Where availability of suitable space allows, the drying method shown is probably as easy as any but two alternative methods are to evaporate the water by putting the ash mixture into a metal container and gently heating this; or to use the type of supported textile bag shown earlier in the drying of a clay body slip into a plastic body.

A final word of warning about ash should be noted. Dry wood ash, whether in the raw or prepared state, is a potentially hazardous material. It contains light particles which easily make airborne dust and contains silica and, in the raw state, caustic material. When ash is handled in the dry state this should be with due care, avoiding the creation of airborne dust. There are those who advocate the use of unwashed ash and its preparation in the dry state which obviously involves dry sieving. If this is undertaken it should only occur outside or in extraction booths fitted with adequate fans, and dust masks should be worn.

The preparation of found raw materials for use in glazes

Apart from clays and wood ash the preparation of found materials for use in glazes is often thought to necessitate the use of heavy equipment such as plate mills, jaw crushers and large ball mills. Sometimes, however, quarry waste may be available that requires only simple preparation. Cutting work in granite, sandstone, marble, limestone and other quarries generates considerable quantities of dust and this is frequently regarded as waste though sometimes it is sold. In quarries, small streams of rain water begin a natural grading of this material. If fine material is available its preparation is simple.

The material is mixed with a proportionally large quantity of water and the fine material is poured into a second container leaving the coarse material behind, exactly as with ash preparation in figures 215 to 217. This fine material is then progressively sieved. Whether or not it is worthwhile grinding up the material retained during sieving is questionable and depends on equipment and time available – trying to reduce the size of a hard material in a pestle and mortar is very slow work. For normal purposes a 100 mesh sieving should be thought of as the minimum necessary – bought materials are considerably more finely prepared than this. After sieving, the material is dried and stored for use – as with wood ash, labelling should indicate the sieve mesh used in preparation.

While using found materials can be instructive and rewarding it should be remembered that the time involved in finding and in preparation makes such materials more expensive than bought ones. The motivation for doing such work is discovering materials which, because of 'impurities', give distinctly different qualities to glazes than can be achieved with purer bought materials.

Egyptian paste

The difficulty of placing a description of Egyptian paste in a book very simply divided into well known and accepted classifications of pottery materials underlines the fact that Egyptian paste is something of a ceramic oddity: it contains very little clay; it contains soluble fluxes; and it is self glazing. Though the description is placed in the section on glaze, Egyptian paste is not a glaze but a body. It is, however, so low in clay that it can hardly be called a clay body.

As a body, Egyptian paste is short and forming processes which can be used with it are limited.

As its name suggests Egyptian paste was used extensively in Ancient Egypt. It was mainly used to make relatively small objects: small vessels, small figurines and, very extensively, to make beads, often very small beads, strung together into large and quite complex arrangements.

The theory of Egyptian paste is that the body is very open, containing just sufficient clay to enable it to hold together in the raw state. Soluble soda fluxes are dissolved in the water which the body contains. The body is composed almost wholly of silica, ideally of variable particle size, coarse as well as fine. As the body dries out much of this soluble material is carried to the surface and is deposited there as a whitish scum. On firing this surface melts into a glassy coating, the pure soda combining readily with the silica of the body. Beneath the surface the lesser amounts of soda which do not reach the surface also react with the silica helping to give strength to the body.

Egyptian paste can be coloured by incorporating pigmenting material into the body. In Ancient Egypt the commonest colour was a greeny turquoise resulting from the response of copper pigment to the predominantly soda flux. Nowadays, using body stains as well as the pigmenting oxides, a wide colour range can be evolved.

The mixing of Egyptian paste

In the sequence of photographs which follows and the text which accompanies these the recipe used is:

Felspar	32
Flint	30
China clay	10
Ball clay	6
Sodium bicarbonate	6
Soda ash	6
Silica sand	10
Copper oxide	2

Though this book is concerned with principles rather than recipes the recipe is quoted because this is necessary to make the principles of mixing clear. 1000 g of this recipe was mixed.

To mix up large amounts of Egyptian paste could be daunting but, as large amounts are rarely needed, mixing it is not a problem provided it is remembered that the water, which the body contains, itself contains the soluble fluxes which form the glaze, so an over-wet mixture cannot be brought back to a 'plastic' state by drying it on plaster of paris as this would result in the loss of some flux material into the plaster. (The term *plastic* is hardly appropriate for Egyptian paste which tends to have poor plasticity.)

About 200 ml of water to 1000 g of dry ingredients are needed to mix Egyptian paste to a workable consistency.

238 The first stage is to add the weighed amounts of soluble flux (sodium bicarbonate and soda ash, in this case) to the measured amount of water. The materials are more readily dissolved in warm water

239, 240 The mixture is poured repeatedly from container to container to assist the formation of a solution. The solution is in fact a concentrated one and not all the flux material may dissolve. This does not matter

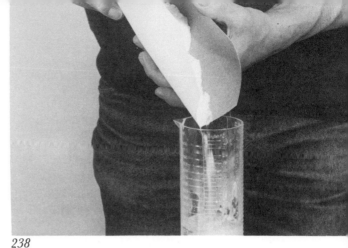

238

239

240

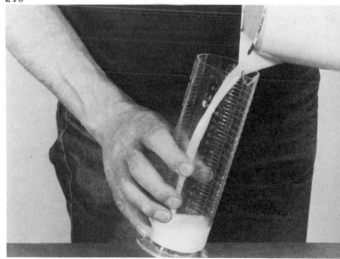

241

242

243

241 The solution is then put into a wide container. Then some of the dry materials are added: first the ball clay then, in any order, the copper oxide and about two thirds each of the felspar and flint. The quantities of felspar and flint actually added do not need to be exact but what is not added should be put on one side for later addition. The materials are then allowed to soak into the solution of fluxes for a few minutes. This thickish mixture is then either stirred up and sieved through at least an 80 mesh sieve or it is scooped into a pestle and mortar and ground

242 Grinding in a pestle and mortar is probably the quicker of the two alternatives but the consistency of the mixture is rather thicker than would normally either be sieved or ground. The intention of whichever action is chosen is to convert this half of the paste mixture to an intimately mixed fine condition. Using bought materials the only actual grinding which occurs is of any crystals of undissolved flux – this on balance makes grinding the preferred of the two alternatives if a suitable size of pestle and mortar is available

243 After a couple of minutes of firm grinding the dollop of paste is scooped into the middle of a sheet of 8 mm plate glass. The mixture will be quite thick and needs spreading out so that the remaining material can be sprinkled on its surface. The plate glass should rest on a firm flat board. If plate glass is not available a formica covered board will suffice though this is liable to become scratched. If a formica covered board is not available a sealed plywood board will do, but this needs to be cleaned meticulously after use

244, 245 The remaining dry materials are then sprinkled over the damp finely mixed material in the following order: first the china clay, second the balance of the felspar and flint and lastly the silica sand

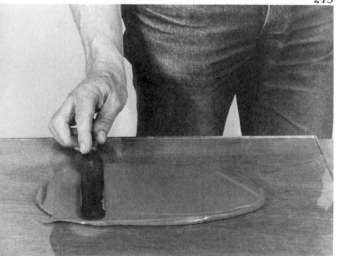

244

245

246

247

248

246 Mixing then commences by folding the damp mixture into the dry materials and chopping and stroking the mixture with the flat scraper. The palette knife is used to keep the flat scraper clean of any material which sticks to it

247, 248 Initially, the task may seem hopeless but the chopping and stroking actions must be continued and the temptation to add more water at this stage must be resisted

249, 250 After two or three minutes when the additional materials have been worked in and have become damp the paste will become a more homogenous mass. Only if the paste is dry and crumbly at this stage should more water be added and, for a 1000 g batch, half a teaspoonful is the most that should be added at one time, this being well mixed in before any more is added. If the mixture is too soft it can be spread out on the glass to dry for an hour or two and then thoroughly folded over and remixed

The logic of the two separate additions of dry materials is that in the first the plasticiser (the ball clay) is thoroughly wetted and the flux material is as fully dissolved as possible and that these are finely mixed with some of the mass of the paste. This fine fraction is then less finely mixed with the remainder of the paste mass and with the coarse material (the silica sand). The sand itself inhibits fine mixing in the second stage. Being neither sieved nor ground, nor indeed copiously wetted, some of the second addition of felspar and flint does not break down to a size much smaller than the sand. The body therefore has a fine fraction and a coarse fraction well intermixed. This and the sand itself gives an openness to the body allowing the soluble fluxes to be carried to the surface more readily than would be the case in a very fine close body. Additionally, the two stages allow the paste to be brought to a useable consistency without the need for any drying out.

Depending partly on the recipe, and partly on the intended quality, Egyptian paste is usually fired in the range 850°C to 950°C, sometimes slightly higher.

The layer of soluble flux which forms on the surface of Egyptian paste during drying varies in quality from a tough coat to layers so dusty that they need careful handling not to dislodge them. In both cases during firing, the flux forms a strong

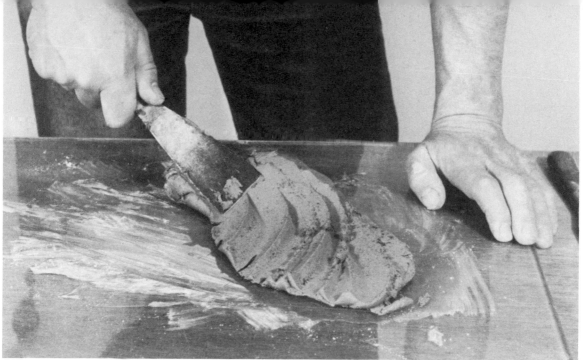

249

250

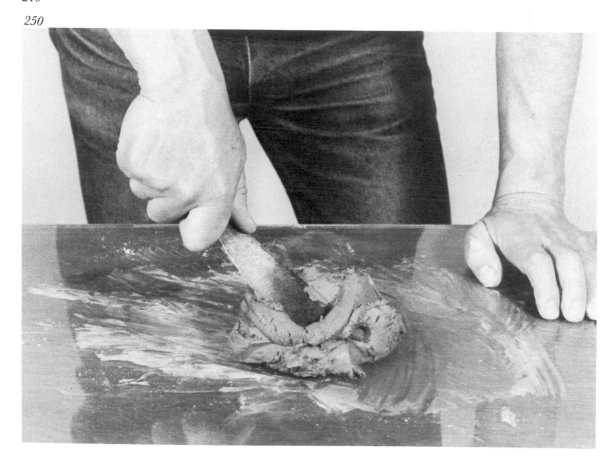

bond with any kiln furniture it touches. Kiln shelves, therefore, need to be protected with batt wash which can then be covered with a thin layer of silica sand. The adhesion of Egyptian paste is minimised if the parts of objects which rest on shelves are lightly rubbed to remove the flux from the surface. Beads can be fired suspended on Kanthal or nichrome wire, the wire itself resting on refractory clay supports.

As an open body which dries out fast, Egyptian paste batches must be kept very tightly wrapped in polythene.

SECTION FOUR

SLIP

The words 'slip' and 'engobe'

Throughout this section the word 'slip' is used to cover suspensions of a wide range of pottery materials. As there is some confusion in the use of the word and how it relates to the word 'engobe' it seems sensible to begin by clarifying these terms and their usage.

'Engobe' is the French word for slip and words with the same root exist in other European languages. In American usage the words 'slip' and 'engobe' both exist but they are used interchangeably, and 'engobe' is the word more frequently encountered.

In Britain in both industrial and non-industrial contexts both words exist but 'slip' is the one much more frequently encountered. In industrial contexts in Britain the term *slip* simply means a waterborne suspension and is imprecise unless qualified, for example, as a 'clay slip' or a 'body slip' or even a 'glaze slip'. In non-industrial contexts some people use the word 'slip' and others 'engobe', while yet others use both words making some distinction between the two. Where this latter is the case 'slip' is usually applied to suspensions which consist solely of clays or are high in clay material, while 'engobe' is applied to suspensions which are lower in clay material. In this case, where the dividing line is, if there is one, and, if not, what mixtures in between should be called, is the subject of further confusion.

One word should cover the whole range of possible mixtures. The fact that here the word is 'slip' may seem rather arbitrary, but the importance of having one word is that it aids understanding of the possible variety of slip mixtures.

The nature and function of slips

Slips are clay based suspensions. They may consist solely of a clay or clays or may have large or small additions to their clay basis. In use they are applied to clay bodies as coatings to cover and thereby change the surface and colour of the body. A slip must have affinity for the clay body which it covers. Slips can be adjusted to suit different clay bodies and be applied to bodies at different stages: biscuit fired and dry as well as plastic and leatherhard.

Slips may be poured or dipped so that they cover only parts of a form: areas of a slip coating may be resisted or be removed by scraping. Slips may be trailed both into a layer of wet slip or onto touch dry slip or directly onto a clay body. Slips may be painted. Thus though defined as coatings on clay bodies slips are frequently applied with decorative intentions as less than total coatings.

Slips may be glazed or unglazed but are distinct from glazes in that they do not form a glassy coating on the clay body.

The origin of slips

Slips were in common use very early on in the evolution of pottery, long before the discovery of glaze. Very early pottery was mostly made of open textured bodies presumably because these survived contemporary firing practices better than close textured bodies. These somewhat coarse bodies were frequently covered with a thin layer of fine slip – often exceptionally fine – which made the ware both smoother and less porous. These slips were usually reddish brown in colour being based on common clays and reached remarkable standards in the separated slips used on Ancient Greek and Roman pottery. Rather

139

than refining red firing clays, some cultures took other directions and used light firing clays as the basis for slips which were pigmented to give a range of colours. Once glaze was discovered the use of white or light firing slip took on a new importance. Most pottery was still made of common clay, usually buff to brown firing, on which translucent coloured glaze could not develop its full potential but if the clay was covered with a light or white firing slip far richer glaze colour was possible and, furthermore, glaze brought out the colour of pigmented slip more fully. Even in industrial practice the possibilities of slips have been widely used.

Universally, throughout history, from the time it was first used to the present day, slip as an allover coating has been used to give qualities and colour to clay bodies which, for economic or technical reasons, would have been difficult or impossible to achieve in the clay body itself.

The theory of slips

The two major technical concerns in applying slip to clay bodies are the *adhesion* and the *fit* of slips. The adhesion is obviously a factor of importance both while the slip dries and during the firing. The fit of a slip is the similarity of its shrinkage to that of the clay body to which it is applied. Of the two factors adhesion is much the more important. Good adhesion will overcome poor fit to a considerable extent so a slip with good adhesion may be used on a range of different bodies. If the slip adhesion is poor, even a well fitting slip may be lifted off a clay body during or after firing by the tensions of a glaze. Technical work with slips, with the exception of work done in industrial contexts, is necessarily much more empirical than such work with glazes, but an understanding of the different qualities of various materials and the oxides they contain – an understanding of glaze theory and indeed the theory of clay bodies – is a great help in developing an understanding of what to do when constructing and correcting faults in slips.

In some instances it is possible to use clay bodies as slip coatings. If, for example, it is intended to coat a white earthenware clay in the leatherhard state with a coloured slip, the simplest solution may well be to mix the same body as a slip with some suitable colouring addition. As the body and slip are identical, except for the colouring addition to the slip, adhesion, both before and during firing, and fit, will be good. Somewhat different in principle heavily grogged stoneware bodies, if fired to a low biscuit, can often be successfully coated with porcelain bodies in a slip state.

Most frequently though, slips are mixed from dry powdered ingredients and comprise clay and non-clay parts.

Though mixtures consisting only of clays or solely of a clay body may sometimes be used as slips it is more helpful to an understanding of these if slips are considered as mixtures which, while always containing clay as their basis, also usually contain fluxing material and flint or quartz and sometimes other materials as well.

The two major problems in coating clay bodies with slip are flaking and peeling. Both these faults are exaggerated by the application of excessively thick slip layers and both occur when adhesion is poor.

In considering adhesion it is important to recognise that it has two distinct aspects: the adhesion of the *raw layer* of slip; and the adhesion of the *fired layer*. The adhesion of the raw layer is easy to ensure by the use of plastic clay in appropriate proportions as one of the slip ingredients. The adhesion of the fired layer is much less frequently considered unless it becomes problematic and is more dependent on the chemical than the physical nature of the slip ingredients.

Fired clay bodies and glaze adhere to one another by the formation of an interface layer. No such distinct layer is formed between clay bodies and slip but it is important to remember that clay bodies contain fluxes which, in becoming active, ensure that bodies harden at their optimum firing temperature. If, in relation to the firing temperature of a clay body, a particular slip is short of fluxes, the activity of the fluxes in the body may not effect a very good adhesion of the slip layer. If, however, a slip contains fluxes which give it a body-like hardness at the same temperature as a particular body the adhesion between body and slip will be greatly enhanced.

The ideal with all slips is that they contain sufficient flux material to mature at or somewhat below the maturing point of the clay bodies they coat.

Against this ideal the notion of a general purpose slip, good for all contexts, is clearly impossible. But slips are much more tolerant mixtures than glazes and when faults occur, or when contexts of use are altered, a few tests with simple alterations are usually all that is required.

Theory in practice - compounding slips

Many recipes for slips are published but not all include clear information about the particular context of use so it is as well to be confident about how theory translates into practice.

Perhaps the first thing to re-emphasise is that all slips are based on clay and that the strength of the raw unfired layer and its adhesion to the clay body is almost always due to the inclusion of a proportion of a plastic clay in the recipe. The example given earlier of a porcelain body used as a slip on a heavily grogged stoneware body is a rare example of a slip containing non-plastic clay, but that is exceptional.

Two types of clays are frequently used to provide the plastic clay content of slips: *ball clays* and the *common clays*. Red terracotta clays have excellent adhesion, both raw and, in most contexts, fired adhesion, and are a good basis for brown and black slips but such slips form a distinct type and are dealt with separately. In the rest of this section the slips discussed are those based on ball clay.

In practice virtually all slips contain both china clay and ball clay – the ball clay being the essential ingredient for adhesion. The usual aim of such slips is whiteness, either whiteness for its own sake to cover or contrast with a darker clay body to which it is applied, or whiteness as a good basis for colour additions. China clays are the whiter of the two types but give poor adhesion both raw and fired. Ball clays detract from whiteness but give better fired adhesion than china clays and excellent raw adhesion. In practice the two types are variably blended to suit particular contexts.

Materials which introduce fluxes are included in recipes to assist in reducing the maturing point of the slip to, or just below, that of the body.

Because white slips without additional fluxing material are inevitably somewhat refractory at earthenware temperatures, the inclusion of fluxing material in white earthenware slips is important. The common problem of white slip flaking at earthenware temperatures would be avoided if the need for fluxes were more widely understood. At stoneware temperatures, materials which may be included in slips to introduce fluxes are china stone, felspar and nepheline syenite. These materials are less effective at earthenware temperatures and should be partially or wholly replaced with leadless frits.

The inclusion of flint is more complex. Flint additions will make slips more refractory and they do reduce the shrinkage of the slip. When glazes are used on top of slips, increased flint in the slip gives the molten glaze silica with which to react, and can lessen the penetration of slip by glaze leaving the slip layer more opaque.

On the whole, mixtures of the materials so far mentioned can be proportionally varied to make slips to suit most contexts, but there are various other materials, apart, of course, from colouring pigments, which may be added to slips. In earthenware slips both whiting and talc can be considered when additional flux material is needed. Molochite, which is calcined china clay, is a useful material to substitute for china clay if the overall shrinkage of a slip needs to be reduced without altering its clay content. If slips lack opacity tin, titanium or zirconium oxides or any commercial opacifier may be added. If the unfired strength of a slip layer needs to be improved, for example to make it stronger as a surface for painting or some other treatment, and it is not possible to increase the plastic clay content of the slip, then a commercial glaze hardener may be added in the recommended amount.

Slips based on common red earthenware clay

Because they are usually fine and plastic and, therefore, as slips, offer excellent adhesion, common red clays have good potential as a basis for slips where the colours which derive from iron oxide are desired. They can be used as they are or can be blended with a light firing or white slip to lighten their tonality. Where black slips are wanted, red clays offer a simple and economical

141

basis, economical because smaller oxide additions are necessary.

Thick layers of red clay slips, especially if these have no additions, may have a tendency to peel especially if applied to somewhat dry bodies and particularly if these are white. But, with appropriate additions, and at appropriate thicknesses, slips based on red clays can be applied to bodies in any state, just as with slips based on china and ball clays.

To make black slips from a red clay basis up to about 6% of iron oxide may be added, plus up to 6% of manganese. The precise amounts needed depend on the darkness of the original clay, the extent to which ball-clay, china clay, flint or other slip ingredients have been added to the red clay and on the firing temperature. The actual quality of the black can be modified with other oxide additions, such as small amounts (up to 2%) of cobalt or copper.

Most red clays are fusible at stoneware temperatures and the addition of materials to the clay basis to form slips needs to acknowledge this, especially when oxides are added to darken the slip as these further increase fusibility. For use as slips at stoneware most red clays need the addition of around 30% of refractory material, flint and china clay being the materials most commonly used. The use of felspar to assist fired adhesion between body and slip is completely unnecessary with such slips.

If a powdered red clay is available this is obviously the most convenient basis for actually mixing slips. Failing this a plastic body should be rolled out thinly, be thoroughly dried, then crushed to granules of 6 mm or less in which state it is easy to weigh and from which state it readily breaks down into slip when put in water.

The correction of flaking or peeling slip

These two faults need to be considered separately and each needs to be considered in relation to different stages of application and completion.

Flaking of slip is caused by clay body shrinkage being greater than slip shrinkage.

When slip which has been applied to leather-hard clay flakes off prior to firing the immediate remedy is to increase the plastic clay content of the slip which has the twofold effect of both increasing slip shrinkage and improving adhesion.

When slip which has been applied to leather-hard, dry or biscuit fired clay, flakes during firing the remedies to try are either an increase in plastic clay content, or the addition or increase of fluxing material. Fluxing material assists fired adhesion.

When slip, applied at any stage, flakes when glaze is applied over it this is caused by the strength of the interface layer between glaze and slip and the tensions in the glaze being stronger than the adhesion between slip and clay body. With slips applied to leatherhard or dry unfired clay an earlier application may help but this fault is usually an indication that the slip is too refractory for the clay body and the inclusion or increase of fluxing material in the slip is the remedy. At stoneware temperatures china stone, nepheline syenite or felspar are the usual materials used and at earthenware temperatures leadless frits alone or together with small amounts of the above materials are used.

Peeling of slips occurs when slip shrinkage is much greater than body shrinkage and is much the rarer of the two faults. Slips with a relatively high shrinkage have high plastic clay content which should give good adhesion and the fault is either one of much too late an application or of an ill-designed slip recipe. The fault, in which the slip develops surface cracks and peels away from the clay body, usually becomes evident as the slip dries. The remedy is to decrease the plastic clay content of the slip and to increase the less or non-plastic material. The fault if the slip has been applied thickly at a very late leatherhard stage may be corrected by an earlier thinner application but whenever it occurs the indications are that the material balance in the slip is seriously wrong and needs substantial modification.

The mixing of slips

Slips contain a far higher proportion of clays than glazes and this fact creates minor differences in mixing procedures. The larger proportions of clay in slips makes them suspend in water far better than glazes and, because they are not subject to the sort of problematic settling that can occur with glazes, slips never need to have a suspension agent incorporated into the mixture. For much the same reason greater care needs to be taken not to use excess water in the initial mixing of slips because while glazes which have been mixed up too wet can be allowed to settle and have the water decanted, this process is so slow with slips that it is inconvenient and should be avoided. Slips are, therefore, better mixed to a thickish consistency which is then thinned for use.

As with glazes slip containers should be clearly labelled. With slips it is important that the temperature range and the condition of clay for which they are intended should be stated on the label.

The application of slip, mainly by pouring and dipping, to clay bodies at different stages

As seems appropriate in a book about materials, the main concentration in this section is on the application of an even, overall layer of a single slip. Slip can, of course, be used, and very frequently is, with quite different intentions to this. At different stages various means of application can be used to create areas and lines of slips with decorative intentions which are outside the scope of this book. Though pouring and dipping can be used for decorative purposes to create less than an even layer of slip they are two of the methods which do enable overall layers to be applied to forms and detailed description is, therefore, of these methods. Of the other two possible methods *spraying* is excluded from detailed description as a mechanical process, and painting is excluded both because it hardly requires detailed description and because its main potential is not in creating an even overall layer of slip.

The most important single factor in slip application by pouring and dipping (and in fact by other processes) is the appropriate adjustment of the fluidity of the slip suspension. Slip should be slightly creamy but should have a fluid mobility. In adjusting slips to the right consistency it is important to remember that all that is required of the slip layer is a reasonable opacity. The physical thickness of layer which will do this depends on the composition of the slip, the nature of the underlying clay body, whether or not glaze is applied over the slip and on the nature of any glaze applied. It is a common tendency for beginners to use suspensions which are too creamy and, therefore, to create slip layers which are unnecessarily thick.

In thinning down slip suspensions a crucial point is reached where a slight increase in slip fluidity quite suddenly diminishes the thickness of the layer which a clay body will retain. This is usually just beyond the point at which the slip consistency was in fact right. Because slips settle so slowly and are, therefore, difficult to thicken up from an over-fluid state, it is a sensible practice to retain some of a slip batch in an over-thick state so, if the remainder is accidentally made too thin, it can be made less fluid by adding some thicker slip.

Checking the condition of previously mixed slips prior to their use is much less time consuming than with glazes. Slips have little tendency to settle. If a little water has gathered on top of the slip, as often occurs, it is better to decant this, though usually it will have to be mixed back into the slip. Under this thin layer of water most slips remain as very even suspensions for long periods and simply pouring the slip from one container to another two or three times is all that is usually needed. If the slip has become lumpy or uneven mixing can be effected quickly if it is poured through a 40 or 60 mesh sieve a couple of times. As soon as it is of even consistency it is, if necessary, adjusted to the right thickness by adding a little water and is remixed evenly to incorporate the additional water.

As should be clear from earlier parts of this section on slips, slips for application to different states of bodies and often to different bodies, are not interchangeable so care should always be taken to ensure that the slip is an appropriate one both for the body and its state.

Applying slip to bodies in a plastic state
An all over coating of slip is only applied to bodies in a plastic state if they can be supported by some means. Thus its use is limited to rolled or cut sheets of clay intended for tiles, or for forming in or over moulds, or to clay already supported in a mould. As clay bodies in this state have little power of water absorption the slip needs to be a creamy, but not too mobile consistency, if a reasonably thick layer is to be retained but it must have a ready fluidity if the layer is to be even.

251

252

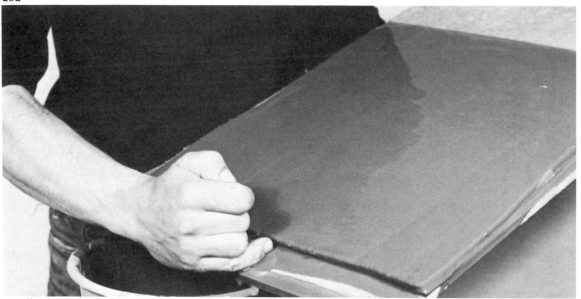

Application to large sheets

251 Application is very straightforward. The clay is supported on a board. The board is tilted at about 45 degrees or a little less and is supported over a container. Pouring along the top edge of the clay the slip is poured evenly by moving the jug steadily from one end to the other. If a wide container is not available the board can be moved and the jug held still so that the excess slip runs into the container. Pouring slip over the top edge of the sheet should be avoided if possible as this tends to penetrate between the board and the clay and tends to stick the sheet to the board making subsequent handling difficult

252 As soon as pouring is complete slip should be wiped off the board at the lower edge and the sides and should be cleaned back to the edge of the clay with a dryish sponge to prevent the sheet from sticking to the board. It is better to make such sheets of clay rather larger than actually needed as edges tend to be slightly prone to cracking and are best trimmed off by about 2 cm when the slip is touch dry

144

Application to tiles

There is a limit to the size of cut or rolled clay which can be well and conveniently handled in the plastic state. Depending a little on the size of one's hand, pieces up to about 18 cm square are, however, relatively easy to handle without risk and when, in view of some intended treatment, slip has to be applied prior to the leatherhard stage this is entirely possible.

253, 254, 255 The cut or rolled tile is simply supported on the palm of one hand with thumb and fingers well spread out and the tile is tilted and rotated while the slip is gently poured. Being soft the tile will bend a little but this is unimportant. When the slip has been applied the edge of the tile furthest from the body is put onto a board with the tile held at a shallow angle and then the hand is quickly withdrawn. As the tile drops onto the board it reassumes its original flatness. Because a little distortion is inevitable in tiles slipped like this they should be made about 12 mm oversize to allow for final trimming when they are firmer

253

254

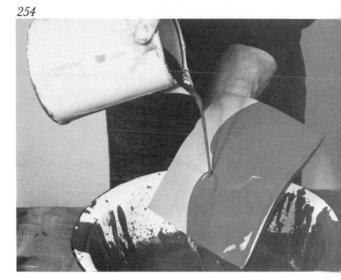

255

256

Application to dishes formed in moulds

Slip application to dishes can be done at the leatherhard as well as the plastic stage. At the leatherhard stage the firm dish is removed from the mould, is slipped and is then immediately returned to the mould so that the form is again supported. This is necessary because of the softening effect which the layer of slip has on the leatherhard clay. The alternative, as here, is to slip the form in the plastic state as soon as it has been formed and before the clay form begins to release itself from the plaster of paris

256   Sufficient slip is poured into the dish

257   The mould is then picked up and tilted and rotated to coat the entire clay surface. This usually involves getting some slip onto the flat edge of the mould

258   The whole surface is steadily covered and then the excess is tipped out. If the slip consistency is right there is no need to tap or shake the mould to remove excess. If tapping is necessary it means that the slip should be made slightly more runny. Plastic clay has no absorption power to hold the layer of slip and tapping or vigorous shaking will create an uneven rather than an even layer

259   Because of the drying power of the plaster of paris, slip on the flat surface of the mould edge will dry long before the dish and, to avoid unwanted flakes of dry slip, the mould edge should be wiped clean. This is easier to do if it is done immediately

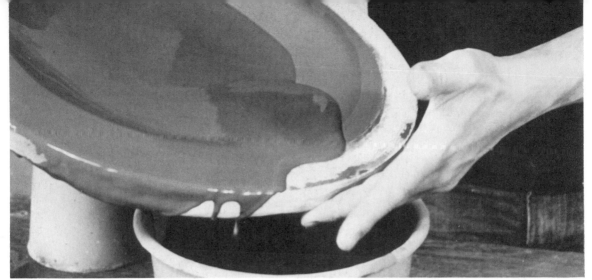

257

258

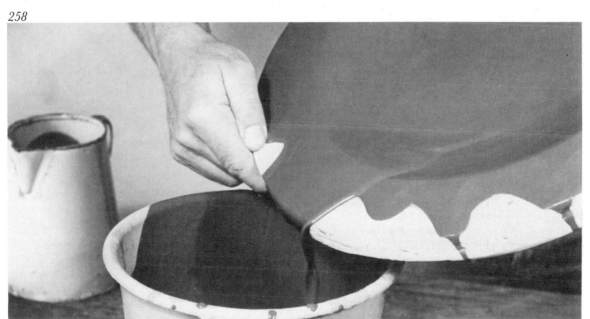

259

Applying slip to bodies in a leatherhard state

Where an even overall layer of slip is intended, certainly with small and medium sized forms, the leatherhard stage is the one at which this work is most commonly done, and pouring and dipping are the most convenient methods. Leatherhard clay has a slight but gradual power to absorb water, so slip is retained by forms far more by virtue of its own consistency than because of the slight water absorption of the clay. For real control of the thickness of the applied layer the adjustment of the fluidity of the slip suspension is crucial.

Slip suspensions which are somewhat too thick are, in fact, more difficult to apply evenly than thinner suspensions and have a much greater softening effect on clay. This latter fact may seem odd as thick suspensions contain less water than thinner ones but it is so because thick suspensions adhere to the clay surface in a thicker layer and there is more water to be absorbed by the clay in a thicker layer of a thick suspension than in a thinner layer of a thin suspension. As further explanation, water itself hardly adheres to clay and dipping a leatherhard form into water has a less softening effect than either a thick or a thin suspension of slip. The water from slip is absorbed slowly by the clay body and problems may show up five to ten minutes after application. When leatherhard forms soften and distort or collapse after a slip application this may be an indication that the form was too soft but it is almost certainly an indication that the slip suspension was too thick. When leatherhard forms soften and crack after a slip application this indicates that the form was probably too dry but may also indicate that the slip suspension was too thick.

Application to the outside of small vertical forms

260 The leatherhard form is held firmly as close to the base as possible and, keeping it level, it is steadily pushed down into the slip

261 It is then withdrawn from the slip and either very gently shaken or twisted to remove any drops from the edge

262 In a steady, gentle swinging motion the form is returned to the vertical position and can then be slid onto a clean work board

Historically, application of slip in this way to the outside of forms was a very common way of covering common red clays with a white ground as a basis for decoration. It was used at many different times, with various subsequent processes by many cultures. So far as an overall coating is concerned, the problem with the process is that the necessity of holding the form near its base makes it difficult or impossible to cover the entire outside of the form – if the fingers which hold the form are themselves immersed in the slip during dipping, it is all too easy to lose a grip on the form and in any case finger marks of uneven slip are left. Treating necessity as a virtue, many examples can be found where the contrast between the unslipped lower area and the slipped upper parts constitute an element of decoration.

260

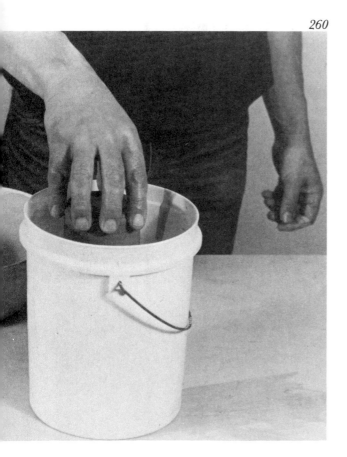

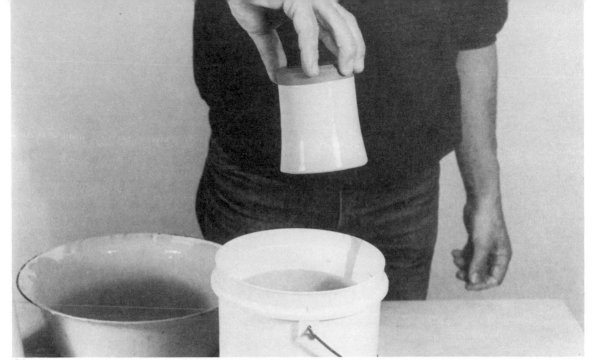

261

262

263

264

265

Application to the inside and outside of small vertical forms

Covering both the inside and outside of small vertical forms is not done very often but it is very straightforward.

263, 264 The inside is slipped first by almost filling the form and then tipping out the slip with a rotating movement

265, 266 As, in the previous example, the form is then held at the base with the fingers evenly spread out, and is dipped in the slip

267 The form is then returned to the vertical position as in figure 262 where the action is described as a 'steady, gentle swinging motion'. When holding softish or firmer leatherhard forms in ways which initially may not seem or feel very secure, successful handling is much more to do with fluent unhurried movements than with fast jerky movements. A tense overstrong grip and sudden movements are far more likely to result in dropping a form than a steady hold and smooth relaxed movement

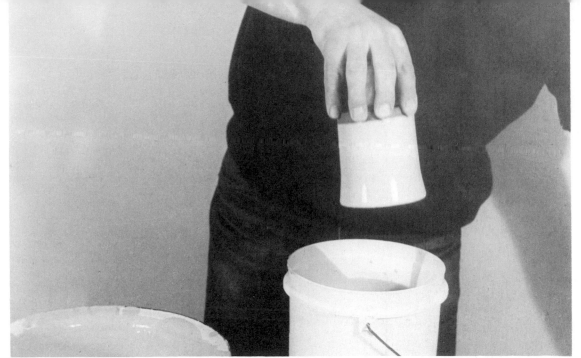

266

267

Application to shallow forms

The application of slip to shallow leatherhard forms can be difficult. The problem is that the softening effect of the slip can make the form distort badly or even collapse. For this reason, with some forms, it may be better to apply the slip at a later stage or, by painting or spraying the slip, to apply a number of thin layers allowing the form to stiffen between applications. Thrown forms can be slipped before they are turned which overcomes this problem.

268, 269   The slip is poured into the form and the form is tilted and rotated. Where forms have clearly defined detail it is often easy to spread the slip very precisely. Here the overall coating is only of the inner part of the form but as the outer edge of the rim has as precise a detail it would have been possible to spread the slip to this edge. Where edges are very rounded it can be difficult to spread the slip to a precise even edge, and the risk of slip running back over the edge is considerable. The slip can, of course, be cleaned off the back but the risk is that, if any gets on the hands, it becomes very difficult to hold the form safely

270, 271   When application is complete the form is tipped up to pour out the slip. With the right consistency of slip this is all that need occur. The form should not be shaken

270

152

272, 273 The layer of slip is wiped off any unwanted areas immediately. A finger or thumb can be used to clean off the main thickness of the layer but will leave smears which have then to be cleaned off with a sponge or chamois leather. Sponges can tend to pull the grog out of grogged bodies so with these, at least as a final cleaning treatment, a chamois should be used because it does not drag out the grog

When the slip has been applied and any necessary cleaning done, the form is put aside until it is firm enough to turn. Deeper forms can be slipped on the inside after they have been turned but the softening effect of a slip application must always be considered when open forms are to be slipped either inside or outside. Practical experience is the sure guide to exactly what is possible with different clay bodies, with different consistencies of slip, and at various points of leatherhardness.

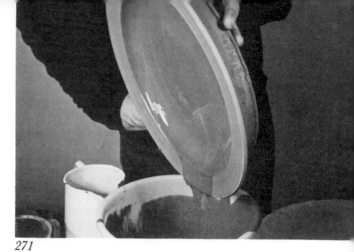

271

272

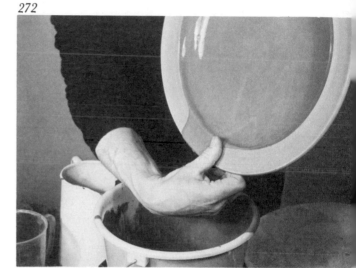

273

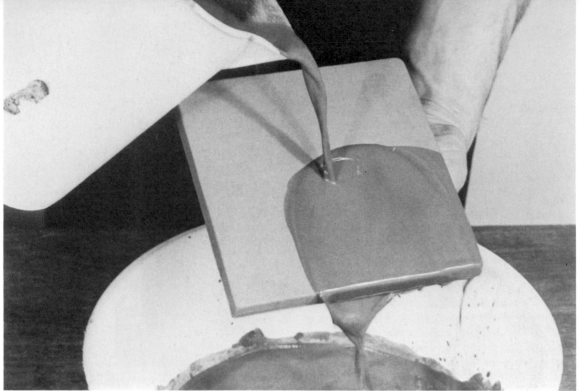

274

275

276

277

Application to tiles

The application of slip to leatherhard tiles is very straightforward. The tile is supported on the finger tips.

274　In this illustration the finger tips have been rotated as far in a clockwise direction as possible and the tile is tilted so that the slip flows off the furthest corner of the tile. As soon as pouring commences the finger tips start to rotate the tile anti-clockwise

275, 276　As the tile is rotated the angle of tilt is also changed and in this way the entire tile is slipped. The jug is virtually stationary throughout the sequence

277　The pouring can be stopped as soon as the tile is coated and, when any excess has drained off, the tile can be slid onto a work board. As well as facilitating quick, even application of slip the rotating action means that no slip goes onto the wrist or supporting fingers, so any number of tiles can be slipped like this with the supporting hand remaining clean and dry throughout

Application to the outside of larger vertical forms

Slip can be applied to larger vertical forms using the same method as shown in figures 260 to 262 and, if the size necessitates it, the base can be held with two hands rather than one. With forms that are wide enough to allow the hand to go inside, pouring rather than dipping may be more convenient and does permit the application of a layer over the whole of the outside.

First of all the form is stood on thin card and the base is drawn round. This shape is then cut out, leaving a short tab.

278 The card is then dampened and placed on the base of the form

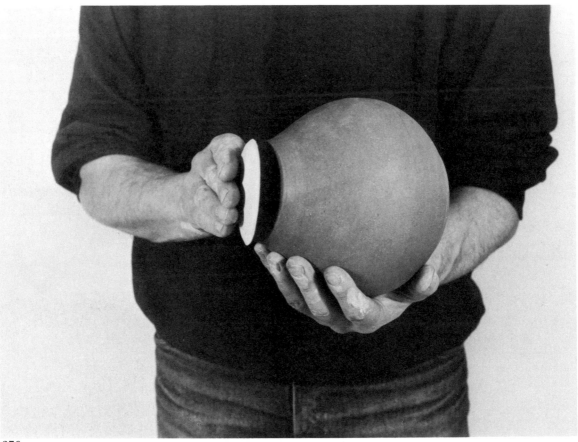

278

156

279 It is firmly fingered down onto the base and it is important that it is damp enough to adhere

280 The lower 7 to 10 cm are then dipped into the slip

281 With one arm inside the form holding it the card disc is removed holding it by the tab

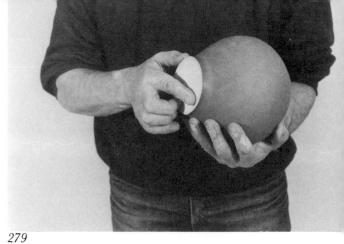

279

280

281

282

282, 283, 284 The function of the card is to prevent any slip going onto the base. If a little slip creeps under the card this should be cleaned off immediately with a dry sponge, but if the card is well attached in the first place this should not occur. The form is then held upside down and slip is poured into the dipped layer, working round the form until the entire surface is coated

283

284

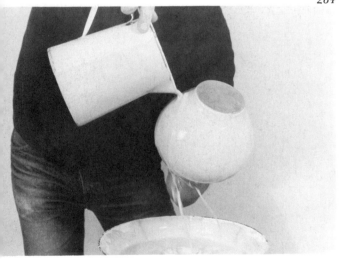

285 Holding the form firmly between the inside hand and the fingers of the other hand, spread out on the base, it is tilted until excess drops have left the top edge

286, 287 A small board is then placed on the base and again holding the form between inside and outside hands it is returned to an upright position

285

286

287

Application to the inside and outside of a larger open form

Where slip is to be applied to the inside and the outside of larger more open forms this needs to be done in stages with an interval between slipping the inside and the outside to allow the inside slip to become touch dry. The sequence which follows is a relatively unusual example but the point of it is not so much that the particular example is possible but, provided a manageable sequence is worked out and body state and slip consistency are exactly right, that slip can be applied to leatherhard objects, by dipping and pouring, in more varied contexts than might at first sight seem to be the case.

288   The slip is poured into the inside of the bowl

289   The bowl is rotated gradually pouring out the slip

290   All slip on the outside of the bowl is removed immediately as is the slip on the very edge of the bowl which will unavoidably get a second layer when the outside is slipped. While the main thickness of the slip layer must be removed to prevent a double thickness occurring it is unnecessary to sponge back to the clay body cleanly

The form is then stood upright and left until it is firm enough for further slip application. Fairly slow drying conditions are best for this because it is important that the slip inside is touch dry otherwise it will be easily smudged. An interval of at least a day in slow drying conditions is to be expected.

291   When the form has returned to the state in which the inside was slipped a card disc of the sort shown in the previous example is cut out for the foot. It is dampened and pressed into place

292   The next action is to dip the edge of the bowl. This is done so that when the slip is poured onto the outside of the bowl it will flow evenly over and off the edge precluding the possibility of it covering some parts of the edge and not others

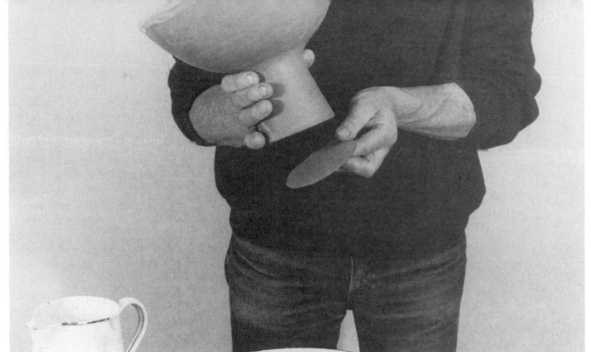

291

292

293

293, 294, 295   There is no need to drain the slip off the edge. The form is immediately but steadily turned over to dip the foot

294

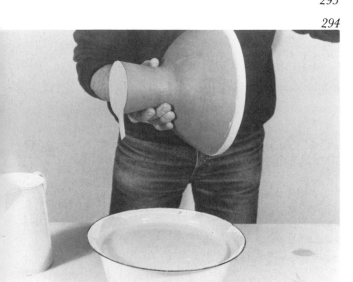

295

162

296 As soon as the foot has been dipped the card disc is peeled away

297, 298 The form is then again turned upside down and is supported on one hand. A folded piece of dry cloth or a dry sponge can act as a pad to prevent fingernail damage to the inner layer of slip. Pouring then commences into the dipped layer of slip on the stem

296

297

298

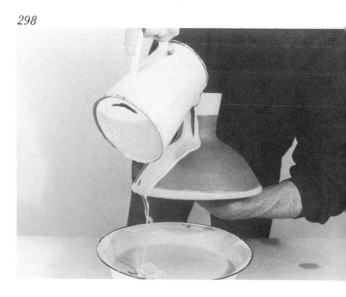

299, 300 Pouring jug and form are then rotated until the entire outside surface is coated

301 A small board is then placed on the base and with a little presure between the two hands the form is tilted and rotated to remove the drips of slip from the top edge

302, 303 Keeping a steady firm pressure between the two hands the form is then rotated to an upright position

302

303

Applying slip to dry bodies

Pouring and dipping are not methods of much use for the application of slip to dry bodies and partly for this reason the dry state is not one in which all-over slip layers are often applied. When slips are applied to dry bodies this is usually done by painting and most usually with specific decorative intentions. Where a flat opacity of colour is the intention it is easier to build up a layer of slip in two or more thin coats than attempting this in a single painted layer. Slip can be used on a dry clay as a thin painted wash, deliberately creating a layer which is not opaque. Varied and subtle qualities can be achieved like this.

Applying slip to biscuit fired bodies

Appropriately compounded slips can be applied at the biscuit stage by pouring and dipping. Application procedures are the same as with a glaze application and the sequences shown for this are equally relevant to slips. Overall coatings of slips are, however, not very frequently applied to biscuited bodies. When slips are applied to biscuited bodies this is most usually done by painting and with specific decorative intention. The biscuit state is a rather more convenient ground for such work than either the leatherhard or dry states because the porosity of the body allows a greater range of thicknesses to be applied with more control. Building up a thickness in two or three layers is usually unnecessary because the porous biscuit will hold a thicker application. Where opacity is not the intention a controlled thin layer can be applied by watering down the slip.

Some further factors relevant to slip application

The main and obvious potential of painting with slip is not in creating an even overall layer. When such coating is wanted on large objects painting is, however, the obvious method for doing this especially where spraying equipment is not available. Industrially, until relatively recently, extremely large structures, mainly in the sanitary ware industry, were made of relatively coarse fire clay bodies and then painted with densely opaque slips. These slips, which both gave the objects whiteness and a fine smooth surface, were applied with broad soft brushes in three or four separate layers at either the dry or biscuit fired states.

When slip is to be applied to large objects, whether as an overall coating or with other intentions, painting is the method to consider first. The dry or biscuit fired states are convenient and, due to the open nature of bodies used for large forms, are entirely possible.

When, at the leatherhard state, slip is applied by spraying, it is easy to forget that, while spraying diminishes or removes any problems of holding the form, the slip itself still has a softening effect on the clay body and, if applied without due consideration can lead to the distortion or collapse of forms as readily as is the case with ill-considered applications by pouring or dipping.

When dry or biscuit fired bodies are sprayed with slip somewhat granular surfaces can build up. Such surfaces may, of course, be wanted but it is as well to remember that when such surfaces occur with glaze spraying they fuse and flatten out but that this does not occur with slips.

Though it has been stated before it seems right to end this section by re-emphasising that though the focus of this section has been on the use of slip as an overall coating of bodies, slips have a decorative potential which extends considerably beyond this.

Casting slips

Casting slips are a vast and complex range of materials outside the scope of this book. They are, however, worthy of mention for their possible use in a context other than that for which they are intended.

Casting slips are clay bodies which have been made more fluid by the addition of deflocculants and water. Deflocculants make a clay body of a soft slurry condition into a fluid slip by having the quality of making the individual particles of the body repel one another. Thus, though a casting slip may be as fluid as an ordinary slip, in fact it contains less water and therefore has less shrinkage. Casting slips frequently have very good raw adhesion even to dry clay bodies. As poured layers they tend to be difficult to apply evenly because of their particular fluidity but as painted layers on various states of clay they have some possibilities. On dry clay bodies they are difficult to apply as a flat layer but can be used to build up very distinct texture.

Separated slips

The nature of separated slips

The process of separating different sizes of material in a moving watery suspension of material has been and is widely used in the grading and preparation of clays. Sandy clays can be cleaned of sand if they are mixed to a watery slip and allowed to run through a series of troughs, each of which overflows into the next – the troughs at the beginning of the series contain the sand and those furthest from the slip source contain the clay of the finest particle size and no sand. China clay has long been cleaned by similar methods. The same process occurs in nature – seams of ball clay and common clays being obvious examples of fine material separated from coarse as the material is transported by water.

This process of separation of fine particles from coarse in a moving suspension occurs because of the greater ability of fine particles to suspend in water and this ability exists in stationary as well as moving suspensions. The making of separated slips simply exploits this ability on a relatively small scale.

Some clays will yield separated slips which have exceptional gloss and, fired to their optimum temperature, very low porosity. If separated slips are overfired they lose their gloss. Discovering the optimum firing temperature of any particular slip is a matter of trial and error. Most separated slips are at their best somewhere in the temperature range of 980°C to 1080°C but a few will retain their gloss as high as 1120°C.

Separated slips can be made from any clay but not all clays contain a sufficient quantity of clay material of ultra-fine particle size to develop the fine gloss which is their particular quality.

Common red clays are the traditional raw material for separated slips so the traditional colour range is of the earthy colours which derive from these clays. But ball clays also have a high proportion of ultra-fine particles and more recently experiments have been made using ball clays to produce pale firing separated slips. These can be coloured with body stains. When body stains are added it is important that these are ground as finely as possible otherwise their particle size will detract from the gloss of the slip. Such work is time consuming and impracticable with a pestle and mortar so a small ball mill or vibro energy mill is really essential. If the slips do not have added stains the need for such equipment does not arise.

The mixing of separated slips

The mixing of separated slips is an easy matter involving only the pouring-off, or siphoning-off, of the top part of a watery slip. Sieving is not relevant because the finest commonly available mesh, 200, allows particles through which are coarse enough to diminish or destroy the fine gloss which is the particular quality of separated slips.

Essentially, the process of separation is one of suspension and the wateriness of suspensions should be such that coarser particles sink quickly while the finer ones remain suspended. Clays which separate readily, and subsequently form a high gloss, can often be effectively separated in ordinary water. Various substances may, however, be added to water to aid or prolong the suspension of fine particles. Wine, vinegar, brewing sediments, proprietory water softening powders and casting slip deflocculants may improve the suspension capacities of tap water. In all these cases the amounts added to water need only be small as it is the slight change in nature of the water, not the strength of the solution, which may aid suspension. When they are effective the additions make the suspension more fluid without it being more watery by reducing the natural tendency of the clay particles to cling together. The effect of whatever is added to water is relative both to the particular clay in question and to the nature of the particular tap water used. Rainwater usually promotes suspension and separation more readily than most tap waters.

In work with separated slips it should never be forgotten that the gloss which is sought may or may not be inherent in the clay. Separation will reveal a clay's gloss-forming potential but if a glossy slip does not result from separation this may be because of the nature of the clay and not a sign of inadequate separation.

Any serious enquiry into separated slips, as with all work in testing, should involve keeping careful records not only of clay used but also of water used, the relative amounts of these, and of the nature and amounts of any additions to the water.

304

305

306

304, 305 First of all, any soluble additions are mixed with and dissoved in the water, then the dry powdered or crumbled clay may, as here, be added to the water. Just as with ordinary slips it is far more convenient and far quicker to mix the slip from dry powdered or finely crumbled dry clay. The clay should be added to the water slowly so that neither on, nor below, the surface is there any build up of pockets of unwetted powder. In this instance 1000 g of powdered clay was added to 2 litres of water in which 5 g of *Calgon*, a proprietory water softener, has been dissolved

306 After several minutes, when all the clay material has had a chance to become thoroughly wetted, the slip is thoroughly mixed by rotating the jar vigorously to disperse the clay evenly in the water. The jar is then put on one side to settle

What occurs next may vary considerably but the advantage of glass containers is obvious. If the clay is one which forms a fine glossy separated slip the separation is usually clearly evident within minutes. Sometimes the finer suspended slip can be separated in less than an hour but it is usually advantageous to leave mixtures much longer to allow the coarser of the fine particles to settle. With longer settling times a number of layers can sometimes be seen and the coarseness of the lower layers may be clearly evident, while the upper layers are graded by differing colours. Occasionally, with slips which separate readily and develop a high gloss, a distinctly more watery layer may form between the suspended fraction of slip at the top and the settled slip at the bottom of the container.

When settlement is judged to be sufficient the suspended fraction of fine slip may be separated. This separation may be achieved either by gentle pouring or by siphoning. Occasionally the settled fraction settles fairly firmly but more usually, and especially if effective additions to the water have been made, it is fluid and is easily disturbed so siphoning is much the preferable method.

307 The principle of siphoning is that the liquid is transferred from a higher level to a lower level through a tube entirely filled with liquid. The flow is created by differential pressure at differing heights and the complete absence of air in the tube. Initially the tube has to be filled by sucking – a mouthful of slip is least likely if the tube is

168

reasonably long. The flow of liquid continues as long as the input end of the tube is immersed in the liquid – once air is admitted to the input end of the tube the flow ceases. To control accurately the position of a flexibile polythene or rubber tube it helps if the tube is taped to a suitable length of wood which enables the end of the tube to be held against the glass where it can be seen

307

308

308 Sufficient containers for all the separated slip should be at hand so the performance of restarting the flow by sucking does not need to be repeated unnecessarily. The suction created by the siphoning action is surprisingly strong and the end of the siphon should not be allowed much nearer than about 25 mm to the upper layer of settled sediment or it will start to suck this up with the separated slip. To overcome this problem it is better if the flexible siphoning tube is quite soft so that it can be pinched to diminish the strength of the suction. If some quantity of work is to be done it is worth buying a siphoning tube with an upturned end. These are made of glass or rigid plastic and are readily available from shops specialising in home brewing accessories where they are sold to overcome the identical problem in siphoning cleared wine from spent yeast and other sediments. The turned up end creates a downward rather than an upward sucking action and the sediment is, therefore, left completely undisturbed

Sometimes the fine separated slip will show a sediment a day or two after separation and when this occurs it can be resiphoned. Almost always a freshly separated slip is too thin for immediate use and needs thickening by evaporation. If excess water is evaporated by heat great care should be taken not to overheat it or lumps may form which are difficult to redisperse. It is much better to pour the thin slip into a wide, shallow container and to cover this with a board propped 25 to 50 mm above it. The wide container will facilitate evaporation and the board will prevent dust and anything else contaminating the slip. Placed near a radiator or other steady heat source sufficient evaporation will occur in a day or less.

Once they have been brought to a usable consistency separated slips should be kept in well sealed containers to prevent contamination and further evaporation.

The application of separated slips

Separated slips are usually and necessarily applied in very much thinner layers than other slips. To develop their particular quality all that is needed is a thin layer. Because they derive from clays of fine particle size and high plasticity, separated slips are extremely plastic and have very high shrinkage but, deriving from their plasticity, they have strong powers of adhesion.

If separated slips are applied too thickly to dry or biscuit fired clay bodies they tend to peel off as they dry but thinly applied, as they should be, they will adhere excellently both as raw and fired layers and can be successfully applied to leatherhard, dry and, surprisingly perhaps, to biscuit fired clay bodies. When applied to dry or biscuit fired bodies they are usually brushed. When this is done the slip should be laid on with a broad soft brush avoiding overbrushing as much as possible. Additional layers can be added once the previous layer is dry. When applied to leatherhard clay separated slips may be applied by pouring or dipping as well as brushing.

Separated slips do not need burnishing, though they will respond to this, but a gentle rub with a soft cloth, or simply in the hands, usually enhances the shine and this improvement is retained during firing.

Extensions to slips

It is difficult and perhaps impossible to be clear about where precisely one type of material ends and where another begins. What, exactly, for example, is the dividing line between earthenware and stoneware, between stoneware and porcelain or between a coloured slip and a pigmenting oxide (or body stain) blended with some frit and some clay? It is perfectly possible to be clear about definitively normal mixtures but when mixtures are substantially modified precise terminology is not always available. It is argued at the beginning of this section on slip that one word should cover a wide range of clay based mixtures to assist in the understanding of the nature of these and their possible diversity. It is not a part of this argument that there is a clear point at which slips, either for compositional or behavioural reasons, abruptly cease to be slips.

It is important to an understanding of slips to acknowledge that both glazes and pigments may be applied at all the stages at which slip application is possible. Provided that factors of raw and fired adhesion are acknowledged it is, therefore, possible to modify slips very substantially to achieve qualities distinct from those which occur through the use of definitively normal clay-based slips.

To modify slips towards glazes within any temperature range the proportion of fluxing materials in the slip is increased beyond the proportion required to ensure a sound fired adhesion between slip and clay. Slips then begin to approach glazes in composition and quality. Two possibilities for testing exist: either a known slip can be modified with increasing quantities of fluxing material or a known slip and a known glaze can be mixed in a line blend. Not all such tests will work, ie producing qualities that an individual finds useful, but the point is that there is no material reason to see a very sharp dividing line where slips end and another line where glazes begin. Between the two, and whether one thinks of the activity as being the modification of glaze or of slip, mixtures can be compounded which offer very distinct, particular qualities which are different from those associated with 'normal' glaze or slip.

Somewhat similarly to painting onto clay, fired or unfired, very useful colours can be made with mixtures of about one third body stain (or oxide), one third clay and one third of a mixture of flint and fluxing material – the proportions of this latter depend on the temperature of firing, the type of fluxing material and whether the pigmenting third has fluxing power. With as much as over 30% pigment and as little as 30% clay, with perhaps little or no plastic clay, such mixtures are hard to think of as conventional slips. Such mixtures can be applied with a body and a colour intensity quite distinct from both underglaze colours and conventionally pigmented slips. Being slip-like they can be applied thickly for complete opacity but can also be diluted with water to apply more translucent marks with considerable control. Between mixtures like this and blended and underglaze colours a considerable range of materials of different qualities can be mixed.

170

SECTION FIVE

COLOURING MATERIALS

Colouring pigments: metal oxides and their derivative colours

Almost all ceramic colour is derived from the use of metal oxides. The term 'pigment', as used in ceramics, is a non-specific one being used loosely to cover metal oxides, blends of metal oxides with other materials and with each other, and with various commercially prepared colours.

The importance of context

Not all the metal oxides are pigmenting but the non-pigmenting oxides can have a strong modifying effect on the colours produced by the pigmenting oxides. Indeed the colour resulting from any pigmenting oxide or prepared colour is dependent on the many and variable factors which comprise its precise context of use.

Chromium oxide is a good example of a pigmenting oxide which can produce a diverse range of colours: in low fired lead glazes it will produce bright red, orange and yellow; across a wide temperature range in various glazes it will produce a variety of greens; in calcined blends including zinc oxide it produces browns; and in calcined blends including tin oxide it produces a range of colours based on the 'chrome tin-pink' reaction ranging from crimson through mauve to pink. This range is exceptional but it does underline the importance of context.

Metal oxides

The number of metal oxides which have value as pigmenting oxides is relatively small and knowledge of their use is ancient. The increase in the range of ceramic colours which has occurred since the industrial revolution is far less to do with the discovery and isolation of a few new elements and their oxides than with increased understanding, as a result of scientific experiment, of ways in which the colours produced by metal oxides can be modified and stabilised.

Pigmenting oxides may be used as a source of colour by incorporating them in clay bodies, slips and glazes and they may be painted onto clay, with or without subsequent application of glaze, and they may be painted onto unfired glaze.

It is extremely important to understand that the pigmenting effect is not the only effect resulting from the use of metal oxides as each has its own response to heat and to other materials with which it is mixed or in contact. Some are highly refractory and some, in forming eutectic mixtures, act as strong fluxes. Additions of pigmenting metal oxides to ceramic materials cannot, therefore, be considered solely from the point of view of colour.

An important example of one side effect of a metal oxide is that additions of copper oxide to earthenware lead glazes can change a glaze which passes a lead release test into one which fails it dismally and is, therefore illegal. (See Section 7 *Sound practice in the use of materials*.)

Another important aspect of pigmenting oxides which must be understood is that their relative strength as pigments varies considerably. Cobalt oxide, for example, is relatively strong, and iron oxide relatively weak. In practice the relative strength of both strong and weak pigments is conditioned by the exact context of use, which may have a strengthening or weakening effect on the tonality of particular oxides in addition to its effect on actual colour. (See colour plate 4b.)

One further but purely semantic factor needs to be mentioned. Potters and potters' literature are imprecise in their use of the word *oxide* and casual in the omission of it. This is often a source of confusion to beginners. *Oxide* may be taken to mean the oxide form of a metal and the common use of, for example, *manganese oxide* or *vanadium oxide* is not a reference to an unusual material not listed by suppliers but merely reference to the oxide form of manganese – manganese dioxide – and vanadium – vanadium pentoxide. Where, for example, reference is made solely to *manganese* or *vanadium* this may be taken to be reference to the oxide form. Further confusion is created by the occasional use of Latin names: for example, *Chromic oxide* is not a different material to *Chromium oxide*. Latin names, rather than confusing, should assist in clarifying as, for example, when more than one oxide form exists, as with *cuprous* and *cupric oxides*. Where stated, chemical formulae constitute the most precise mode of communication. Confusion among beginners, though recurrent, is rarely long lived as they slip into the traditional imprecisions.

Counted among the pigmenting 'oxides' are the carbonate forms of copper, cobalt and manganese.

Suspension and solution colours in glazes

Where pigmenting oxides are added to glaze a distinction must be made between suspension colours and solution colours. Suspension colours occur when refractory pigmenting oxides remain suspended in glaze. Even when used in clear shiny glazes suspension colours tend to have an opacifying effect. In most glazes the greens derived from chromium oxide are opaque and are a common example of suspension colour. Small proportions of most pigmenting oxides produce solution colours, for example small percentage additions of iron, manganese, copper and cobalt oxides produce solution colours in most clear glazes at most temperatures leaving glazes with a coloured but unopacified translucency. If the proportion of oxide addition is raised then opacity is reached by virtue of tonal strength but a saturation occurs and no more pigmenting oxide can be held in solution. The larger additions of oxides which create this condition result either in suspension colours or, if the undissolved oxide crystalises on cooling, crystalline effects such as those frequently found in stoneware glazes with a high iron content.

Blended colours from metal oxides

In every context of use the pigmenting oxides may be mixed with each other to produce a blend of colour extending the range which single oxides will produce.

In clay, slip and glaze oxide blends are simply added to the material though, to avoid specking, separate mixing and sieving of the pigments are frequently done before these are added into the batch, and are evenly distributed throughout the material.

Because oxide blends intended for painting are used on, and not in, clays or glazes their composition can be more elaborate and the possible colour range is broader. The relative isolation of their use allows the effect of non-pigmenting modifying oxides to be relatively greater so these are more frequently included. Furthermore, as oxides alone are, potentially, tonally strong as painted material other materials may be added to assist the control of painted tonality. Any additions need to acknowledge the refractory or fluxing nature of the pigmenting oxides and can be included to affect colour, surface, tonality and paintability. Materials which are frequently used are clays (plastic clays, particularly, improve the flow of a painting mixture) flint, china stone, felspar, frits and glaze. Oxides and oxide blends painted onto clay tend to be dark, and matt or metallic in surface depending on the oxide, unless they are glazed which brings out their colour. Blends of pigmenting and non-pigmenting materials intended for painting are prepared for use either by grinding in water using a pestle and mortar, where quantities warrant this, or by crushing as a thin paste on a glass slab or tile with a palette knife.

Calcination

The immense increase in the range of available colour in pottery which has occurred since the Industrial Revolution is due largely to developments in the process and understanding of calcination. This has been evolved to produce and stabilise colours in isolation from as many of the variable factors of context as possible.

Calcining consists of grinding together the pigmenting materials and the modifying materials with any fluxing materials included. The ground material is then dried and fired during which various factors are important including the surface area of the mass of material and the schedule, final temperature and the atmosphere of the firing. After firing the material, which may be a fused or merely a sintered mass, is reground. Sometimes this single cycle is all that occurs but calcination may occur more than once with water grinding between each firing and sometimes with the addition of uncalcined material at intermediate stages. The grinding at initial and intermediate stages is usually to a finely controlled size. The exact procedures of the process are as important as the recipes in the production of consistent colours.

Calcination produces a vastly wider range of colours than that which is available from uncalcined blends. Calcined colours, though far more stable than uncalcined, are not wholly inert and the resulting colour is somewhat conditioned by the context of use. Manufacturers usually stipulate the optimum conditions, such as temperature and type of glaze, needed for the production of specific intended colours. Calcined colours are available as underglaze colours and glaze and body stains, and exist in most ready made coloured glazes which can be bought.

It is as true of calcined colours as it is of oxides and oxide blends that the breadth of the possible colour range decreases as the temperature of use increases.

Individuals do not normally consider experimenting with producing calcined colours. It would be very time consuming and demands sophisticated control of a level largely unavailable in non-industrial contexts. In any case a wide range of calcined colours are readily available.

Underglaze colours

These colours are manufactured for industrial application by both printing and painting and are compounded to be used under glaze, as the name suggests, on high fired biscuit with a low hardening-on firing at about 850°C to burn away the media and to harden the colour prior to the glaze firing.

In non-industrial use as painting material they will produce consistent results if applied to leatherhard or dry clay as well as to biscuit though a subsequent high biscuit firing may alter the colour which would be produced by the expected industrial usage. A hardening-on firing may be avoided if glaze is applied directly onto the

unfired colour though to prevent contamination of glaze this is usually done only if glaze spraying equipment is available.

Underglaze painting colours are usually mixed with gum or glycerine water-based media rather than oil based and should be well mixed with a palette knife on a tile before use.

The glaze applied over underglaze colours will affect the actual colours which result. The effect of any glaze intended for use should be tested. Some glazes will dull the range of colours and suppliers should be asked to recommend glazes for their range of colours. Thin applications of glaze are normal in industrial practice. Despite the intentions of colour manufacturers and the conventions of industrial practice eminently usable effects can be obtained by breaking with industrial conventions.

In spite of their name many underglaze colours can be applied successfully over unfired glaze. Occasionally colours used in this way may develop a rather dry surface when they are fired and if this occurs a small proportion of frit or clear glaze added to the colour usually cures the problem.

Underglaze colours are mostly commonly available in dry powder form but some suppliers offer underglaze crayons, felt tip pens and ready-mixed colour in tubes.

Glaze and body stains

Some manufacturers supply universal stains which can be added to glazes or bodies but where separate stains for glaze and body are available these are formulated to have a minimal effect on glaze maturing and body vitrifying temperatures respectively. Suppliers stipulate maximum temperatures for stains and to exceed these will usually result in loss or change of colour. Maximum percentage additions, often surprisingly large especially with body stains, are also stipulated and where this is the case the stipulation gives some guide to tonal strength.

As would be expected, the use of stains extends very considerably the range of colour which is possible with the use of metal oxides and uncalcined mixtures. Stains, however, are not cheap and while the use of stains in glaze does not greatly increase costs, the use of stains in clay bodies can be extraordinarily expensive so for this reason stains are used in slips rather than bodies where this is possible.

Stains are not inert so, like other pigmenting materials, their effect is always conditioned by their context of use. Both the strength and colour of given proportions of glaze stain will differ depending on the chemical nature of glazes. Body stains only develop their strongest tonality for given proportions when bodies are vitrified. The use of glaze over body stained slip or clay always strengthens the tonality of the colour, and different glazes will result in slightly different colour.

Except when used in small proportions glaze stains tend towards the opacity of suspension colours rather than the translucency of solution colours.

Outside the precise conventions of the pottery industry, underglaze colours and glaze and body stains are often successfully used as interchangeable materials. When this works there can be no objection; when it does not it should be remembered that the various calcined colours have been evolved for particular contexts of use and that use outside these is, therefore, a bonus.

Enamels

Enamels may be thought of as being like very low firing glazes. They are composed of low temperature fluxes, silica and colouring pigment, but are low in, or devoid of, alumina. Conventionally, enamels are applied onto a fired glazed surface, usually white, which allows their bright colour potential to be most fully exploited. Both historical and modern examples may be found of enamel applied to unglazed surfaces but this is the exception rather than the rule. Depending on their particular composition, enamels are fired somewhere within the temperature range of 700°C to 900°C, usually around the middle of this range.

Enamels were evolved because of the desire in both Oriental and European cultures to produce hard, durable and brightly coloured wares. The hard, durable ceramic was most easily produced at relatively high temperatures while firing at low temperature considerably widened the palette of colour available for decoration. Thus the practice arose of a final enamel firing to decorate plain or partly decorated higher fired ware.

Two distinct qualities of enamel can be found

in historical examples. At one extreme are thinly applied, semi-opaque coloured enamels usually finely and precisely painted; at the other extreme are thickly applied, glassier enamels, usually applied in freer, broader marks. The use of both qualities of enamel can be found, separately and in combination, in Oriental and in European traditions.

Concerns for consistency of result and related modern techniques of repetitive application have meant that enamels prepared for industrial use have tended more and more to be relatively opaque in quality and to require only thin application.

The commercially prepared enamels available from suppliers are compounded for industrial use within the industrial tradition which has evolved and, as such, offer good colour response with thin application and permit a good retention of fine detail. As they are specifically intended for thin application, prepared enamels are relatively strongly pigmented and if used thickly they tend to develop a dense rather sticky looking quality. Used thinly as intended they are consistent. They exist in a wide range of colour.

Until relatively recently commercially prepared enamels were most commonly available in powder form and required mixing with a medium. Increasingly, ranges of enamels for painting are now available ready mixed in tubes or small jars.

For those who wish to use the more glaze-like translucent quality which is not a usual attribute of industrial enamels there are two alternatives. Either the quality of commercially prepared enamels can be modified by the use of translucent enamel flux. This is not listed by all suppliers and when not listed may be available on request. Blended with enamel colours this does enable thicker application and the use of a deeper, more glaze-like quality. Or, and probably better, if a rich translucent depth of colour is wanted, enamels can be mixed from raw materials.

Mixing enamels from raw materials necessarily involves the use of raw lead oxide or the making of one's own frits. It is perfectly possible, though rather time consuming, to make one's own enamel frits because these are not needed in large quantities. Mixed enamels readily achieve a translucent depth of colour but the range of colours and the consistency of result will not match that available with commercially prepared

174

enamels. This should be clear before anyone decides to embark on making frits.

There are two problems associated with enamels.

The first is that enamels have relatively poor resistance to abrasion. This is obviously only of minor importance in purely decorative work which is not subject to abrasion but in tableware it is obviously a serious drawback.

The second is that many enamals do not conform with current safety legislation on metal release for tableware. Enamels are at risk from the acids present in food and drink, particularly fruit juice, and from the alkalis used in detergents. If the enamel surface is attacked chemically or becomes worn through physical abrasion then the greatly increased surface area of the dulled surface is even more prone to chemical attack so the two problems are in fact related.

Much industrial research has been devoted to solving these problems in recent decades, the twin aims being to improve the resistance of enamels to abrasion and to reduce or eliminate their lead oxide content. Suppliers of commercially prepared enamels will advise on intended contexts of use and factors related to metal release. Anyone who makes enamels from raw materials and uses these on ware which could be used with food or drink should have their work tested regularly for metal release.

Lustres

Various means of producing lustrous effects in and on glaze exist. This brief section outlines the two types of lustre which can be applied on glaze. Both depend on the reduction of a thinly applied mixture.

Of the two types the commercially prepared lustres offered by most suppliers are the more convenient. These exist in a wide range of effects from the almost colourless but strongly irridescent 'mother of pearl' types to quite deep tones of colour. They are supplied as a ready-mixed liquid and are applied thinly to fired glaze surfaces. The compositions of these lustres are not published but they are made from metallic salts, most commonly of copper, gold, silver and bismuth mixed in a medium which contains or, in part, constitutes a reducing agent. Prepared lustres are simple to

use but they have to be applied thinly, as applications which are too thick tend to adhere poorly and to dust off when fired, also prior to application, the fired surface should be free from greasy finger-marks as these are also a cause of poor adhesion. As they are self-reducing they can be fired in an oxidising atmosphere and firings should be well ventilated to clear the fumes from the kiln.

Being prepared primarily for industrial use they develop their intended quality most fully on clear shiny glazes on white bodies. Used in contexts other than this they tend to produce effects rather less related to manufacturers' descriptions but these can be rich and varied.

The precious metals, gold and platinum, are supplied in the same form as other lustres and may be applied at the same time. They are applied fractionally thicker than other lustres – gold, particularly, should not be applied too thinly (a pinkish purple colour occurs if it is applied too thinly). *Silver* lustre is in fact *platinum*. Though present in some lustres silver is not used as a precious metal as it tends to oxidise and blacken after firing. 'Bright' gold and platinum emerge from the kiln finished, but matt or 'burnished' gold and platinum require burnishing after firing with fine, mildly abrasive burnishing sand.

Fibre-tipped pens containing gold and platinum are available and work well if used frequently but do not store well after they have been used as the fibre tip ceases to produce a good flow. If the flow of a pen diminishes it can often be restored by removing the tip and soaking this in lustre thinners.

All commercial lustres should be kept in airtight bottles as they tend to thicken rather rapidly on contact with air. Lustre thinners can be used to restore the original fluidity provided a lustre has not thickened too much.

Considering the amount of attention which has been afforded to many firing processes in recent decades it is surprising that more work has not been done on lustres based on ancient Persian and Hispano-Moresque types. These are based on forms of various metals such as silver nitrate, silver chloride, silver sulphate, silver carbonate, bismuth sub-nitrate, copper carbonate, copper oxalate and copper sulphate which are mixed with ochre and applied to the fired glaze surfaces. The ochre

175

with a water-based medium to form the painting material. The ochre acts solely as a vehicle for the application of the metal. At the highest point of firing and during the initial stages of cooling the kiln is reduced. This reduction fixes a thin film of metal to the glaze surface. The low temperature of the firing means that the ochre and the glaze do not adhere to one another. When the work is cool it is washed and rubbed with a very mild abrasive to remove all traces of the ochre. Crucial to the success of the practice is the control of the temperature and atmosphere of the firing. Too little temperature and very little happens; too much temperature and carbon penetrates the glaze; too thick an application of lustre, together with too much reduction, and lustre flashes erratically, spreading onto unlustered areas.

Any work with this type of lustre, until confidence and experience are acquired, should aim to have as many carefully recorded firings as possible. In addition really careful record keeping of clays and glazes used, of biscuit and glaze firing temperatures and, obviously, of lustre mixtures is essential.

Lustres of the second type have a depth and richness which is different from the more colourful but more superficial qualities of commercially prepared lustres.

Mixing pigments into clay bodies

The first fact to understand about pigmenting clay bodies is that it is far easier to make them darker than it is to make them lighter. Pink or yellow stain does in fact show when added to a red earthenware body but a great deal of stain has to be added and the colour is far from pure. In practice, therefore, white or very light firing clay bodies are those most usually coloured with metal oxides or stains. Red earthenware or buff firing or fireclay bodies may be used where dark or black firing bodies are wanted.

Tests with, or recipes for, pigmented clay bodies may be either of dry weighed or plastic weighed bodies to dry weighed pigment. Obviously results over a period will be more consistent if both body and pigment are weighed when dry but, provided care is taken to ensure that a closely similar consistency is used, weighing plastic clay body and dry pigment leads to acceptably consistent results partly because clay bodies are less sensitive than glaze to small variations in percentage additions of pigment. To work with plastic weighed bodies and dry weighed pigment is certainly the more common practice.

White clay bodies coloured with stains are one way of achieving pure flat colour in ceramics which has a distinct quality. If the colour is to be even, steps have to be taken to disperse the stain finely through the body.

One last factor to mention before describing mixing procedures is that of *cost*. It should be noted that adding metal oxides or stains to clay bodies may make what is generally and correctly thought of as a relatively cheap raw material into a surprisingly expensive one. This is less the case with metal oxides as the more expensive oxides are also the strongest and as oxides anyway are usually added in quite small percentages. But with body stains, which may be added in relatively larger proportions, the price increase may be considerable. To quote actual figures could be misleading as oxide, and therefore stain, prices fluctuate. Proportionately though the prices of clays and clay bodies, metal oxides and stains stay in relatively similar relationships. The price of body stains do vary somewhat from colour to colour but, to give some indication, a small addition of a medium priced stain may much more than double the price of a clay body, while a stronger addition of a rather more expensive stain may increase the body price more than tenfold. Some other materials in ceramics are expensive but most of these go a long way in use so this aspect of coloured bodies is mentioned as being exceptional. Used well, stained clays offer colour possibilities not widely exploited within the traditions of ceramics.

Stained clay bodies being used in processes such as inlay and agate are not often needed in large amounts and the mixing processes used depend on two factors: firstly whether a fine even mix is needed and secondly on the actual amount being mixed.

When a certain amount of specking is acceptable a very quick way of adding metal oxide or body stain to a clay body is to *knead* it in. The weighed amount of pigment is simply spread out on a board well away from the near edge and the weighed body is kneaded so that it steadily picks up the pigment.

309 Kneading should be done at the edge of the area of pigment not in the middle of it so that only a little is picked up in each kneading movement. The kneading action needs to be such that picking up pigment is alternated with short spells of kneading away from the pigment so that what has been picked up is worked into the clay mass

310 Ideally the clay should be at the soft rather than the firm end of the plastic state because the addition of dry powder tends, at least temporarily, to make a firm body rather crumbly. To overcome this tendency it helps if an area of the wedging surface is kept slightly damp so that while the pigment is being kneaded into the mass the outside retains a slightly sticky surface. Repeated sponging of the wedging surface will be needed to achieve this but the surface should never be left actually wet from the sponge as this will make the clay skid around and make kneading difficult

Eventually all the pigment will be picked up and it is important then to continue kneading to mix the pigment thoroughly into the clay body. Especially if the pigment addition is large, clay pigmented by this method loses some of its previous plasticity. At least some of the plasticity can be restored if the pigmented body is left wrapped in polythene for a day or two and then rekneaded. When kneading is complete the kneading surface should be very thoroughly cleaned. If much of this work is undertaken it can help to have a number of loose marine plywood boards so that rather than pigmenting bodies on a general work or kneading surface this is done on boards kept specifically for the purpose.

When dry pigment is to be added to pieces of clay which are too small to knead the same principles of picking up pigment and mixing it into the mass are applied by whatever means seems most convenient to the quantities in question.

309

310

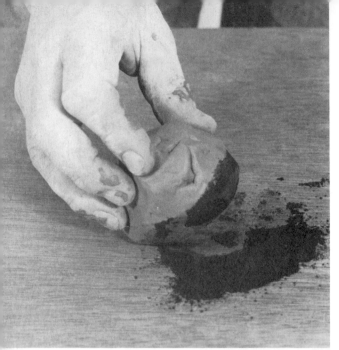

311 The small ball of clay is rolled into the pigment repeatedly to pick up a quantity of pigment

312 A convenient way of mixing this into the mass is to extend the ball of clay into a coil and then double this back on itself and reroll it repeatedly. If this, as in the previous example using kneading, is done on a slightly damp surface the clay body will tend to lose less of its plasticity. Hand wedging can be the final action to distribute the pigment evenly throughout the body but this should not be done until there are no signs of dry pigment on the clay surface, otherwise the force of the action will tend to send the pigment all over the place

311

312

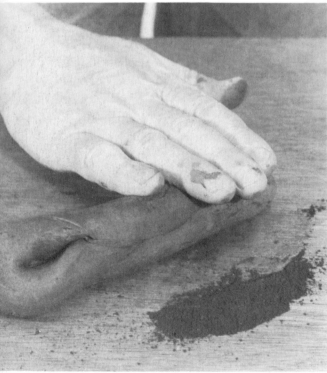

Where the intention is to avoid all specking, the pigment must be ground in a pestle and mortar and sieved through a 200 mesh sieve.

Initial work is likely to be with relatively small amounts of clay but even this can be a messy process. The secret of avoiding mess is to keep the wet pigment off the fingers as much as possible. The procedure depends on whether small, say under 5%, or larger quantities of pigment are to be added to the clay.

Smaller proportions have a less softening effect on the clay and can usually be conveniently added to a ball of clay pinched into a thick-walled, hollow form.

313   The metal oxide or stain is first ground and sieved and then allowed to settle. The clear water should then be poured off the top

314   The pigment is then scooped from the mortar with a rubber kidney into the hollow of the lump of clay

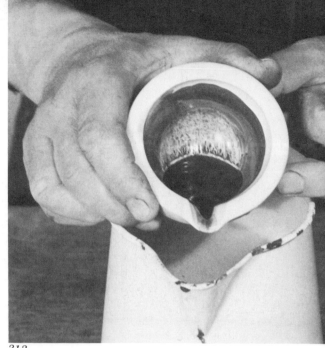

313

314

179

315 The pigment is then mixed with some clay by stirring it round in the hollow. The tool should cut into the clay to mix it with the pigment but should not cut in too deeply

316 When as much mixing as possible has been done with the wooden tool the thick walls should be thumbed downwards into the pigmented slurry

315

316

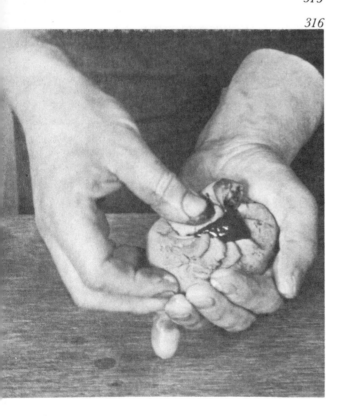

317, 318, 319 This process of folding layers of clay downwards is then repeated a number of times until the slurry is well distributed through the lump in a number of layers. The pinching thumb inevitably picks up some neat pigment but no pigment need be lost by getting slurry mixture all over the hands

Once the pigment and clay are well intermingled further mixing is done by hand wedging – repeatedly halving the lump and squeezing it together again, or alternatively the lump can be rolled into a coil and then be repeatedly rolled and doubled over until mixing is complete. With large enough lumps, and it is perfectly possible to use this process with quite large lumps, provided the percentage of pigment added is not large, final mixing can be completed by kneading.

181

When larger proportions of pigment are added these have such a softening effect on the clay that working the pigment into a hollowed ball of clay is not possible. In this case the clay is mixed on a flat work surface. Marble, slate and close grained marine ply are all appropriate surfaces but soft, uneven or open grained wooden surfaces are not suitable.

320 The clay is initially spread out on the work surface and is scored or impressed with fine linear marks to increase the surface area which the pigment can reach

321 As before, the pigment is ground, sieved and allowed to stand until clear water can be poured away. It is then scooped into the clay. A slight pinched wall helps to retain the pigment

322 Using a paint scraper the pigment and clay are then chopped together. The palette knife is used to scrape off the clay and pigment which repeatedly builds up on the paint scraper throughout the mixing process

320

321

322

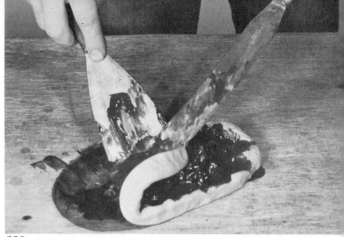

323 Eventually the clay and pigment slurry in the middle will break out over the edges and from this point the whole mass should be repeatedly chopped up and stroked through with the paint scraper and needs to be lifted off the work surface and turned over at intervals

324 With high proportions of pigment mixing can appear somewhat hopeless at this stage. To work effectively it is important that the scraper is cleaned frequently with the palette knife. The actions of chopping and stroking are continued and quite quickly a more manageable, homogenous mixture will be formed

323

324

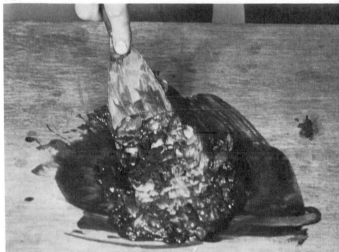

325 As a more homogenous mixture is achieved the nature of the chopping and stroking actions become clearer. Here the chopping action of moving the scraper through the clay mass with a regular up and down motion is shown

325

326

327

326 The alternative action of stroking the corner of the scraper through the clay is illustrated here

327 When each cycle of chopping or stroking motions is complete the clay is scraped off the work surface and returned to a more compact mass before it is again spread out. Chopping or stroking continues until all signs of uneven striations have gone. With high proportions of pigment the clay is usually much too sticky to use and has to be put on one side to stiffen up. When pigment is mixed in by this latter process no unevenness of colour mixing should be left as evenness is far more quickly achieved by mixing at the sticky soft stage than by kneading. Kneading will be necessary to produce an even consistency after the clay has stiffened but should not be needed for colour mixing

Where a larger quantity of clay body needs body stain or oxide added to it without the specking which would result from kneading the pigment in, and especially where quite large additions of colour are involved, a variation of the previous method can be used.

328　The ground sieved pigment is mixed with a relatively small amount of the weighed clay body. This is done, as shown previously, with a metal scraper and a palette knife shown here in use on a large sheet of plate glass which is an excellent base for such mixing

329　The pigment is thoroughly blended into the clay body

330　The remainder of the amount of the body is then cut up into a number of slices and the piece of clay is reassembled sandwiching a layer of the very soft, highly pigmented mixture between the unpigmented slices

328

329

330

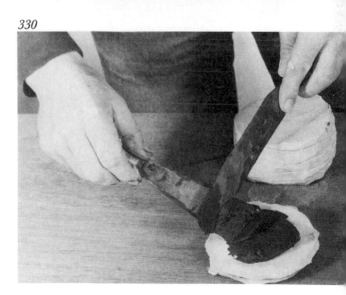

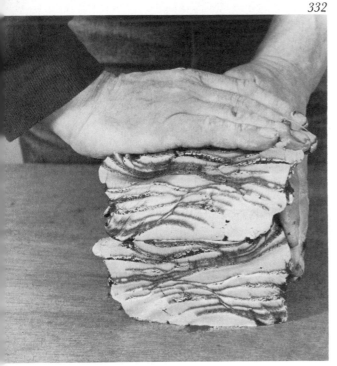

331 On no account can normal wedging be undertaken or the soft clay mixture will splash out. (In fact if the sandwiched reassembled piece can be wrapped up and left for a while the mass will become rather more even in consistency.) The whole piece is then cut up as if for wedging but rather than throwing the two halves together they are simply placed one on top of the other

332 The clay mass is then firmly squashed down and the action repeated until the mass is kneadable

The preparation of colours for painting

The marketing of ready-to-use tube colours has eliminated the need for preparation with some types of colour. Colour manufacturers are only likely to manufacture colours and types of colour in ready-to-use form which, in their judgement, will be most saleable in worthwhile quantities. So for those with some particular intentions knowledge of the preparation of colours, as well as their composition, is likely to remain necessary.

A range of options exists for the preparation of small amounts of colour which involves the use of palette knives or glass mullers on tiles or plate glass slabs and the use of pestles and mortars. Only part of that range is shown and from this the variations should be obvious.

The range of processes has an effect which varies from the purely blending action of a palette knife on a tile which only mixes the powder with the medium, through the blending and grinding action which can occur between the two ground glass surfaces when a glass muller is used on a ground glass slab, to the stronger grinding action of a pestle and mortar. A glass muller is a heavy hemispherical or conical glass tool with a handle formed at the top and a flat, ground glass working surface at the bottom. Lighter mullers are now manufactured by inserting a glass rod into a thickish glass disc. These are inferior to, and much less comfortable to use than the heavier type.

Which of the various options is appropriate in any given instance depends upon whether the material being prepared is already finely ground and only requires mixing with some medium, or whether the material does need to be ground, and whether a very finely ground painting mixture is in fact required.

Mixing colour on a ground glass slab with a palette knife

In the photographs which follow powdered enamel colour is being mixed with an oil based medium. Bought powdered enamel colours are very finely ground but unless they are thoroughly blended with some medium the painted colour may develop speckling due to tiny pockets of unwetted colour.

333 The medium is first put in the middle of the ground glass slab

334 Sufficient powder is then sprinkled onto the medium to form a fairly viscous mix

335 The powder is then stirred into the medium and before proper mixing starts more powder or a drop or two more medium are added if necessary to bring the mix to the right consistency

333

334

335

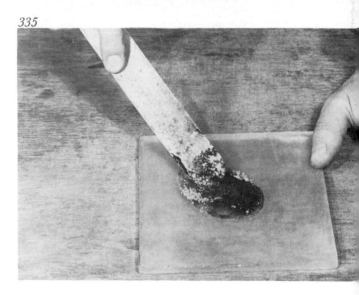

187

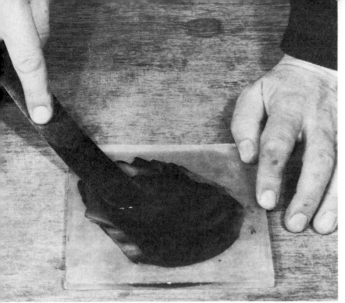

336

336 The action of mixing is to exert some pressure onto the springy palette knife to bring at least 25 mm into flat contact with the glass slab and then to work the knife backwards and forwards across the tile in fan shaped movements. If the action spreads out the colour too much, or if it is not viscous enough, the material can be scraped back into the middle with the knife. Very thorough blending of powder and medium and crushing of lumps of powder can be achieved quickly by this method

337 The thickly prepared colour is then scraped onto a glazed tile or into a shallow dished container for use where it will require further dilution with medium

337

Mixing colours with a glass muller
In this example powdered enamel colour is mixed with an oil based medium.

338 Unless a true grinding effect is intended a glass muller can be used on plain as opposed to ground glass. The initial action is to rotate the muller lightly on the powder and medium until the two begin to mix

339 The subsequent and main action exerting a downwards pressure, is to move the muller round and round in small circles. This tends to spread the colour mass as it mixes it but it can be returned to the centre by holding the muller stationary at the edge of the colour, and rotating it, which draws the viscous colour back to the middle, or by lifting the muller and drawing it across the ridge of displaced colour towards the centre

338

339

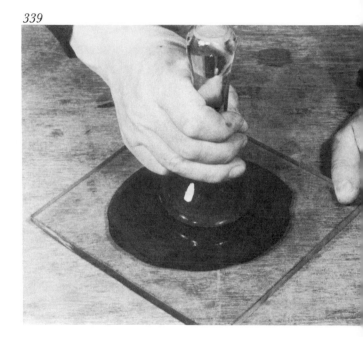

189

340

341

Mixing colours using a pestle and mortar

Pestles and mortars exist in a variety of sizes from 8 cm diameter to at least 35.5 cm. The smaller and medium sizes are those most useful for colour grinding. Pestles and mortars are made of unglazed porcelain and give decades of service. These expensive items will chip or break if dropped and, therefore, should be handled with care. Their ability to grind material is based on their form and their hardness but porcelain will, of course, only effectively grind materials softer than itself. All bought oxides and colours fall into this category so the only wear in use is the exceptionally slow wear of the two surfaces rubbing against each other.

Virtually all prepared colours are sold ready ground and, therefore, require only crushing and blending with a medium but some oxides are sold without being very finely ground and these, if a smooth fine painting mixture is required, do need to be ground further.

In this example a slightly granular manganese dioxide mixed with a little cobalt oxide is ground in water.

340   Water is put into the mortar first of all, then the oxides are added, followed by more water to bring the mixture to a suitably watery consistency

341   The action of grinding is a simple circular motion rotating the pestle around the base of the mortar. The pestle may be tilted or held vertical or this position may be alternated with each rotation. The action is not fast and is done with firm downward pressure. As the majority of effective grinding occurs in the lower part of the mortar, between this and the end of the pestle, the mixture should be sufficiently watery to return the material to the base of the mortar. Some material is inevitably left on the sides of the mortar where it cannot be effectively ground by the pestle and this should be occasionally wiped back to the bottom with a rubber kidney. If much material is left on the sides the mixture may need additional water

190

342, 343 When the mixture has been sufficiently ground it is first wiped off the pestle and then from the sides of the mortar

344 The mixture may then be poured and wiped with a kidney into a suitable shallow container or, if an excessively watery mix is not wanted, the mixture can be allowed to settle and the excess water carefully poured away, taking especial care not to lose any of the finest, most suspended part of the mixture

343

342

344

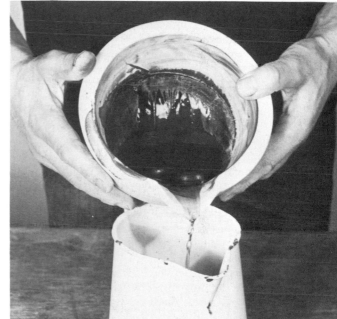

Some further factors related to preparing colours

The methods described can all be used with bought underglaze or onglaze colours, pigmenting oxides, blends of pigmenting oxides with other colours, bought enamel colours and enamels made from mixed frits, but the use of pestles and mortars is usually kept for occasions when considerable grinding is necessary and is done with waterborne mixtures. Blending and grinding colour on a tile or glass slab with a knife or muller can be done as readily with colours which are purely waterborne or mixed with water based media as with oil based media, but the initial mixture should be in quite a viscous condition whatever the medium or uncrushed tiny pockets of material can escape the crushing action of mixing by floating outwards in too fluid a mixture.

Oil based colours are generally put onto a tile for use and, in use, a few drops of medium are put next to the viscous mixed colour which is blended to the desired thinness in the area between the colour and the medium. Because oil based colour tends to dry out hard quite quickly it is usual to mix only sufficient for immediate use.

Water-based colours are better kept in dished containers which allow thicker colour to gather in the middle so that thin or thicker colour can be picked up with control. Ideally each colour should have its own brush or brushes and water container. Water is then added to the mix by brush from this container which is also used for the initial rinsing of brushes before these are properly washed under a tap. In time quantities of fine particles of colour build up in the water container and can be decanted and returned to the colour container.

When an oxide which needs grinding is to be mixed with other materials and when clay is one of these materials – and this may often be the case with oxide painting mixtures – the clay should not be added to a very watery mix as it will make it difficult to thicken the mixture by decanting water. In such instances the mixture should be ground in a watery condition without the clay and the clay should be added only when grinding is complete and the excess water has been decanted. The clay can be blended into the mixture by grinding this to a paste-like consistency.

Enamel colours made with home made frits

benefit from grinding. This can be done either with a glass muller on a ground glass slab – the glass of an enamel frit is much softer than commercial glass – or in a pestle and mortar but the small quantities needed usually make the former the more convenient method.

Making small amounts of enamel frit

In the series of photographs which follows 300 g of dry materials were used. The recipe is:

Lead carbonate 48   Borax 18   Flint 34

When the ingredients have been weighed out they are dry mixed using a pestle and mortar. This is the most practical way of ensuring an intimate mixing of the materials. All the materials listed are hazardous as airborne dust, so care should be taken to avoid this. The materials must be mixed dry because of the solubility of borax. A large pestle and mortar enables the work to be done very quickly as it is the mixing rather than grinding which is important. If materials and working conditions are very dry the materials can be very lightly sprayed from a hand sprayer which will minimise any risk of airborne dust.

A small thick walled, low fired, biscuit bowl of rounded form is needed to contain the materials during firing. Before the frit materials are put into this it must be coated on the inside with an even and quite generous layer of flint or quartz. This is mixed with water and brushed on. It is important that flint or quartz is used and not alumina or battwash because some of the material with which the bowl is coated sticks to the frit and alumina, or the zirconium oxide frequently present in battwash both have a detrimental effect on the frit, while the additional silica which flint or quartz will bring merely increases the silica in the frit slightly.

The bowl containing the frit is then fired to between 850°C and 900°C.

345 When the fired frit emerges from the kiln it will be seen to have pooled in the base of the bowl and will be adhering to the flint wash. The function of the flint wash is to minimise the adhesion of the frit to the bowl. If there are any bare areas or thin areas in the flint wash frit will adhere very strongly in these places. Very occasionally the melted pool of frit can be lifted away from the bowl but this is rare. More usually the first step is to break the bowl. This is best done by gently tapping with a heavy hammer. The heavier the hammer the better because the aim is to free the frit while breaking the bowl into a few large pieces. Here the bowl has just begun to crack

346 The first large piece of the bowl has come cleanly away from the frit leaving some of this projecting into space

347 With the bowl inverted this projecting piece of frit is tapped to free it

345

346

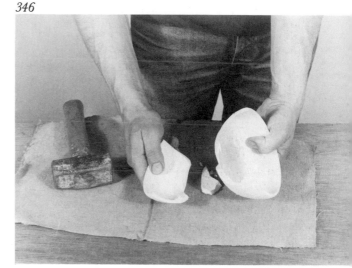

347

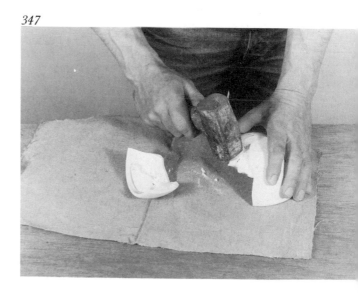

348

349

348 Exactly what happens each time is, of course, different but the aim is to avoid contaminating the frit with fragments of clay body and this is best achieved if the bowl and frit initially are broken into as few pieces as possible. Here the pieces of frit have been separated from the broken bowl and the flakes of flint wash. The bowl is then discarded

349 The pieces of frit are then wrapped in a closely woven thick cloth, placed on a heavy flat piece of metal and firmly hit with a hammer. The cloth obviously prevents the frit flying all over the place

350 After about six or eight firm blows with the hammer the cloth can be opened

351, 352 The frit pieces are then graded by size, the larger ones being subsequently returned to the cloth for further breaking and the smaller ones, of 6 mm and less being placed from the cloth onto the metal surface

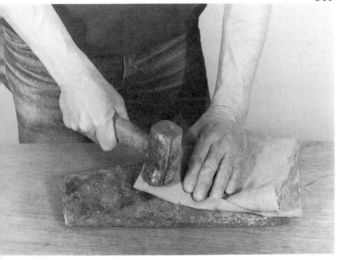

350

194

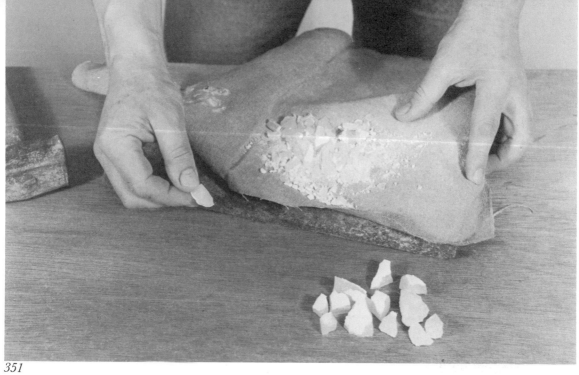

351

352

353 Note: this illustration shows a clear view of an action normally done underneath a thin piece of textile which both eliminates the hazard of flying fragments and the dispersal of the frit

Hammers of the type shown in this sequence are known as *lump hammers* and have a convex face. Their convexity enables them to be held on a flat surface and rocked backwards and forwards. Flat faced hammers can be used but the action is more awkward and crushing is much slower. This firm rocking action quickly reduces the frit from small fragments to a fine granular state. The aim is to crush the frit until the largest granules are no larger than about 1.5 mm. When this has occurred much of the frit material will be very much finer than this. The crushed material is put into a pestle. It is quicker to work on a small amount of frit at a time. The cloth which covers this action throughout should be about 45 cm square and of fine texture. It should be draped over the hand so that it covers the actual work area

The sequence of figures 350 to 353 is repeated until all the frit is reduced to a fine granular state. The thick cloth in which the frit is smashed will become cut and should be discarded but the fine cloth used to cover the crushing action should suffer no damage.

The next step is to grind the granulated frit using a pestle and mortar. A heavy large one is much easier and quicker to use than a small one. The mortar shown here is 30 cm in diameter.

Dry grinding granulated frit is extremely hazardous as tiny fragments can fly a metre or so into the air, so grinding is always done wet as this removes the hazard completely.

It is difficult to be precise about how much water to use and, to some extent, this is a matter of feel but it does depend on the size of the pestle and mortar and on the amount of material being ground. The important thing to remember is that the most efficient grinding occurs at the widest point of the base of the mortar where this curves up into the wall. The pestle is so formed that, rotated at this diameter, a very strong crushing action occurs between it and the mortar.

Enamel frits tend not to suspend so if the grinding mixture seems too watery grinding has only to cease for a minute or so for clear water to be poured off the mixture.

354 It is as well to start the grinding with a watery mixture. In this state, only the very finest material does not run back down the walls, and the mass of material is mobile enough for the rotating action of the pestle to move new material into its path. Even with a watery mix an occasional movement across the middle of the mortar should occur simply to ensure that all the material is affected by the steady circular grinding action

355 If a considerable proportion of water is decanted, the mixture assumes a thinnish paste-like consistency and this can be a good condition in which to achieve fine grinding. With this consistency it is essential to wipe the material regularly with a rubber kidney, down the wall of the mortar back into the grinding area of the base

354

355

356

357

358

356, 357 Enamel frits are in fact not very hard material and a mobile state, as here, neither paste-like nor very watery, is the most convenient state in which to complete grinding

358 The final actions are to sieve the frit and dry it out. Test sieves are much more convenient for small amounts of material and, if available, should be used. Sieving should be through a 100 or 120 mesh sieve, any material retained by the sieve being returned to the mortar for further grinding. The easiest way of drying out small amounts of frit is to let it settle, decant the water and then dry out the material on a paper towel. Once dry the frit is ready for use in enamel colour recipes

As stated earlier, frits of this type do enable a quality of enamel to be made which is very different from the enamel colours which can be bought. It is as well to remember, however, that these should not be used on the type of functional items covered by legislation regarding metal release unless they have been laboratory tested.

SECTION SIX

TESTING

Testing

The need for testing

To some extent the need to make tests is constant but, after initial experience, the need is variable from individual to individual.

For the beginner the need to test is clear and has three distinct functions. Firstly, making tests gives useful experience in the mixing of the various types of materials used in pottery. Secondly, a programme of sensible diversity gives useful awareness of the breadth of qualities possible in ceramics. Thirdly, testing gives useful initial experience in the different thicknesses and consistencies which are possible with and appropriate for different materials.

For the experienced the need to make tests is far more variable. Some people quickly discover a range of materials which gives them the surfaces, colours and qualities they need for their ideas and creates little or no need for different or developed materials. Others are constantly experimenting to develop new or refined materials with which to realise their ideas.

Testing to confirm

Testing is by no means limited to those who are learning about basic possibilities or who are evolving refinements of materials. Tests to confirm the nature of materials and mixtures are common and it is as sensible to do these with mixtures bought in ready-to-use form as it is with mixtures weighed up in the workshop.

It is sensible practice to test each new batch of any material as it is received and before it is put to extensive use. Suppliers do, of course, test their materials as their reputation and, therefore, their business depends on the supply of materials of consistent quality. It is wise, however, to be aware that variations can and do occur as ultimately the consistency of raw materials is only as consistent as their source, and the composition of rocks and clay beds do vary so both raw materials and ready-to-use mixtures based on them can also vary from batch to batch. Most ceramic materials are fairly common and concerns of diminishing resources are not as pressing as in many other fields. Particular deposits of any material can, however, become exhausted and alternative supplies may be noticeably different.

Confirming that the labelling of materials is correct is another aspect of the continuing need for testing. Incorrect labelling of materials is fortunately uncommon but even with all the systematic monitoring undertaken by suppliers it can and does occur. If it goes unnoticed until the material has been used in batches of mixtures it understandably causes severe and distressing problems.

A further aspect of testing to confirm is that once any batch of glaze, slip, colour or anything else has been weighed up and mixed it should be tested *before* it is put into extensive use to make sure that no errors in weighing have occurred.

With experience, the look and feel of the many apparently very similar materials used in ceramics give a clue as to whether there should be cause for concern but confirmation that all is correct only occurs with fired results.

In many fields the final appearance of materials is evident during the making process. It is the physical and visual changes that occur during firing which make some form of continuing testing essential to the controlled production of pottery.

For anyone, beginner or experienced, one function of making tests is to ascertain or confirm the nature of a material in a less time-consuming context than that of actual use. Saving time is actually only one aspect of this, for what can go wrong if serious mistakes are made or if materials of quite unknown quality are used can be expensive in terms of damage to other work, kiln furniture and kilns.

359 This illustration is of some glaze tests and clay body tests. As can be seen, at the temperature of firing, two of the body tests have melted violently. Some of the clay flowed onto the kiln shelves below but as the clay was only of test size serious damage was limited. Had the 'test' been a large form, the molten clay would have flowed until it could flow no further and would have damaged other work, other kiln shelves and the kiln bricks

359

The use of test kilns

Test kilns are very small, intended specifically for the convenient speedy firing of tests. A typical size of electric test kiln is 13 cm wide, 13 cm high and 22.5 cm deep but they are made both larger and smaller. With test kilns, fired tests can be available in a matter of a few hours.

However, the very speed which makes them convenient itself makes test kilns of limited use for some purposes. They tend, for example, to be more reliable to confirm the fluxing of a glaze than to test the qualities of a body because the speed of firing does not allow the more complex and subtle changes which occur during the firing of bodies to occur fully – body colour is particularly unreliable in a test kiln. Given the choice it is better to have a test kiln than not to have one but they should never be relied on to predict precisely the results which would occur in a larger kiln. For this reason it is as well, whenever possible, to fire tests in a normal firing.

The form of tests

There is some variety of practice in the form taken by tests and, while this must be a matter for individual decision, the practice of making test tiles deserves some mention.

Test tiles of, say, 7.5 cm by 10 cm have the advantage that they are easy and quick to make and economical of firing space. In time they build up into a manageable, if physically heavy, record of testing done. If made with a hole they can be pinned up for reference. In the case of glaze tests, tiles have the disadvantage that if fired flat they show little of the flow characteristics of glaze but this disadvantage can be overcome by firing them supported in a toast-rack-like structure built of slabs. Both to fire and store tiles take up much less space than small forms and small, but not too small, tiles seem the most sensible form for tests.

Tests by definition do not duplicate the actual context of use and, though this may not be to do with the form of tests, it does seem important to say that tests done by beginners are far too frequently seen as separate from making actual objects. Usually such tests are only of glaze, often only of glaze at a single thickness and only on a single clay body. This may be to do with a mental separation between the activity of making tests – thought to be good and necessary – and that of making real objects. While testing does have a

relevance for beginners in introducing the diversity of the range of possibilities, it is important that a link between testing and other work is quickly established because ultimately testing should be directly linked to current or intended work. Tests range from being quite time consuming to being quite quick to do but, in either case, it is as well to remember clearly that, in addition to providing a technical verification of materials and mixtures, they provide visual information and the more of this they can provide the more relevant they may be.

The making of tests: some general points

Record keeping

It is time consuming to mark tiles with full details of amounts, materials and temperature of firing but the alternative of marking tests with some sort of numbering system which relates to a notebook record is extremely risky. While a numbering system does have the attraction of initial speed, if the notebook record is lost the tests themselves immediately become useless and all the time apparently saved will be lost. Marking tests fully need not preclude the keeping of fuller records in a notebook and it is wise in such a record to write in what firing schedule the tests were fired, how they were mixed and so on. Space is at a premium on tests so, for this reason and to save time, it is a good idea to devise a simple shorthand code for materials and this obviously facilitates recording the maximum information on the test itself.

It is obviously important that tests should be marked distinctly in some way that neither rubs off after firing nor blurs during it. If the test is marked on the part that rests on the kiln shelf during firing it is also important that the marking mixture neither sticks the test to the shelf nor leaves a reversed imprint on it. In most contexts a marking mixture of 5 parts iron oxide and 1 part manganese dioxide neither rubs off nor blurs. However, no universal marking mixture exists and what will be best in any specified context has to be decided in each case.

Care in testing: test amounts

Because tests involve small amounts of materials they should be done with as much accuracy as possible. This demands care and the availability of scales designed for measuring sufficiently small quantities. It should be remembered that an error of 1 g in a test of 100 g is equivalent to an error of 50 g in a batch of 5000 g. Care in the weighing of colouring additions is particularly crucial otherwise the difference between a test and a batch can be alarming.

The nature of materials and intentions varies so much that it is difficult to be specific about what are sensible quantities for tests. Relevant to the question is the fact that weighing and mixing are a time consuming part of the making of tests and this time is put to best use if the test material is tried in several contexts. For example, it seems sensible to mix enough of a test glaze to try it on several bodies or enough of a test slip to try it on several bodies and with several glazes and so on. Very broadly it hardly seems worthwhile making much less than 5 kg of a clay body test or less than 100 g of a slip or glaze (or of a coloured body intended for inlay) but it is entirely sensible to mix 10 g or less of a test blend of pigments for painting. Certainly though, economy is not a sound reason for mixing up tiny test amounts. These only permit tiny tests which convey very little information, technical or visual.

Mixing procedures: blending
Unless these are of bought ready-made materials, tests of individual mixtures *unrelated* to any others clearly have to be weighed, mixed, sieved and tested individually. Where, however, tests are of *related* mixtures some short cuts are possible. An example will clarify this.

If, hypothetically, the decision has been made to test percentage additions of iron oxide to a particular glaze recipe at 1% intervals between 1% and 10%, at least four methods are possible. In this example the glaze base is the same in all the tests, as is the pigmenting oxide, and only the amount of this varies.

Firstly, all the ingredients for each of the ten amounts of glaze may be weighed separately, each with the differing amounts of iron oxide, and be mixed up, sieved and tested.

Secondly, a batch of unpigmented glaze may be mixed thoroughly, sieved and then divided by liquid measurement in ten equal amounts (filling identical containers to the same level is an adequate way of doing this). The separate pigment additions are then put in turn into the ten containers and each mixture is sieved to disperse the pigment thoroughly.

Thirdly, a batch of unpigmented glaze may be mixed up, sieved and then dried. The dry mixture may then be weighed into ten separate amounts and the differing proportions of oxide added. Each separate mixture is then sieved to disperse the pigment.

Fourthly a batch of unpigmented glaze is mixed up and divided into two equal quantities. One of these is left unpigmented and the other has 10% of iron oxide added to it and is resieved. The same tests can then be made by mixing together measured volumes of fluid glaze. A mixture of nine parts of clear glaze to one part of pigmented will give 1% iron oxide and so on. Care has to be taken to ensure the glaze is kept well stirred as each volume is measured and the water content of the two halves of the original mixture must not be altered after the amount is divided into two. Depending on the amounts involved any suitable measuring container may be used but domestic measuring spoons are very convenient for test amounts.

The time and labour involved in these four methods is obviously very different and one or other of the methods is relevant in contexts quite different from the hypothetical example given.

In the above example the series of tests is of a type known as a line blend. A *line blend* is a series of tests in steps between one material and another. Line blends may be used to investigate and vary all sorts of qualities as well as the tonality and colour of oxide additions. (See colour plates 3(b) and 3(c).)

Triaxial blends are stepped blends of three materials. (See colour plate 3(a).)

Putting testing to the test
Testing can be vitally relevant in many different ways, for example in broadening an awareness of possibilities, in furthering an understanding of the behaviour of materials and their constituent oxides, and in achieving the particular visual qualities intended, but it can also be an alluring study in itself. That allure can be a hindering diversion for beginners. There is far more to using tests than may be obvious at first sight. If the main focus of work is the total quality and content of objects it is at least as important to put tested materials to use as it is to have made the tests.

SECTION SEVEN

SOUND PRACTICE IN THE USE OF MATERIALS: HEALTH AND SAFETY

Anyone who uses ceramic materials has to be concerned with some practices concerning known health hazards; potters who make certain types of functional pottery have to be concerned with specific hazards arising from their use. In most countries the need to recognise both these hazards is now reinforced by law. The concerns relevant to the use of materials and those relevant to products are separate and can be described separately.

Health hazards in the use of materials

The health hazards associated with ceramic materials can be linked to three groups of materials, the most common of which are listed at the end of this section. The first group comprises those materials which contain silica where the hazard is silicosis, which is a respiratory disease caused solely by the inhalation of silica dust. The second group comprises various materials which, because of their effect on the human system, are classed as toxic. The third group comprises all lead compounds where the hazard is lead poisoning. This latter group could be seen as part of the second group but is usually considered separately because it is an extreme hazard, has long been recognised as such, is the subject of specific legislation and is, in addition, related to the hazards of glazed products.

With the first group of materials the specific danger is the inhalation of fine silica dust. Particles of one micron size and less are the most hazardous. The accumulated effect of exposure to this dust is silicosis, a particular form of a group of respiratory diseases known as pneumoconiosis.

With the second and third group the toxic nature of the materials, though varying in degree

from material to material, is general, and the hazard is poisoning of one sort of another. With one or two exceptions (not relevant to mention here because the practice of their use should be no different) they are all toxic regardless of the way they enter the human body whether by breathing as airborne dust, by entering the digestive system or by entering the bloodstream through cuts or abrasions in the skin.

The health hazards with all three groups of materials are most serious in contexts of frequent or continuous exposure where the effects are cumulative.

The three groups of materials are:

GROUP 1   Materials containing silica, hazardous as airborne dusts

Ball clay (all types)	Flint
Bentonite	Frits
China clay	Nepheline syenite
Clay (all clay bodies)	Quartz
Cornish stone	Talc
Felspar (all types)	Woolastonite

So far as the specified disease of silicosis is concerned, the degree of hazard varies in direct relationship to the percentage of free crystalline silica which is fine enough to be airborne. This is not related to the actual percentage of silica shown in oxide percentage analyses of materials. In relation to the hazard of pneumoconiosis the sensible practice is to handle all dry materials with equal care whether they are silicates or not. Some less frequently used silicate materials are not included in the list above. Talc, the basis of talcum powder, is a material about which questions might be asked. Talc is magnesium silicate containing over 50% silica but, in theory at least, having no free silica. Talc has been liberally powdered onto faces, and elsewhere, for centuries which in this context must raise questions. Notwithstanding this it should be handled with similar care to all silicate materials and the non-silicate ones not listed.

GROUP 2. Toxic materials, hazardous as airborne dusts, as powders and in liquid suspensions

The list of materials below begins with a list of elements. Some of these are encountered in one form only as an oxide or carbonate but others may be encountered in several forms even as soluble salts. In whatever form they are encountered they are toxic.

Antimony	Copper
Arsenic	Lithium
Barium	Manganese
Boron	Nickel
Cadmium	Selenium
Chromium	Vanadium
Cobalt	Zinc

All body and glaze stains.
All on and underglaze colours.
All overglaze enamels.
All liquid metals and lustres.

The degree and nature of hazard varies with the materials listed above. Some are more toxic as dusts than in liquid suspensions. All should be handled equally carefully in either state.

While commercial frits render materials safe to within the legal limits of low solubility in the human system if they are accidentally ingested, common sense dictates that frits are handled with the care accorded to the rest of the list above.

The presence of some of the materials from the GROUP 2 list above in medicines should not be seen as casting any doubt on the seriousness of this section. Doctors and their precursors have administered small doses of known poisons for centuries in the treatment of certain illnesses and conditions. The essential difference between accidental consumption and the administration of a medicine is in the control of the form and amount of the poison.

GROUP 3. Lead compounds, hazardous as airborne dust, as powders and in liquid suspensions

Lead carbonate:	Lead peroxide:
white lead	red lead
Lead oxide:	Lead sulphide:
litharge	galena

The hazard with these materials is lead poisoning.

The above forms of lead are referred to as 'raw' lead and are more toxic than the fritted forms of lead which are lead bisilicate and lead sesquisilicate.

Lead poisoning is cumulative and if exposure continues is severely debilitating and eventually fatal.

Sound practice in the use of materials

The measures which should be taken to combat these hazards are straightforward and should be rigorously observed. They are:

1 In the attempt to eliminate the creation of airborne dust wet processes rather than dry should be used whenever possible. For example, fettling of glaze should be done as soon as possible within the touch dry state by scraping and sponging, not by rubbing or scraping in the dust dry state; spillages of glaze or slip should be sponged up immediately they occur; all work surfaces should be sponged clean after use; all clay cutting processes – incising, carving, fettling, etc – should be done within the leatherhard stage, not when objects are dry. Where work with dry material is unavoidable this should be done in a booth designed for the process and fitted with efficient filtered extraction.

2 With the sole exception of work with clays and slips which have no added pigment or other toxic materials no work should be done if the hands or lower arms have cuts, abrasions or open wounds of any sort.

3 Part-used packets or bags of materials should be emptied into rigid metal, plastic or ceramic containers which should be clearly labelled. Most dry ceramic materials are supplied in paper or paper and cloth packaging, sometimes with polythene linings, designed for transport and

whole-pack storage. When put to workroom use as part-pack containers such packaging tends to be both dust producing and dust harbouring. When dry materials are transferred from a manufacturer's packaging into workshop containers this should be done making every effort to avoid the creation of dust. From all points of view it is essential that they are clearly relabelled. In contexts where there is a considerable use of materials necessitating frequent replenishment of containers there should be a booth designed for this purpose, fitted with efficient dust extraction.

4   All buckets, jars and other containers of glaze, slip and all types of colour should be clearly labelled with a complete list of all ingredients and their amounts.

5   Either work clothes or overalls should be worn. Industrial employees are required to wear terylene overalls for all dry work and waterproof overalls for all wet work. These and all workroom towels should be changed and washed regularly. Whether 'regularly' means daily or weekly must be decided by common sense in relation to the type of work.

6   When work is finished hands should be washed thoroughly and work-clothes or overalls removed.

7   The floors and, when appropriate, the walls of workrooms should be cleaned regularly either by using a vacuum cleaner with an efficient filter or by a wet process.

8   Meals and drinks should not be consumed in workrooms where toxic materials are stored and used.

9   There should be no smoking in workrooms where toxic materials are stored and used.

Legislation which has to be observed varies from country to country and is based mainly on hazards in industrial contexts. Deciding exactly how this legislation should apply in the different usage of non-industrial contexts, such as small workshops and studios and educational institutions, is usually delegated to local officials, and interpretations understandably vary. Most local officials are highly conversant with regulations concerning electrical and mechanical hazards but away from centres of industrial pottery production they are not always conversant with the specific hazards of pottery materials. The sensible approach for anyone responsible for safe practice is to adopt and adhere to procedures which acknowledge material hazards (of which dust is the most problematic) in as thorough a manner as is appropriate to the particular context. Whatever their own expertise, local officials can and, if asked, will contact colleagues who have specific expertise in ceramics and if there is doubt it is far better to consult the responsible local official than to ignore the problem. Suppliers of materials can also be consulted about aspects of the safe use of their products.

Further factors relating to the safe use of materials
Four other aspects of the use of ceramic materials need to be mentioned.

Firstly, rather like the industrial worker, the individual potter, in doing particular work with a particular range of materials, may be considered as a specialist who may be exposed to unrecorded hazards. 'Safe' materials are only those not known to be hazardous. The only sensible answer is to handle all materials with the respect they deserve – centuries of use have established that plastic clay is harmless, centuries of use have established that some materials are toxic and with increasingly specialised use that list is still growing.

Secondly, there is the fire hazard associated with some of the media used for decorating. Some of the newer synthetic media have fumes which also constitute a health hazard. The amounts used in ceramics outside the industry are so small that the hazard is not great but the normal precautions about extraction of fumes should be observed and all paper and rags contaminated with media should be removed from buildings so that the danger of spontaneous combustion to buildings and people is avoided. A particular danger attached to spraying with media is that most wet-spray booths, designed for water-borne glaze spraying, do not have isolated motors and many media have a volatile content which could be ignited by an electric motor. Booths specifically designed for spraying with such media are available. In most countries manufacturers supplying flammable or toxic media are bound by law to advertise this fact and to mark containers as such, giving details of the flashpoint and recommended conditions of use. Liquid precious metals and lustres are usually supplied mixed with flammable media.

Thirdly, in that the use of any ceramic material

involves firing, these are some procedures to observe in the use of kilns. Manufacturers should be consulted about the safe general operation of kilns but in the context of a book on materials there are three specific aspects to mention. The first is the various fumes given off by the clay itself when it is biscuit fired. These are generated at different stages. Sulphurous fumes are obnoxious in any amount and toxic if concentrated. Secondly, there are the fumes given off by wax and decorating media. These fumes are obnoxious but unlikely ever to be generated by a kiln in toxic concentration. Thirdly, there are the fumes of reduction-carbon dioxide, carbon monoxide and, if reduction is excessive, airborne particles of carbon. Carbon monoxide is a highly dangerous gas but combines with oxygen so readily that, except with an extremely badly fired, badly designed kiln situated in a very enclosed space, in practice it constitutes no hazard. In all cases electric kilns should be situated in well ventilated rooms, ideally fitted with ducted extraction, and in such contexts there is no problem. Flame kilns exhaust biscuit and media fumes with the burnt fuel gases in their flues and with these only the fumes of excessive reduction are a problem. Flame kilns are best situated in very airy rooms and a sensible siting, together with efficient operation should completely remove any inconvenience and all danger from fumes but in some situations either general extraction from the room or ducted extraction may be necessary.

Fourthly, the practice of going outside buildings to do various dust generating operations so that workrooms are not contaminated needs a brief mention. Where this solely involves clay bodies there can be no objection to the practice though the person concerned may be well advised to wear a dust mask. Where mixtures containing toxic materials are concerned the practice has to be totally condemned. Materials toxic to humans are usually no less so to other living organisms and when the environment is polluted, even in a small way, this is sheer irresponsibility.

The hazards of materials have been highlighted by the industrial age and much modern legislation is a very belated response to problems which were all too clear in the last century when increased specialisation created increasing exposures to specific hazards. Ironically, increased legislation has created a vicious circle in that building regulations and minimum heating levels have created drier, more airy, warm conditions in which dust is more easily generated with the result that, to comply with regulations, as more and more possibly dusty air is extracted from work areas more and more heat has to be pumped in.

The damp earth floor has some aspects to recommend it.

The proportion of ceramic materials which have to be listed as hazardous is high and if this and the lists of precautions seem daunting it should be stressed that the practices outlined are little more than the dictates of sound common sense and, rather than inhibiting work, frequently contribute to convenience and efficiency. It should be remembered that throughout the world potters have a long established reputation not only for being long lived but for enjoying full and active old age. Only the specialised conditions of modern industry have spoiled that reputation.

Hazards in the domestic use of ceramic articles

These have been the source of increasing international concern and legislation in recent decades. Knowledge of the possible hazards is ancient. Legislation varies from country to country but there is increasing pressure for the establishment of internationally agreed standards.

The specific hazard is metal poisoning caused by metal release from the glazes of vessels used for the storage, cooking or consumption of food and drink. Acids present in food and drink – fruit juices, cooking juices and vinegar particularly – can dissolve metals from an imperfect glaze in quantities which are sufficient to be fatal. Recent industrial records in this are good but there have been fatalities caused by the use of non-industrial vessels. The amounts involved are tiny and the tests measure the metal release in parts per million or milligrammes per litre.

Regulations prescribing the maximum permitted levels of release vary depending on the type of ware. In Britain the relevant legislation is contained in *British Standard 4860* Parts 1 and 2 and the release of lead and cadmium are specified. It is worth noting that significant release of lead from a glaze containing no intentional inclusion of a lead compound or frit is virtually impossible but that significant cadmium can be released where it is only present as an impurity in glaze materials.

The most serious and common problem is that of *lead release*. There is a common misapprehension that the use of a lead frit eliminates all possibility of the problem. This is not the case. In fact, a well fired, well compounded glaze using a 'raw' form of lead can give negligible lead release figures very well within the legal limits, and a poorly fired or poorly compounded glaze, whether frits or 'raw' lead are used, can give figures well over the limit. Poor firing and ill-advised additions are two factors which can have extremely detrimental effects on previously tested 'safe' glazes. Technically, underfiring arrests the formation of the glassiness of a glaze before the solution of silica and flux is complete which results in a more matt, softer surface with a vastly increased surface area open to attack and, because of its incomplete glassiness, more susceptible to attack. Additions to make a glaze more matt can have a similar effect and colouring oxide additions, even if the glaze surface appears unaltered, or even shinier, can have an extreme effect. The effect of copper oxide as a catalyst of lead release is a well-known example of this and even small additions of copper oxide of 1.5% to 2% will increase the lead released by 'safe' glaze to a disproportionate and usually illegal extent.

Because of the fear of the possibility of lead release lead glazes suffer from bad publicity. This perhaps is to be expected because if, through ignorance or irresponsibility, things go wrong the effect can be fatal. However, to be objective it must be stated that well-mixed lead glazes of sound composition, which are well fired, completely overcome the problem of lead release and, as well as being safe, such lead glazes are extremely durable. Cadmium release from such glazes where the cadmium is present as a trace impurity in materials is not a problem.

The *release of cadmium* from glazes in which it is intentionally included is an entirely different matter. To date, cadmium-containing glazes have not been discovered which conform reliably to the legal standards set for cadmium release. The attraction of using cadmium glazes is that cadmium facilitates the achievement of bright colour, particularly red. Cadmium-containing materials are not available from potters' suppliers because of their toxicity, but ranges of glazes containing cadmium are widely marketed. While catalogues are very explicit about glazes which must not be used on domestic articles, this fact is not always stated on individual packaging so great care must be exercised. As far as cadmium release is concerned, the only course of action to follow is to be aware of the problem and observe closely manufacturers' guidelines for the safe use of their products.

Lead and cadmium are not the only metals that can be released by glazes but are the ones legally identified as hazardous. Research on metal release has concentrated on glazes fired in the earthenware temperature range, on the effect of coloured decoration in that range, and on lower fired decoration. Leadless earthenware and stoneware glazes, which are bound to be free of the major problem of lead release, have received less attention. It is for obvious ease of cleaning rather than metal release, though this latter is not inconceivable, that heavily pigmented matt glazes of any type should not be used on vessels intended for food and drink.

The problems of metal release are fortunately rare. The sensible steps to take for anyone who produces domestic vessels are to be aware of relevant current legislation and any changes to this which occur, to consult suppliers about materials where there is doubt, to submit lead glazes for laboratory testing, to adhere to tested recipes and established firing temperatures and schedules, and only to alter tested materials after thorough experiment and further laboratory testing.

APPENDICES

GLOSSARY

This glossary includes no terms not contained in the text of this book

Ball mill. A ball mill is a machine used for the fine grinding of pottery materials – for reducing fine granular material (of 2 mm and less) to fine dust. The grinding occurs in a cylindrical container, either made of or lined with porcelain, which is supported horizontally and which rotates on its axis. The grinding medium is porcelain balls. In use the cylindrical container, usually called a jar, is loaded with about half of its volume of balls, a quarter of its volume of the material being ground and up to a quarter of its volume of water. Because the granular material can fill the spaces between the balls and the water can do this and fill the spaces between the particles of the granular material such a load leaves the jar between half and three quarters full. The precise proportions are not important and in any case depend on the size of the balls (which in turn relate to the size of the jar) but it is important that jars are not overfilled as this greatly lengthens grinding time. The speed of rotation is crucial and must relate to the size of the jar and be such that as the machine rotates the balls cascade down over one another continuously.

Blunger Blungers are used for mixing materials into a slip state. A blunger consists of a hexagonal or octagonal container within which, on a central spindle, a number of paddles rotate. Blungers are usually used for mixing up clay bodies into a slip state from dry powdered materials or for mixing up casting slips either from powdered materials or from plastic bodies but they may also be used for mixing glaze or slip. Blungers are filled through a hatch in the top and emptied through a tap at the bottom. Many blungers are made so they can operate at two speeds, a high speed to accomplish thorough mixing quickly and a slower speed to keep the mixed materials suspended.

Deflocculants Deflocculants are materials added to suspensions, particularly casting slips, which reduce the tendency of particles to cling together thereby increasing the fluidity of suspensions without increasing their water content. Very small proportions of deflocculents are needed and excessive amounts cause thinned suspensions to rethicken. The traditional deflocculants are sodium silicate (waterglass) and sodium carbonate (soda ash) but more convenient proprietary brands are now available the commonest of which is sodium 'dispex'.

Fettling Fettling is the general cleaning up of clay ware and glazed ware prior to firing. With clay ware it particularly applies to slip cast work in which the marks left by mould seams have to be removed by scraping and/or sponging. When this is done to dry work it should be done in an extraction booth or, failing this, over a shallow dish of water, in each case the intention being to prevent the dispersion of clay dust. Glaze fettling is the rubbing down of blemishes in a layer of glaze (which likewise should occur with all steps taken to avoid the creation of dust). With good glazing the need for fettling should be minimal.

Filter press A filter press is the standard machine used industrially for removing water from body slips and thereby converting them into plastic bodies. A filter press comprises a reservoir of slip which feeds a pump which forces slip, under high pressure, into the press itself. The press consists of a series of cloth lined plates clamped together. Traditionally the hollow plates were made of cast iron but though many of these are still in use the plates are now made of lightweight aluminium alloy or plastic. Once the pump has filled the press it continues to force slip into it thus building up great pressure and forcing water out through the filter cloths which, being finely woven and tightly clamped between the edges of the plates, retain the clay. When pumping has continued for long enough the plates are unclamped and the plastic body can be peeled off the filter cloths. Slabs of filter pressed clay are firm round the edges and soft in the middle.

Fly ash Fly ash is the term given to the fine wood ash which is carried from the firebox into the chamber of wood fired kilns. This, anything from marginally to quite noticeably, affects glazed surfaces to which it adheres. On forms directly in the flame path fly ash alone can create glazed areas on unglazed clay.

Hand blunger Hand blungers are designed to rest on the edges of a bin. In this position two fixed arms extend downwards and support a flanged disc. Extending downwards from the motor on top and between the two arms and penetrating through the disc is a central rotating shaft which ends in a small impeller. The impeller rotates beneath the disc and within the flanges. The flanges on the underneath of the disc prevent the rotating impeller touching the bottom of any container in which it is used which is less deep than the length of the arms. Hand blungers are sometimes called portable mixers and this is a much more accurate description of their use. They are excellent, durable and time-saving pieces of equipment for mixing slips and glazes prior to sieving and for re-mixing stored mixtures of this type. Neither the size of motor nor the form of the impeller are intended for the very different operation of transforming a plastic body into casting slip or indeed lump clays into body slips.

Hand wedging Hand wedging is a miniaturised version of the wedging process described. Quite simply the piece of clay is repeatedly halved and thrown together in the hands. Methodically done this very quickly achieves thorough mixing of small amounts of a clay body too small to prepare by wedging or kneading on a bench.

Jaw crusher This is a substantial machine used for crushing hard material into small pieces.

Low solubility When the term 'low solubility' is applied to a glaze or frit this is an indication that as a finely ground material it does not release lead in a soluble form over specified maximum limits. Regulations concerning the low solubility of frits and glazes are designed to ensure the health of those who work with those materials not those who use the fired products whose health is designed to be protected by separate legislation concerning the release of toxic materials from fired products.

Mesh The mesh of a sieve is simply its size grading. 100 mesh, for example, specifies that there are a hundred apertures per linear 254 mm. British Standard Specifications apply to mesh sizes (with a 100 mesh sieve the aperture is stipulated as 0.152 mm which in turn specifies the wire thickness used in the woven mesh). Other countries have similar standards.

Plate mill This machine has hardened steel plates and is used to crush small pieces of hard material to a fine granular state from which it can be ground to a fine powder in a ball mill.

Pugmill A pugmill is a machine in which angled blades project from a central rotating shaft located in a tapered tube. As the shaft turns the projecting blades force clay down the tapered tube. The machine mixes clay to an even consistency. A de-airing pugmill in addition forces the clay through a vacuum chamber and in doing so both mixes it and removes all the air from it.

Vibratory sifter This is a machine to which a sieve may be fixed. The sieve is vibrated laterally but very slightly at high speed. Sieving is incomparably easier and faster than with a sieve brush and a static sieve and wear and tear on the mesh is minimised.

Vibro-energy mill Like a ball mill this machine is used for the fine grinding of materials. The machine operates with jars and balls like those used with ball mills but instead of being rotated the jars are vibrated fractionally sideways at high speed. Compared to ball mills vibro-energy mills are noisy (and ball mills are far from silent) but grinding time is considerably reduced.

Wasters Wasters are items which break or suffer other irreparable damage during a firing. Clean wasters (those which are not seriously overfired or contaminated with colouring pigment or glaze) are, in the industrial context, frequently crushed for subsequent use as grog.

LISTS OF MATERIALS AND THEIR OXIDES AND FUNCTIONS

With the main exception of Table 5 most of the data in this appendix is primarily of use to those who wish to undertake calculations as a means of studying glazes.

Table 1
Common elements in pottery

Though pottery is concerned with oxides rather than elements a list of the elements which form the commoner oxides is a useful reference for those studying materials from a theoretical point of view.

Element	Symbol	Atomic weight
Aluminium	Al	26.98
Barium	Ba	137.34
Boron	B	10.81
Calcium	Ca	40.08
Lead	Pb	207.19
Lithium	Li	6.94
Magnesium	Mg	24.31
Potassium	K	39.10
Silicon	Si	28.09
Sodium	Na	22.99
Zinc	Zn	65.37

As oxides the above elements are all combined with oxygen.

Oxygen	O	16.00

Some materials contain other elements, which appear as part of the unfired formulae of materials but are lost as gases during firing. These elements are listed below. With some materials some oxygen is similarly lost.

Carbon	C	12.01
Fluorine	Fl	18.99
Hydrogen	H	1.01
Nitrogen	N	14.01
Sulphur	S	32.06

While these elements are released from materials in firings of normal duration and with a clean, oxidising atmosphere, very fast firing or particular reduction conditions may result in some of these elements or these combined with others as compounds being trapped within the fired material. This may be done intentionally as for example when carbon is trapped in clay bodies in some types of low firing but if done accidentally indicates extremely inappropriate and uncontrolled firing schedules and leads to problems.

Table 2   Further common elements found in pottery

Oxides of the elements listed below are commonly found in pottery and have various responses to heat, some being unreactive and refractory and others being strong fluxes. All have a distinct pigmenting effect.

Element	Symbol	Atomic weight
Chromium	Cr	52.00
Cobalt	Co	58.93
Copper	Cu	63.55
Iron	Fe	55.85
Manganese	Mn	54.94
Nickel	Ni	58.71
Tin	Sn	118.69
Titanium	Ti	47.90
Vanadium	V	50.94
Zirconium	Zr	91.22

In various types of prepared colour and in ready-made glazes, oxides of the elements antimony, beryllium, cadmium, praseodymium, selenium, uranium, also occur but these are excluded from the list above because they are very rarely used except in some ready-mixed form.

Alone among common ceramic materials lustres do not exist as oxides. Various elements listed above occur in lustres as do bismuth, gold, platinum and silver.

Table 3(a) Common oxides in pottery materials

The following oxides are the main ones which occur in the materials from which clay bodies, slips and glazes are mixed. Of the oxides listed below clay bodies and slips contain mainly alumina and silica (mainly as clay mineral but with some free silica) and contain only minor amounts or none of the other oxides. Glazes, however, may contain any of the oxides as major constituents.

The molecular weights listed are primarily of use in glaze calculation.

Oxide	Formula	Molecular weight
Aluminium oxide (alumina)	Al_2O_3	101.96
Barium oxide	BaO	153.34
Boric oxide	B_2O_3	69.62
Calcium oxide	CaO	56.08
Lead oxide	PbO	223.19
Lithium oxide	Li_2O	29.88
Magnesium oxide	MgO	40.31
Potassium oxide	K_2O	94.20
Silicon oxide (silica)	SiO_2	60.09
Sodium oxide	Na_2O	61.98
Zinc oxide	ZnO	81.37

Table 3(b) Common oxides and their functions in glazes

The layout below is the same as that shown on page 56 and is the one common to all expressions of glazes by the unity formula method.

Flux	Stabiliser	Glass former
Barium oxide BaO	Aluminium oxide Al_2O_3 (alumina) (Boric oxide or B_2O_3)	Silicon oxide SiO_2 (silica) (Boric oxide B_2O_3)
Calcium oxide CaO		
Lead oxide PbO		
Lithium oxide Li_2O		
Magnesium oxide MgO		
Potassium oxide K_2O		
Sodium oxide Na_2O		
Zinc oxide ZnO		

The oxide of boron, called **boric oxide**, is a slight oddity in the table above. It has a low melting point and is an extremely useful glaze making oxide. Where to place boric oxide in unity formula expressions of glazes has long been the subject of academic dispute and this dispute is understandable: like alumina it lends viscosity to glazes; like silica it is a glass former; like the fluxes it lowers the melting point of glazes. Some authorities class it with alumina and others with silica but none class it with the fluxes. As long as its many faceted role in glazes is understood it does not really matter very much whether it is placed with alumina or silica because in any specific glaze or frit the relative amount of it present is perfectly clear in either position.

Table 4 Further common oxides in pottery materials

The oxides listed below are important as pigmenting oxides. Some of these may occur as impurities in materials which primarily contain the oxides listed in Table 3.

Though the molecular weights are given these are only rarely used in glaze calculations.

Oxide	Formula	Molecular weight
Chromium oxide	Cr_2O_3	152.00
Cobalt oxide	Co_3O_4	240.79
Copper oxide	CuO	79.55
Iron oxide	Fe_2O_3	159.70
Manganese oxide	MnO	70.94
Nickel oxide	NiO	74.71
Tin oxide	SnO_2	150.69
Titanium oxide	TiO_2	79.90
Vanadium oxide	V_2O_5	181.88
Zirconium oxide	ZrO_2	123.22

NOTE Some of the oxides above may change form during firing either as a result of a reducing atmosphere (as in the case of copper and iron oxides which, respectively, change to Cu_2O and FeO) or simply through the application of heat (as in the case of cobalt oxide which changes to CoO).

Table 5 Common materials: notes on their main functions and contexts of use

Both Tables 5(a) and 5(b) include a few materials not listed later in Tables 6 or 7 and in all cases these are marked with an asterisk.

Table 5(a) Non-pigmenting materials

Alumina (calcined) is used in glazes when clay is an inconvenient or problematic way of supplying the alumina which is necessary, as, for example, when

216

crawling has occurred. Its main use is as a wash to protect kiln furniture and it is also used in large quantities to support bone china during firing.

Alumina (hydrate) can be used for all the functions of calcined alumina but in glazes the calcined form is to be preferred because this has no chemically combined water to lose.

Ball clays* have important obvious uses in clay bodies due to their good plasticity and are a common material in slips. In glazes, ball clay is sometimes substituted for china clay. In stoneware glazes particularly such substitution may lead to glazes becoming noticably more fluid owing to the fluxing impurities present in ball clays.

Barium carbonate is a glaze fluxing material and is the most convenient source of barium oxide. It is not used as a flux in bodies or slips. When white scumming is a problem on unglazed red terracotta bodies, as is not infrequently the case, **barium carbonate** or **barium sulphate*** can be added to the body. An addition of about 2% of either material will cure the problem.

Bentonite* is an ultra fine highly plastic clay often used in clay bodies and glazes and occasionally in slips. In bodies additions of as little as 5% improve plasticity but there are limits to how much can be used because larger additions detrimentally increase shrinkage and lead to a darkening of the light firing bodies in which bentonite is most useful. Up to 2% of bentonite is sometimes added to glazes to improve their suspension (either as a simple addition or in place of other clays). Because bentonite tends not to sink into water very quickly where powered mixing facilities are not available, bentonite is best carefully dry mixed with some other material from the recipe before it is added to water.

Bone ash* is the principal material in bone china bodies. It provides **calcium oxide** and **phosphorus oxide***. Phosphorus oxide is one of the rarer glass forming oxides (and as such is not mentioned in Table 3(b). Bone ash is occasionally used in glazes.

Bone china* is an industrial body developed for its particularly white, translucent qualities. It has very low plasticity.

Calcined china clay (molochite) is high fired china clay and is available in many size grades, from 200 mesh to dust to coarse grog. In glazes the fine grades can be used when the shrinkage associated with other clays is undesirable. In slips rather similarly it can be used to adjust the shrinkage of a slip without altering its clay content (by partial substitution of it for china or ball clay). In clay bodies it can be added in any size grade depending on the intended texture of the body. Because

it is a very pure refractory material such additions increase the refractoriness of bodies.

China clay is an essential material in white and light firing bodies and is a common one in slips – in these contexts its physical qualities as clay are clearly vital. In glazes its relative freedom from impurities give its chemical nature more importance and it is a most convenient source of the alumina and silica it provides.

Colemanite is a glaze material which does not figure in slips or bodies. It provides calcium oxide and boric oxide and in theory is the only insoluble source of boric oxide. In practice, in fact, colemanite is slightly soluble and this can lead to problems in glaze suspensions. It has a variable composition.

China stone (Cornish stone) provides the fluxes potassium, sodium and calcium oxides combined with alumina and silica. It is very commonly used to provide fluxes in both bodies and glazes. As a material it varies in composition and a number of named varieties exist. It is similar in composition to nepheline syenite and the felspars but has a higher proportion of silica.

Dolomite provides calcium and magnesium oxides. It is mainly used to contribute these to high temperature glazes.

Felspar is a mineral which provides a fluxing oxide (or oxides) in combination with alumina and silica. It has various forms for which ideal formulae exist – **orthoclase**, **albite** and **anorthite** respectively, providing potassium, sodium and calcium oxides (in theory). In practice, felspars are of somewhat variable composition and the three named types tend to contain the named oxide predominantly with small proportions of the other two – combined of course with alumina and silica. Felspars are found in earthenware and stoneware glaze recipes, are used as body fluxes and occur sometimes in high temperature slips. Potash felspar is **orthoclase**, soda felspar is **albite** and lime felspar is **anorthite**. When a recipe simply specifies 'felspar' this can be presumed to be potash felspar.

Flint is a convenient source of virtually pure silica and as such is used in glazes, slips and bodies.

Lithium carbonate is useful wherever lithium oxide is required in glazes and it provides only this. It is occasionally used in small amounts in slips to increase the fluxing content, mainly in the earthenware temperature range.

Lead carbonate and **lead oxide** in various forms were once extremely important as the materials which provided lead oxide whenever this was required in glazes and, as lead oxide was the most important glaze fluxing oxide in most earthenware traditions, the various forms of raw lead were extremely important.

217

Almost exclusively lead frits are now used in place of raw lead oxides. The use of raw forms of lead still occurs if some very low temperature glazes are used and if enamel frits are mixed up. Lead oxide (either raw or in fritted form) is not used as a flux in slips or bodies.

Magnesium carbonate is useful whenever magnesium oxide is required in glazes and it provides only this. It is mainly used in high temperature glazes.

Nepheline syenite is a felspathic material which, like the felspars, is somewhat variable in composition. It provides sodium and potassium oxides combined with alumina and silica. It is distinct from the felspars in that the proportion of fluxes to the combined proportions of alumina and silica is higher than with the felspars. It is, therefore, more powerful as a fluxing material. It is used very commonly for its provision of fluxes in glazes but is also important as a body flux and can be used in slips, particularly at higher temperatures, for this effect.

Petalite contains lithium oxide combined with alumina and silica. Its main use is as a glaze flux particularly at high temperatures. It is, in fact, also a body ingredient of some specialised bodies with exceptional resistance to thermal shock.

Quartz is a convenient source of virtually pure silica and as such it is used in glazes, slips and bodies.

Sand* can be added to clay bodies to impart a fine, granular texture. However, being relatively pure silica, sand additions must not be overdone or the silica content of the body may be increased to the point where the body becomes prone to cracking during the cooling cycle of firings. **Silver sand*** (sometimes called silica sand) is sold as a very clean, pure and white sand and is the type most usually added to bodies. Silver sand is also sometimes used as placing sand on kiln shelves instead of battwash. Yellow sands contain clay and iron oxide as impurities and are much more fusible than silver sand. Yellow sand should never be used as placing sand and should be carefully tested before it is added to large amounts of a clay body. Sand is too coarse to be of use in glazes.

Spodumene contains lithium oxide combined with alumina and silica, and is similar to petalite. Its main difference from petalite is that the proportion of silica to lithium oxide and alumina is lower and it is, therefore, less refractory. Like petalite it is used in the production of some highly specialised bodies but outside that context its use is as a material to provide lithium oxide as a flux in glazes.

Talc provides magnesium oxide combined with silica. Talc is the mineral **steatite** pulverised and ground to a powdered state. Steatite, better known as soapstone, can itself be fired. Talc is a major body ingredient of various specialised bodies with good electrical insulation qualities and thermal shock resistance and has been used in some white firing tableware bodies. Bodies in which talc is included in high proportions tend to lack plasticity and largely because of this disadvantage its main use outside specialised contexts is as a glaze material in the middle and high temperature range. Talc tends to float on water and to resist attempts to mix it in so, where power assisted mixing is not available, it should be dry mixed with another glaze material before it is added to water.

Whiting provides calcium oxide and its commonest use is as the usual source of this in glazes. It is sometimes used to provide calcium oxide as a flux in bodies and, because of the lime-alumina-silica eutectic, its effect is very noticable at temperatures much above 1120°C, even in relatively small proportions.

Woolastonite provides calcium oxide combined with silica and with adjustments to the recipe to compensate for its silica, may be used instead of whiting as an alternative source of calcium oxide. Woolastonite tends, however, to result in a higher level of impurities than is the case with whiting and where this is important whiting is to be preferred.

Zinc oxide is the sole source of zinc oxide when this is required in glazes. Glazes are its sole context of use in which it functions as a flux.

Table 5(b)   Pigmenting materials

NOTE 1   The precise colour effect of the pigmenting materials is profoundly affected by their context of use. Many of the non-pigmenting materials in fact have an important effect on the colours which the pigmenting materials produce.

NOTE 2   This table does not include materials which are used in the manufacture of prepared colours and stains and are not used raw.

Antimoniate of lead* is a compound which consists of both antimony and lead oxides. It is highly poisonous. **Antimony oxide*** is colourless but in the presence of lead oxide gives good yellows. As a painting material lead antimoniate needs to be mixed with about an equal part of a lead frit otherwise the surface tends to be rather dry. In glazes in which lead is a major flux about 5% of lead antimoniate will give an opaque yellow. The colour is unstable above 1100°C. Prepared stains and colours are now normally used instead of antimoniate of lead.

Chromium oxide is a refractory pigmenting oxide which is green in the raw state and produces greens in many contexts. In many glazes it produces a saturation green colour in amounts over about 3%. Chrome red and chrome yellow are forms of lead chromate used as pigments in the paint industry and, in glazes in which lead oxide is the sole or major flux, a range of colours from yellows through orange to reds can be produced at temperatures below 1000°C. Used with other oxides chrome oxide assists in the formation of dense opaque blacks. An unstable reaction known as the *chrome-tin-pink reaction* occurs when chrome oxide is painted onto or incorporated in glazes opacified with tin oxide. Chrome oxide is an important oxide in the production of calcined stains and colours.

Cobalt carbonate* is, weight for weight, less powerful as a colouring pigment than cobalt oxide. This is true of other oxides for which carbonate forms exist. All carbonate forms of oxides are less prone to specking and require less work to eliminate specking than do the oxides themselves.

Cobalt oxide is the strongest of the colouring pigments. In virtually all glazes at all temperatures less than 1% is needed to give strong blue. Though by itself it is refractory cobalt oxide forms eutectics with other glaze making oxides, readily entering into solution in the fired glaze. Cobalt oxide makes glazes less abrasion resistant and for this reason is rarely used industrially to pigment glazes used on tableware. In high temperature glazes in which magnesium oxide occurs as a flux cobalt oxide produces blues tinged with pinkish, mauvish colours.

Copper carbonate* is weaker and less prone to specking than copper oxide.

Copper oxide in oxidising conditions, produces greens in most contexts. In glazes in which lead oxide is the major or the sole flux the green colour is a quite bright grass green while in glazes fluxed with sodium oxide the colour is turquoise. 2% of the oxide is usually enough to give strong colour to a glaze and amounts of over 4% tend to overload a glaze with pigment and to lead to the production of metallic black glazes which are prone to run. In reduction conditions copper oxide will produce pinks and reds. Neither the oxide nor the carbonate form of copper should be used in, on or under glazes which contain lead oxide if the items are intended to be used with food or drink because copper oxide has a predictable and detrimental effect on lead release.

Iron chromate* is a compound containing the oxides of iron and chrome. It is not a widely used pigment but can produce greys and browns but these are very sensitive to context and, therefore, somewhat unpredictable. Certainly, much more reliable greys can be obtained with prepared stains. It can be used with other oxides, in the production of dense blacks in slips and glazes.

Iron oxide is the commonest of the pigmenting oxides. All clays contain some iron oxide as an impurity: with china clays the amount is usually between 0.5% and 0.75%; with ball clays it is usually between 1% and 2%; with common red firing clays it is often in excess of 8%. Clay body colour, importantly dependent on the amount of iron oxide present, is always a fundamental factor in the final appearance of objects – just as important when the body is covered in a slip or an opaque glaze as when it is fully evident. In addition to clays many of the non-pigmenting materials listed in Table 5(a) also contain up to about 1% of iron oxide so very few pottery mixtures are without it. In glazes, in oxidising conditions, it produces a range of colours from pale yellow ochres through tan to deep browns and blacks. In glazes, in reducing conditions, at high temperatures, it produces a range from the pale greens and blues, known as *celadons*, to deeper bottle greens and blacks. Where high temperature glazes have upwards of about 8% of iron this can, on cooling, crystalise out of the glaze solution and cause bright flecks of russet red to occur in dark glazes. Most suppliers offer several grades of iron oxide which differ mainly in the way they have been prepared but, once the particular qualities of a type are known, it is wise to be clear whether or not further purchases are of the same type or not as results in some contexts will vary with different types.

Manganese carbonate* is weaker and less prone to specking than manganese oxide.

Manganese oxide gives brown colours in most contexts. In many glazes the brown is modified with a hint of purple. In glazes in which sodium oxide is the major or the sole flux the colour produced is a rich aubergine. Manganese is similar in strength to copper oxide and additions of rather less than 4% are normal in glazes unless, used with other oxides, the intention is to use it to create black. Small amounts of manganese oxide (and often iron as well) are often used to modify the blues produced by cobalt in mixtures for painting. In such contexts, if specking is to be avoided, it is vital that the mixture is finely ground. Manganese oxide is frequently available in alternative forms – coarse or fine – and where this is the case the coarse tends to be finely gritty which is useful for textural effects but is hard to grind to a fine state if specking is not wanted.

Nickel oxide produces a variety of colours in different contexts but it is not one which is commonly used because results are prone to inconsistency.

Rutile* is a mineral of varying composition consisting mainly of titanium oxide with some iron oxide. Used in glazes it produces distinctly mottled tan colours and if used with small amounts of other pigmenting oxides produces various colours with distinct mottling.

219

Ilmenite*, also consisting of titanium and iron oxides, is a similar material with similar effects, but is available in various graded sizes, the coarser ones being useful for speckled effects in slips and clay bodies and if a more irregular, crystalline effect (as distinct from regular mottling) is wanted in glazes.

Tin oxide, in amounts much over 1%, does not enter into glaze solutions but remains suspended. As a very fine white powder it therefore has a whitening, opacifying effect. Depending on the particular nature of the glaze and on the colour of the clay body amounts between 5% and 10% are normally needed. One problem sometimes encountered with glazes opacified with tin oxide is that these can tend to crawl but apart from this it is generally agreed that tin oxide is the best glaze opacifier. It is not, however, a cheap oxide and partly because of this much research has been devoted to evolving alternatives and a number of glaze opacifiers are marketed. Mixed with a frit or, on about a 50:50 basis, with a clear glaze tin oxide can be painted onto coloured glazes. It is occasionally added to slips to assist whiteness and opacity, particularly in painted slips, but its commonest use is in glazes.

Titanium oxide added to glazes in amounts from 4% to 10% has an opacifying effect but this is a creamy white rather than the faintly blue white of tin oxide and is accompanied by a matting effect. This latter effect is due to the potential which titanium oxide has for forming tiny crystals in the cooling glaze. Titanium oxide is an important impurity in clays and its presence in ball clays is the major reason why it is so difficult to make plastic bodies which are white firing because the amount of ball clay necessary to achieve good plasticity brings with it sufficient titanium oxide to detract from the whiteness of the body.

Vanadium oxide produces somewhat textural greeny yellows when added to glazes. Partly because it is highly poisonous and partly because of its expense it is not a commonly used oxide. It is an important oxide in the production of calcined colours and stains.

Zirconium oxide, like tin oxide, is highly refractory and is used as an opacifier in glazes because it remains suspended in the glaze solution. The colour reaction of painting materials used on glazes opacified with zirconium oxide is different from those on glazes opacified with tin oxide (as indeed is also the case with glazes opacified with titanium oxide). 2% to 3% more zirconium oxide is needed to achieve opacity equal to that obtained with tin. Glazes opacified with zirconium oxide develop hard, abrasion resistant surfaces.

Zircon* or **Zirconium silicate*** is a compound containing zirconium oxide and silica. Finely ground it makes a good opacifier of comparable strength to zirconium oxide. Various opacifiers based on zirconium silicate are available. While zirconium oxide makes an excellent battwash, used to protect kiln furniture, the silicate form, being cheaper, is more often used for this purpose.

Table 6
The ideal formulae, molecular and unit weights of common raw materials

Raw material	Ideal formula	Molecular weight	Unit weight
Alumina: calcined	Al_2O_3	101.96	101.96
Alumina: hydrate	$Al_2(OH)_6$	156.02	156.02
Barium carbonate	$BaCO_3$	197.35	197.35
Calcined china clay (molochite)	$Al_2O_3.2SiO_2$	222.14	222.14
China clay	$Al_2O_3.2SiO_2.2H_2O$	258.18	258.18
Colemanite	$2CaO.3B_2O_3.5H_2O$	411.12	205.56
Cornish stone (china stone)	$0.4K_2O$ $0.4Na_2O. Al_2O_3.8SiO_2$ $0.2CaO$	656.37	656.37
Dolomite	$CaCO_3.MgCO_3$	184.41	184.41
Felspar; potash (orthoclase)	$K_2O.Al_2O_3.6SiO_2$	556.70	556.70
Felspar: soda (albite)	$Na_2O.Al_2O_3.6SiO_2$	524.48	524.48
Felspar: lime (anorthite)	$CaO.Al_2O_3.2SiO_2$	278.22	278.22
Flint	SiO_2	60.09	60.09
Lead carbonate (cerussite)	$PbCO_3$	267.20	267.20
Lead carbonate (basic, white lead)	$2PbCO_3.Pb(OH)_2$	775.61	258.54

continued...

Table 6 *continued...*

Raw material	Ideal formula	Molecular weight	Unit weight
Lead oxide (litharge)	PbO	223.19	223.19
Lead oxide (red lead)	Pb_3O_4	685.57	228.52
Lithium carbonate	Li_2CO_3	73.89	73.89
Magnesium carbonate	$MgCO_3$	84.32	84.32
Nepheline syenite	$\begin{array}{l}0.75Na_2O\\0.25K_2O\end{array}.Al_2O_3.4SiO_2$	412.36	412.36
Petalite	$Li_2O.Al_2O_3.8SiO_2$	612.56	612.56
Quartz	SiO_2	60.09	60.09
Spodumene	$Li_2O.Al_2O_3.4SiO_2$	372.20	372.20
Talc	$3MgO.4SiO_2.H_2O$	379.31	126.44
Whiting	$CaCO_3$	100.09	100.09
Woolastonite	$CaO.SiO_2$	116.17	116.17
Zinc oxide	ZnO	81.37	81.37

NOTES

1 *Unit weights*

The molecular and unit weights of materials are relevant to calculations by the molecular unity formula method because this is based on the concept of materials and glazes as molecules.

In calculations it is important that the unit weight not the molecular weight is used (in most cases these are the same but in a few they are different). This is because some materials exist in a form which provides more than one hypothetical molecule of its least common oxide (this is always clear from the formula). With such materials the unit weight is calculated as the appropriate fraction of the molecular weight. In the above table such materials are colemanite, basic lead carbonate and talc (and a few others not listed above do exist but are less common). Some literature refers to molecular weights as formula weights and to unit weights as equivalent weights.

2 *Variations in symbolic expressions*

Particularly with the important and variable group of materials, including the felspars, nepheline syenite and china stone, two types of variation in the expression of formulae occur which can lead to confusion:

(i) sometimes nepheline syenite, for example, rather than being expressed with the formula in the table above is written as $K_2O.3Na_2O$ together with increased molecular parts of Al_2O_3 and SiO_2 – in other words expressing the whole formula as whole molecules rather than part as fractions. When such formulae are used in molecular unity method calculations it is important that the molecular weight derived from that particular formula is used (see Appendix Three, Calculation 1).

(ii) sometimes, again taking nepheline syenite as an example, the potassium and sodium oxides are expressed as $(KNa)_2O$, followed as normal by the molecular parts of Al_2O_3 and SiO_2. This is simply a convenient abbreviation and expresses that both oxides are present without expressing their relative amounts. Where suppliers use such expressions they usually also state a molecular weight calculated on the relative proportions of those oxides present in a percentage analysis.

Table 7 Percentage composition of raw materials based on their ideal formulae

As is mentioned in the text the majority of ceramic literature on glaze theory uses the molecular unity method. (Ironically the closely related study of glass uses the oxide percentage method.) Those who study glaze by the oxide percentage method may, for a high degree of accuracy use manufacturers' published analyses. It is, however, also possible to use the oxide percentage method with the ideal percentage compositions listed below. This of course is no more accurate than using the molecular unity method with ideal formulae but some people find it quicker, clearer and more comprehensible to calculate with percentages

NOTE The percentage compositions listed above, being based on ideal formulae, may vary considerably from the actual percentage analyses available from manufacturers. This is both because minerals vary and because ideal formulae ignore the presence of minor impurities.

Raw material	Ideal formula	Percentage composition
Alumina: calcined	Al_2O_3	100% Al_2O_3
Alumina: hydrate	$Al_2(OH)_6$	65.35% Al_2O_3 + loss
Barium carbonate	$BaCO_3$	77.70% BaO + loss
Calcined china clay (molochite)	$Al_2O_3.2SiO_2$	45.90% Al_2O_3 ; 54.10% SiO_2
China clay	$Al_2O_3.2SiO_2.2H_2O$	39.49% Al_2O_3 ; 46.55% SiO_2 + loss
Colemanite (boro-calcite)	$2CaO.3B_2O_3.5H_2O$	27.28% CaO ; 50.80% B_2O_3 + loss
Cornish stone (china stone)	$0.4K_2O$ $0.4Na_2O.Al_2O_3.8SiO_2$ $0.2CaO$	5.74% K_2O ; 3.78% Na_2O ; 1.71% CaO ; 15.53% Al_2O_3 ; 73.24% SiO_2
Dolomite	$CaCO_3.MgCO_3$	30.41% CaO ; 21.86% MgO + loss
Felspar: potash (orthoclase)	$K_2O.Al_2O_3.6SiO_2$	16.92% K_2O ; 18.31% Al_2O_3 ; 64.76% SiO_2
Felspar: soda (albite)	$Na_2O.Al_2O_3.6SiO_2$	11.81% Na_2O ; 19.44% Al_2O_3 ; 68.74% SiO_2
Felspar: lime (anorthite)	$CaO.Al_2O_3.2SiO_2$	20.16% CaO ; 36.65% Al_2O_3 ; 43.20% SiO_2
Flint	SiO_2	100% SiO_2
Lead carbonate (cerussite)	$PbCO_3$	83.53% PbO + loss
Lead carbonate (basic, white lead)	$2PbCO_3.Pb(OH)_2$	86.33% PbO + loss
Lead oxide (litharge)	PbO	100% PbO
Lead oxide (red lead)	Pb_3O_4	97.67% PbO + loss
Lithium carbonate	Li_2CO_3	40.44% Li_2O + loss
Magnesium carbonate	$MgCO_3$	47.98% MgO + loss
Nepheline syenite	$0.75Na_2O.Al_2O_3.4SiO_2$ $0.25K_2O$	11.27% Na_2O ; 5.71% K_2O ; 24.73% Al_2O_3 ; 58.29% SiO_2
Petalite	$Li_2O.Al_2O_3.8SiO_2$	4.88% Li_2O ; 16.64% Al_2O_3 ; 78.48% SiO_2
Quartz	SiO_2	100% SiO_2
Spodumene	$Li_2O.Al_2O_3.4SiO_2$	8.03% Li_2O ; 27.39 Al_2O_3 ; 64.58% SiO_2
Talc	$3MgO.4SiO_2.H_2O$	31.85% MgO ; 63.31% SiO_2 ; + loss
Whiting	$CaCO_3$	56.02% CaO + loss
Woolastonite	$CaO.SiO_2$	48.27% CaO ; 51.73% SiO_2
Zinc oxide	ZnO	100% ZnO

Table 8 Frit formulae and percentage compositions

The composition of frits is sometimes expressed by manufacturers as a unity formula and sometimes as a percentage composition. Using the methods detailed in Appendix Three, Calculation 2, conversion from either expression to the other is simple.

Because one manufacturer's frits are different from another's and because information is readily available it seems sensible not to quote compositions as these would be of little value except to indicate the variety which exists. Lead frits, however, are fairly standard and theoretical details of these are as below:

Formulae	Ideal formula	Molecular weight	Unit weight
Lead bisilicate	$PbO.2SiO_2$	343.37	343.37
Lead sesquisilicate	$PbO.1.5SiO_2$	313.33	313.33
Percentage compositions			
Lead bisilicate	65% PbO ; 35% SiO_2		
Lead sesquisilicate	71.23% PbO; 28.77% SiO_2		

In fact, manufacturers' details will show tiny inclusions of alumina or titanium dioxide as these additions further diminish the toxicity of lead frits but in all except the most precise calculations the details above are sufficient.

Table 9
Soluble materials used in frits

The following soluble materials sometimes occur in suppliers' catalogues but are in fact rarely used other than in the industrial manufacture of frits. In addition to the materials listed various insoluble materials – silica-providing materials always, alumina-providing materials often, together with other materials – are also included in frits.

The list is included more for interest than for any practical use it may have.

Material	Formula
Borax (crystals)	$Na_2B_4O_7.10H_2O$ (sometimes also expressed as $Na_2O.2B_2O_3.10H_2O$
Boric acid (or boracic acid)	H_3BO_3
Potassium carbonate (pearl ash)	K_2CO_3
Potassium nitrate (saltpetre, nitre)	KNO_3
Sodium carbonate (soda ash, anhydrous)	Na_2CO_3
Sodium carbonate (washing soda)	$Na_2CO_3.10H_2O$
Sodium nitrate (Chile saltpetre)	$NaNO_3$

Soda ash occurs in tiny quantities in some casting slip recipes where it acts as a deflocculent.

CALCULATION METHODS

This appendix is included primarily for those who use calculation as an aid to experiment with glazes. The principles of Calculation 5(i) and 5(ii) are, however, of use with clay bodies as the oxide percentage method is standard in this context. While calculation is an extremely useful aid for those who experiment with and modify and evolve glazes those who use ready made glazes will have no need of it.

Calculation 1 Calculating the molecular weight of oxides and materials

Calculation 1(i) Calculating the molecular weight of a single oxide

The molecular weights of oxides do not need to be worked out each time calculations are undertaken but are tabulated in all literature about glaze theory. The whole procedure of calculation is however clearer if the method by which this was done is shown.

The starting point is the atomic weight of elements. These have been established for all elements and describe the weight of one atom of an element in relation to the weight of one atom of hydrogen. (The atomic weights of elements which occur commonly in pottery are given in Table 1.)

Using aluminium oxide – aluminia – as an example:

Oxide formula : Al_2O_3 (two atoms of aluminium combined with three of oxygen)

Atomic weight of aluminium 26.98
Atomic weight of oxygen 16.00

Element	Atomic weight of element		No. of atoms (factor of multiplication)	
Al	26.98	×	2	= 53.96
O	16.00	×	3	= 48.00
Molecular weight of alumina				= 101.96

Calculation 1(ii) Calculating the molecular weight of a material containing more than one oxide

Using a table which shows the molecular weights of oxides (Table 3 in this book) the principle of calculation is the same as that shown above.

Using calcined china clay as an example:

Material formula: $Al_2O_3.2SiO_2$

Oxide	Molecular weight of oxide		No. of molecules (factor of multiplication)	
Al_2O_3	101.96	×	1	= 101.96
SiO_2	60.09	×	2	= 120.18
Molecular weight of calcined china clay				222.14

The molecular weights of all the materials in Table 6 are worked out by this procedure and for calculation purposes these are simply taken from some source such as this.

Occasionally such calculations do have to be undertaken in preparation for glaze calculation work mainly where the actual rather than the ideal formula of felspar (and related minerals) is used and in the case of frits. When manufacturers publish frit formulae they also usually state their molecular weights but where this is not done these can be calculated using the procedure above. The mathematics is a little longer but quick with a simple calculator.

Using a frit with the formula below as an example:

0.26 Na$_2$O   0.42 Al$_2$O$_3$ 4.21 SiO$_2$
0.14 K$_2$O   0.86 B$_2$O$_3$
0.58 CaO
0.02 MgO

Oxide	Molecular weight of oxide		No. of molecules (factor of multiplication)		
Na$_2$O	61.98	×	0.26	=	16.1148
K$_2$O	94.20	×	0.14	=	13.188
CaO	56.08	×	0.58	=	32.5264
MgO	40.31	×	0.02	=	0.8062
Al$_2$O$_3$	101.96	×	0.42	=	42.8232
SiO$_2$	60.09	×	4.21	=	252.9789
B$_2$O$_3$	69.62	×	0.86	=	59.8732
			Molecular weight of frit		418.3107
					or
					418.31
					(to two decimal places)

Calculation 2 Conversions between formulae and percentage compositions

Calculation 2(i) Calculating the formula of a material from a percentage analysis of it

Where percentage analyses of materials exist converting these to formulae for use with molecular unity methods of calculation is a more precise way of calculating glazes than using ideal formulae and is particularly relevant with the more variable materials such as felspars, especially in high temperature glazes where they often provide a high proportion of the fluxing oxides of a glaze. The method of conversion is simple but is greatly facilitated if a calculator is used.

The first step is to convert the percentage analysis into a statement of molecular parts by dividing each oxide by its molecular weight, as below, using an analysis of a china stone as an example:

Oxide analysis of china stone sample			Molecular weight of oxide	=	Molecular parts of fluxes	Other molecular parts
SiO$_2$	72.05	÷	60.09	=		1.1990
Al$_2$O$_3$	15.10	÷	101.96	=		0.1481
TiO$_2$	0.02		Omitted			
Fe$_2$O$_3$	0.14		Omitted			
CaO	2.06	÷	56.08	=	0.0367	
MgO	0.04	÷	Omitted			
Na$_2$O	4.32	÷	61.98	=	0.0697	
K$_2$O	5.02	+	94.20	=	0.0533	
Total of molecular parts of fluxes				=	0.1597	

The amounts of titanium, iron and magnesium oxides can, for practical purposes, be noted and omitted. Although calculators will show more there is little point in recording more than four decimal places in the molecular parts columns in the list above. The molecular parts of the fluxing oxides are listed separately so that the molecular parts of each oxide can be divided by this to bring the expression to unity on the fluxes in the conventional way:

Thus:

Molecular parts of oxides			Total of molecular parts of fluxes		Molecular parts in unity	
SiO_2	1.1990	÷	0.1597	=	7.508	SiO_2
Al_2O_3	0.1481	÷	0.1597	=	0.927	Al_2O_3
CaO	0.0367	÷	0.1597	=	0.230	CaO
Na_2O	0.0697	÷	0.1597	=	0.436	Na_2O
K_2O	0.0533	÷	0.1597	=	0.334	K_2O

and arranged as a unity formula:

0.230 CaO		
0.436 Na_2O	0.927 Al_2O_3	7.508 SiO_2
0.334 K_2O		

Compared with the ideal formula for china stone (Table 6) it will be seen that this sample has a slightly higher ratio of fluxes to both alumina and silica than is the norm and that the balance between the fluxes is somewhat different.

Calculation 2(ii) Calculating the percentage composition of a material from its formula

To do this the molecular weight of the material must be known or calculated. The molecular parts of each oxide is then multiplied by the oxide's molecular weight and this is divided by the molecular weight of the material and multiplied by 100.

Taking calcined china clay as an example:

Formula : Al_2O_3 $2SiO_2$ Molecular weight : 222.14

Percentage of alumina in material is:

$$\frac{1 \times 101.96}{222.14} \times 100 = 45.90\% \ Al_2O_3$$

(to two decimal places)

Percentage of silica in material is:

$$\frac{2 \times 60.09}{222.14} \times 100 = 54.10\% \ SiO_2$$

(to two decimal places)

The same procedure exactly works with all materials but with complex ones is mathematically rather longer.

In the more complex example below the frit formula has been provided by the manufacturer and the percentage composition is to be calculated. No molecular weight for the material is available.

The first step is to calculate the molecular weight of the frit. This is done by the method shown in Calculation 1(ii).

The published formula for the frit is:

0.62 CaO		1.85 SiO_2
0.34 Na_2O	0.172 Al_2O_3	
O.04 K_2O		0.65 B_2O

The molecular weight of the frit is calculated to be 233.57.

Using the method exemplified with calcined china clay the calculation can be set out as below:

$$\frac{0.62 \times 56.08}{233.57} \times 100 = 14.89\% \ CaO$$

$$\frac{0.34 \times 61.98}{233.57} \times 100 = 9.02\% \ Na_2O$$

$$\frac{0.04 \times 94.2}{233.57} \times 100 = 1.61\% \ K_2O$$

$$\frac{0.172 \times 101.96}{233.57} \times 100 = 7.51\% \ Al_2O_3$$

$$\frac{1.85 \times 60.09}{233.57} \times 100 = 47.59\% \ SiO_2$$

$$\frac{0.65 \times 69.62}{233.57} \times 100 = 19.37\% \ B_2O$$

Calculation 3   Calculating from a glaze recipe to express it as a molecular unity formula

Comparing glaze recipes does not give a very clear idea about how different one glaze may be from another while comparing formulae gives a precise idea of differences in oxide make-up. Converting recipes into formulae is quite quick if a calculator is used.

Tabulation makes the procedure faster, clearer and less prone to errors. The Leach Cone 8 glaze quoted in the text is used below as an example:

STAGE 1   Converting recipe to molecular parts of material

Recipe materials	Percentage amount		Unit weight		Modular parts
Felspar	40	÷	556.70	=	0.072
Flint	30	÷	60.09	=	0.499
Whiting	20	÷	100.09	=	0.200
China clay	10	÷	258.18	=	0.039

STAGE 2   Determining oxide presence and amounts

Material formulae	Molecular parts	Oxides present and amounts			
		K_2O	Al_2O_3	SiO_2	CaO
$K_2O.Al_2O_3.6SiO_2$	0.072	0.072	0.072	0.432	
SiO_2	0.499			0.499	
$CaCO_3$	0.200				0.200
$Al_2O_3.2SiO_2.2H_2O$	0.039		0.039	0.078	
Totals of individual oxides		0.072	0.111	1.009	0.200

STAGE 3   Totalling fluxes

K_2O	0.072
CaO	0.200
Total	0.272

STAGE 4   Bringing all oxide amounts to unity on the fluxes

Oxide amounts			Total of fluxes		Unity formula amounts of oxides
K_2O	0.072	÷	0.272	=	0.265
CaO	0.200	÷	0.272	=	0.735
Al_2O_3	0.111	÷	0.272	=	0.408
SiO_2	1.009	÷	0.272	=	3.710

Which, arranged as is the convention, reads:

0.265 K_2O

0.735 CaO   0.408 Al_2O_3 3.71 SiO_2

Calculation 4   Calculating from a molecular unity formula to a recipe

In calculating from a molecular unity formula to a material recipe it is important to begin with the materials which provide the largest number of oxides so that materials which provide only one oxide, where these exist, can be used to provide the balance necessary. With high temperature glazes most calculations can be done only using mineral materials but with low temperature glazes, and with the exception of lead glazes, many calculations cannot be completed with mineral materials because the fluxing oxides necessary are not provided by these in sufficiently high proportions in insoluble form – hence the need for frits.

In the calculation example below the unity formula for the Leach Cone 8 glaze calculated in the previous example is used but instead of using the original materials woolastonite is chosen instead of whiting.

STAGE 1   Tabulate needs based on formula, select materials and tabulate oxides provided by each.

Oxides needed			**1**						
0.265	0.735	0.408	3.71	*Material*	**3**	*Material*	**2**	*Molecular*	**5**
K_2O	CaO	Al_2O_3	SiO_2	*formula*		*selected*		*parts*	
Oxide amounts provided			**4**						
0.265		−0.265	−1.590	$K_2O.Al_2O_3.6SiO_2$		Felspar		0.265	
0		0.143	2.120						
	0.735		−0.735	CaO.SiO_2		Woolastonite		0.735	
	0		1.385						
		0.143	−0.286	$Al_2O_3.2SiO_2.2H_2O$		China clay		0.143	
		0	1.099						
			1.099	SiO_2		Flint		1.099	
			0						
0.265	0.735	0.408	3.71						

To clarify the procedure above, entries are made in the boxes as numbered.

1 The oxides symbols and amounts needed are entered in box 1. (This glaze formula may, as here, derive from some other calculation or may be taken from some published source.)
2 The materials are chosen and entered in box 2.
3 Working from published data (such as Table 6 on page 220) the material formulae are then entered in box 3. These formulae give the key to the relative amounts of oxides which materials containing more than one oxide provide.

4 Referring to the oxides needed (as shown in box 1) and the relative amounts of oxides provided by each material (as shown in box 3) box 4 is then completed. As the calculation for each oxide is made the amount provided is subtracted from the amount needed. To guard against subtraction error the amounts provided can be added and totalled at the bottom of box 4.
5 Finally, when the calculations in box 4 are complete and checked box 5 is completed as information to carry forward to the second stage of calculation.

STAGE 2   Calculating the parts by weight and then the percentage recipe from the molecular parts.

Material	Molecular parts		Unit weight		Parts by weight		Total of parts by weight		Multiplied by 100		Percentage recipe 100
Felspar	0.265	×	556.70	=	147.526	÷	335.87	=	0.4392 × 100	=	43.92
Woolastonite	0.735	×	116.17	=	85.385	÷	335.87	=	0.2542 × 100	=	25.42
China clay	0.143	×	258.18	=	36.920	÷	335.87	=	0.1099 × 100	=	10.99
Flint	1.099	×	60.09	=	66.039	÷	335.87	=	0.1966 × 100	=	19.66
		Total of parts by weight	335.87					Percentage total			99.99

The final recipe then reads:

felspar	43.92
woolastonite	25.42
china clay	10.99
flint	19.66

and theoretically this recipe is the same as the Leach Cone 8 glaze. It is important to clarify what this means. On a very white body the glaze with woolastonite will show the effects of iron impurities because, unlike with whiting, analyses of woolastonite usually reveal the presence of significant iron oxide (in the region of 1% to 0.75%). Apart from this slight colour difference (probably not perceptible on darker clays) the two glazes will have very similar physical characteristics and very similar reaction to pigmenting oxides.

Calculation 5
Percentage calculations

Various percentage calculations are used in industrial practice and in the analysis of materials but there are two types which may be of practical use.

Calculation 5(i)   Calculating the percentage of oxides present in a material recipe

Calculation of this is simple and is based on calculating the oxide percentage of each material in the recipe and then adding these.

If, for example, a recipe contains 24% of a particular material which itself is known to contain 63% of silica then the amount of silica which that material brings to the recipe is calculated by multiplying 24 by 63 and dividing the result by 100 as below

$$\frac{24 \times 63 =}{100}$$

but when working with a calculator it is more convenient to think in decimal fractions and to proceed as below

$$24 \times 0.63 = 15.12$$

If the original percentage was 6.3% the multiplication factor would be 0.063, and if it was 0.63% the factor would be 0.0063 and so on.

Using a clay body recipe the calculation can be set out as below:

Recipe	Ball clay	50
	China clay	22
	Quartz	15
	China stone	13

Manufacturers' material analyses:
(All except quartz are quite variable materials so the analyses below are only relevant to materials bought with these analyses as a specification.)

	Ball clay	China clay	Quartz	China stone
SiO_2	67.0	48.00	97.40	72.05
Al_2O_3	19.00	37.00	1.30	15.10
TiO_2	1.60	0.04	0.01	0.13
Fe_2O_3	0.90	0.80	0.08	0.14
CaO	0.30	0.05	0.32	2.06
MgO	0.40	0.30	0.02	0.61
Ka_2O	2.00	1.60	0.42	5.02
Na_2O	0.40	0.10		4.32
Loss	8.30	12.20		

(Loss on ignition is invariably recorded with clays but is not always stated with other materials. Even when loss is included not all analyses actually total one hundred. This is not a sign of inaccurate analysis but rather that there are tiny amounts of other material present which other tests have proved to be of no detriment.)

When all analyses are to hand the calculation can be set out as below:

	Ball Clay % × 0.5		China clay % × 0.22		Quartz % × 0.15		China stone % × 0.13		Body
SiO_2	33.5	+	10.56	+	14.61	+	9.367	=	68.037
Al_2O_3	9.5	+	8.14	+	0.195	+	1.963	=	19.798
TiO_2	0.8	+	0.009	+	0.002	+	0.017	=	0.828
Fe_2O_3	0.45	+	0.175	+	0.012	+	0.018	=	0.656
CaO	0.15	+	0.011	+	0.048	+	0.268	=	0.477
MgO	0.2	+	0.066	+	0.003	+	0.079	=	0.348
K_2O	1.0	+	0.352	+	0.063	+	0.653	=	2.068
Na_2O	0.2	+	0.022	+			0.562	=	0.784
									66
									92.996

(All calculations corrected to 3 decimal places)

Because of the loss associated with various raw materials (in clay bodies particularly, but not only clays) the amounts of oxides do not add up to one hundred. It is normal therefore to convert the amounts of oxides which have been calculated to a true percentage. This is done by totalling the oxide amounts, by dividing each oxide amount by the total and multiplying the result by 100.

This done the percentage oxide analysis reads:

SiO_2	73.16
Al_2O_3	21.38
TiO_2	0.89
Fe_2O_3	0.71
CaO	0.51
MgO	0.37
K_2O	2.22
Na_2O	0.84

99.98 (corrected to 2 decimal places)

In this percentage form this oxide analysis provides a basis for comparison.

With clay bodies the clays which provide the majority of the body material are marketed in such variety that it is essential to do such calculations on the basis of manufacturers' analyses if such work is to be of any use in making comparisons. With glazes, depending on the intentions of the work, calculations can be done either with actual analyses, which will show the precise oxide composition of a glaze made with a particular batch of materials, or with the ideal percentage compositions shown in Table 7 which will show the general glaze composition in terms of the major oxides present.

Calculation 5(ii) Calculating a glaze recipe from an oxide percentage composition

The basis of calculations of this sort is simple. The necessary amount of each recipe material is discovered by selecting materials which contain the necessary oxides and by dividing the oxide need of the glaze by the oxide content of the material and multiplying the result by 100, as below:

$$\frac{\text{Percentage of oxide needed}}{\text{Percentage content in material of oxide}} \times 100 =$$

Amount of material needed

Simple as this calculation is the full tabulated calculation will be clearer if it is preceded by examples of this basic calculation as it occurs with different types of materials.

EXAMPLE ONE   A few of the oxides needed in glazes are available directly as materials in 100% pure form. If 5% of such an oxide is needed the calculation is so simple as to be unnecessary:

$$\frac{5 \times 100 + 5 \text{ parts of oxide}}{100}$$

230

EXAMPLE TWO   Many oxides are only available in materials in which they are combined with other oxides or elements. Whiting ($CaCO_3$), a common provider of calcium oxide (CaO), is an example of this. To the ceramic reactions which occur during firing it provides only calcium oxide (apart from minor impurities) but it contains only 56.02% of calcium oxide, the remaining 43.98% of the material being given off as carbon dioxide (CO_2) during firing. If 5% of calcium oxide is needed in a glaze and if whiting is the chosen material the calculation is:

$$\frac{5\% \text{ CaO needed}}{56.02\% \text{ CaO in whiting}} \times 100 =$$

8.93 parts of whiting needed in recipe (corrected to 2 decimal places)

EXAMPLE THREE   Many materials contain more than one oxide which takes part in ceramic reactions. With such materials a second stage of calculation is necessary because when the amount of the first oxide has been calculated by the method exemplified above the amount (or amounts) of the other oxide (or oxides) also provided needs to be known. Felspar, in providing three oxides, is an example of such a material. The ideal percentage composition of felspar is 16.92%, potassium oxide (K_2O), 18.31% alumina (Al_2O_3) and 64.76% silica (SiO_2). If a glaze needs 5% K_2O and if felspar is the chosen material the amount of felspar needed is calculated as above and is 29.55 parts (to two decimal places). The amounts of alumina and silica brought into the glaze in the 29.55 parts of felspar is calculated by multiplying the percentage of these in felspar by 29.55 and dividing the result by 100 but because

$$\frac{29.55}{100} = 0.2955$$

the calculation is done more quickly using decimal fractions and, in this instance multiplying by 0.2955.

In this example, as well as providing the original 5% K_2O, the 29.55 parts of felspar also provide:

$18.31 \times 0.2955 = 5.41\% \ Al_2O_3$
and
$64.76 \times 0.2955 = 19.14\% \ SiO_2$

(both calculations to 2 decimal places)

The above examples show the method which must be undertaken in turn with each chosen material. Just as with the molecular unity method in Calculation 4, to guard against providing too much of a particular oxide it is important to begin calculation with materials which provide more than one oxide.

In the tabulated calculation which follows the oxide percentage composition of the glaze for which a recipe is calculated is:

K_2O	6%
MgO	1.2%
CaO	11.8%
Al_2O_3	13.2%
SiO_2	67.8%

and the materials chosen are:

Felspar providing	16.92% K_2O; 18.31% Al_2O_3; 64.76% SiO_2
Dolomite providing	30.41% CaO; 21.86% MgO
Whiting providing	56.02% CaO
China clay providing	39.49% Al_2O_3; 46.55% SiO_2
Flint providing	100% SiO_2

Consideration of the relative percentages of oxides in the recipe and of those in the materials shows that the materials do not have an inappropriate balance of oxides and that the necessary amounts of materials can be calculated in the order listed above. The calculation is then set out as below:

Parts of material	Materials chosen	Percentages of oxides needed in glaze				
		K_2O 6	MgO 1.2	CaO 11.80	Al_2O_3 13.20	SiO_2 67.80
35.46	Felspar	6			6.49	22.96
		0			6.71	44.84
5.49	Dolomite		1.2	1.67		
			0	10.13		
18.08	Whiting			10.13		
				0		
16.99	China clay				6.71	7.91
					0	36.93
36.93	Flint					36.93
112.95						0
112.95	Total parts of materials					

(All calculations above corrected to 2 decimal places)

Each horizontal line in the calculation above is completed using the processes described in examples one to three. Strictly, perhaps, the whiting, providing only one oxide, should be calculated after the china clay, which provides two, but because, using ideal percentage compositions, there is no overlap of oxide provision this is not crucial. Despite the fact that all the calculations above are based on percentages the total parts of materials, though usable as real weights, do not add up to 100 because of the gaseous loss associated with dolomite, whiting and china clay. To convert the parts of material to a percentage recipe of the amount of each material calculated is divided by the total parts of materials and is multiplied by 100. In this instance, corrected to two decimal places, the percentage recipe is as overleaf:

$35.46 \times \dfrac{100}{112.95}$ = 31.39% felspar

$5.49 \times \dfrac{100}{112.95}$ = 4.86% dolomite

$18.08 \times \dfrac{100}{112.95}$ = 16.01% whiting

$16.99 \times \dfrac{100}{112.95}$ = 15.04% china clay

$36.93 \times \dfrac{100}{112.95}$ = 32.70% flint

If, rather than working with the ideal percentage compositions of materials used above, the actual percentage analyses of materials were used, calculation of a material recipe would still proceed in the same way. However, because of the inevitable impurities present in materials, tiny amounts of oxides not stipulated in the original glaze oxide percentage composition would be brought in . These would simply be noted as additional oxides inevitable with that particuilar batch of materials.

FURTHER READING

Books marked thus * are highly theoretical or technical rather than immediately practical in their approach.

Catalogues

The catalogues and data sheets issued by *English China Clays* and by *Watts, Blake and Bearne* (see suppliers' addresses for both companies) provide detailed information on the clays which they market, giving insight of the particle size distribution and mineralogical and chemical composition of different ball and china clays.

Most material suppliers produce catalogues which contain much useful information on materials. The catalogue of *Potclays Ltd* is distinctive for the quality of information it provides about the many clay bodies which the company markets.

Pamphlets

Ceramists Handbook originally compiled for W Podmore and Sons Ltd by their then Chief Chemist, Arthur Wedgwood. This is now available in revised form from Potterycrafts Ltd and contains much technical data.

Health and Safety in Ceramics issued by The Institute of Ceramics and distributed by Pergamon Press. This is a technical and comprehensive guide to the subject particularly directed at individual studios and small workshops and at workshops in schools and colleges.

Magazines

In Britain *Ceramic Review*, edited by Eileen Lewenstein and Emmanuel Cooper, regularly includes informative articles about materials and their uses.

Dictionaries of ceramics

Dictionary of Ceramics by A E Dodd, Newnes, 1964, is a reference dictionary with brief entries for all terms likely to be encountered in the more technical literature of ceramics.

Illustrated Dictionary of Practical Pottery, Robert Fournier, Van Nostrand Reinhold, 1973

A Potter's Dictionary of Materials and Techniques, Frank Hamer, Pitman, 1975

Books of recipes

Formulario y Prácticas de Cerámica, José L Artigas is very comprehensive, including recipes for bodies, glazes, enamels, frits and lustres, Gustavo Gili S A, 1961 (No English translation is available but translation of the recipes is fairly straightforward)

Potter's Book of Glaze Recipes, Emmanuel Cooper, Batsford, 1980

The Ceramic Review Book of Clay Bodies and Glaze Recipes edited by Emmanuel Cooper and Eileen Lewenstein, Craftsmen Potters Association, 1983

Books on calculation

Calculations in Ceramics, R Griffiths and C Radford, Maclaren, 1977

Ceramic Calculations, A Heath, Webberley, 1937

Selected Books

There are many, many books on pottery which include sections on materials. The list below is selected and includes books which are either wholly devoted to materials or which have substantial sections of particular relevance to this subject.

A Potter's Book, Bernard Leach, Faber, 1940

Pioneer Pottery, Michael Cardew, Longman, 1971

Clay and Glazes for the Potter, Daniel Rhodes, Pitman, 1960

Ceramic Glazes, Felix Singer and W L German, Borax Consolidated Ltd, 1960. This is a concise work on the subject and, in appendices, gives copious information on eutectic mixtures and on glaze compositions, both expressed as percentage compositions and as molecular formulae.

*Ceramic Colours and Pottery Decoration, Kenneth Shaw, Maclaren, 1962

Ceramic Faults and their Remedies, Harry Fraser, Black, 1986

Oriental Glazes, Nigel Wood, Pitman, 1978. This book includes clear descriptions of calculations by the oxide percentage method.

Ceramic Glazes, Cullen W Parmelee, Industrial Publications, 1951

A Handbook of Pottery Glazes, David Green, Faber, 1978

Glazes for the Studio Potter, Emmanuel Cooper and Derek Royle, Batsford, 1979

*Properties of Ceramic Raw Materials, W Ryan, Pergamon, 1977

*The Effect of Heat on Ceramics, W F Ford, (Institute of Ceramics Textbook Series), Maclaren

*Industrial Ceramics, Felix Singer and Sonja Singer, Chapman and Hall, 1963. Though the title of this book accurately reflects its contents much of its encyclopaedic contents are of relevance in non-industrial contexts.

MATERIALS SUPPLIERS IN THE UK

General suppliers of materials and equipment

Deancraft Fahey Ltd
12 Spedding Road, Fenton Industrial Estate, Stoke-on-Trent, Staffs ST4 2ST

Ferro (Great Britain) Ltd
Wombourne, Wolverhampton, West Midlands WV5 8DA

Fulham Pottery Ltd
40–44 Burlington Road, off New Kings Road, London SW6 and at: 8–10 Ingate Place, Battersea, London SW8 3NS

Potterycrafts Ltd
Campbell Road, Stoke-on-Trent, Staffs ST4 4ET

Clay body makers, kiln makers and general suppliers

Potclays Ltd
Brickkiln Lane, Etruria, Stoke-on-Trent, Staffs

Suppliers of clays in bulk

English China Clay Co Ltd
John Keay House, St Austell, Cornwall PL25 4DJ

Watts, Blake and Bearne and Co Ltd
Park House, Courtney Park, Newton Abbot, Devon TQ12 4PS

Other suppliers

E W Good & Co Ltd
Barker Street, Longton, Stoke-on-Trent, Staffs

Suppliers of lustres
Hanovia Ltd
Engelhard Industries, Valley Road, Cinderford, Glos

Suppliers of Filter Cloths and tools
G H Heath and Son (UK) Ltd
Heathcote Works, Burslem, Stoke-on-Trent, Staffs

Kiln manufacturers and suppliers
Cromartie Kilns Ltd
Park Hall Road, Longton, Stoke-on-Trent, Staffs
Kilns and Furnaces Ltd
Keele Street Works, Tunstall, Stoke-on-Trent, Staffs
Laser Kilns Ltd
1 Coopersale Road, London E9 6AU

Kiln furniture and refractory manufacturers and suppliers
Acme Marls Ltd
Clough Street, Hanley, Stoke-on-Trent, Staffs
Diamond Refractories Ltd
Stoke Old Road, Hartshill, Stoke-on-Trent, Staffs

Equipment manufacturers and suppliers
J W Ratcliffe & Sons Ltd
Old Boro Works, Rope Street, Shelton New Road, Newcastle, Staffs

NOTES
1 In many areas local agents now exist and buying from these usually saves all, or a large proportion, of the carriage cost of goods bought from Stoke-on-Trent.
2 The two listed suppliers of clays in bulk do not deal in small orders but delegate these to a national network of agents, whose addresses they provide.

INDEX

The index is selective, only the major mention of topics being included
In all cases page, not illustration, numbers are indicated